A CIVIL TONGUE

Mark Kingwell

A CIVIL TONGUE

Justice, Dialogue, and the Politics of Pluralism

The Pennsylvania State University Press
University Park, Pennsylvania

Library of Congress Cataloging-in-Publication Data

Kingwell, Mark, 1963–
    A civil tongue : justice, dialogue, and the politics of pluralism
/ Mark Kingwell

        p.   cm.
    Includes bibliographical references and index.
    ISBN 0-271-01334-6 (cloth : acid-free paper)
    ISBN 0-271-01335-4 (paper : acid-free paper)
    1. Justice.   2. Dialogue.   3. Etiquette.   4. Courtesy.
    5. Pluralism (Social sciences).   I. Title.
JC578.K56   1995
320'.01'1—dc20   93-48808
                                                          CIP

Published by The Pennsylvania State University Press,
University Park, PA 16802-1003

It is the policy of The Pennsylvania State University Press to use acid-free paper for the first printing of all clothbound books. Publications on uncoated stock satisfy the minimum requirements of American National Standard for Information Sciences—Permanence of Paper for Printed Library Materials, ANSI Z39.48–1984.

Contents

For Gail, with love

Preface and Acknowledgments

This book is about a simple but elusive goal: a vigorous public debate about how a pluralistic society should be organized. Can we address, and possibly settle, our disagreements about abortion, gender equality, public welfare programs, and taxation? Can we ask questions about distortion and manipulation in the existing media of public debate? Can you, a single concerned citizen, make your genuine views known and relevant, both to yourself and to the society you live in?

My central conviction in the discussion that follows is that this vigorous public debate, if we can ever find it, is all the political meaning that the vexed word "justice" should have for us. If true, this significantly alters the role of political theorists. I am convinced, through both experience and reflection, that most citizens do not require further philosophical or moral visions of justice. What they want instead is a convincing characterization—a good interpretation—of the sort of public debate that will address the hard questions of political life. I am also convinced that most citizens find existing versions of public debate inadequate—even, sometimes, positively threatening. The desire for a public conversation that is challenging, lively, decisive, undistorted, and fruitful is widespread. Unfortunately, disagreement about what this conversation should be like, and how it should be defended, is just as widespread. What drives my philosophical study of dialogue and justice is a desire to close this persistent gap between political desire and social reality.

In many ways, this is a book about failure. It begins with a failure in the aspirations of justice theory as they have emerged in the two decades or so since the publication of John Rawls's *A Theory of Justice*. That failure is both normative and psychological: the inability of theory-generated principles of justice to find wide social or moral sanction, but also the related inability of the so-called "rational chooser" to model real human commitments. What I will call dialogic models of justice are a response to these failures. Dialogic models of justice defend not principles of justice but rather conversational spaces in which such principles can be assessed by real citizens. They change the Socratic question "What is justice?" into a new one: "What is just talking?" This book is the result of thinking about the problems and promises of the dialogic response. It constitutes both a survey of the extant theories and an answer to the question of *what kind* of dialogue we require for justice.

Hence a second level of failure: in certain respects, all the theories I examine in what follows defend inadequate versions of dialogic justice. Yet all of them are significant failures, failures that point the way forward. My motivation in offering a critical discussion of them is that we can, by combining their virtues, approach a better answer. So, beginning with the aspirations of liberal political theory, I examine a number of reformations and responses, both North American and continental, to the project of linking justice and dialogue. In the end I argue that the best route to vigorous public debate lies in the conversational virtue of civility. I know that civility will seem an odd, even potentially dangerous, place to locate our hopes for renewed public debate. Yet there are good reasons, as I shall suggest, for seeing this notion as not only superior to other available options but also positively emancipatory in its critical capacity.

In examining the conversation of justice and the implications of civility for its successful performance, I have been torn, like most thinkers about justice, between personal conviction concerning what constitutes the good life for humankind and a philosophical desire to articulate principles or procedures of justice that would be convincing to all rational agents. One thing I have learned in thinking about these issues is that the condition of being so torn is a natural one, and neither side of this choice (if it is a choice) succeeds in saying all we want to say about justice. In other words, the most convincing theory of justice is neither a very "thick" array of principles derived from a single conception of the good life, nor a very "thin" or minimalist decision procedure for testing norms based on universal rational commitments. Compromise here, as in politics, is a fact of life. I think the virtue of civility gives citizens a way of facing the prospect of political compromise with greater confidence and resolve, and with renewed hope for success in finding just accommodation of our differences.

The work of defending this conclusion I naturally leave to the discussion itself. For the moment I merely desire to see justice and civility both served by thanking those persons and circumstances that have influenced me and contributed to the completion of this work.

I first explored many of the ideas in this book in a doctoral dissertation written for the Yale University Department of Philosophy. To the supervisors of that work, Georgia Warnke and Bruce Ackerman, I owe many thanks. My intellectual debts to them are obvious in the pages that follow; my personal debts are not so, but equally extensive. Rüdiger Bittner, Sarah Broadie, Christopher Dustin, Carol Freedman, Mark Gedney, Raymond Geuss, Robert Hanna, Karsten Harries, Chris Kutz, Alasdair MacIntyre, Mark Migotti, J. Donald Moon, Michael Nash, Alex Oliver, Hayden Ramsay, Steven B. Smith, Larry Vogel, and two anonymous readers also provided valuable feedback on early versions of some of this material.

A 1990 conference invitation from Matthew Parfitt provided me with the occasion for linking hermeneutics and civility and prompted helpful suggestions from Robert Schreur and Jodi Mikalachki. Margaret Visser and Cornelia Pearsall provided some useful leads in the etiquette literature. Early versions of some of this work were presented and discussed at meetings of the York University philosophy colloquium (October 1991), the American Philosophical Association Eastern Division (December 1992), and the Canadian section of the International Association for Philosophy of Law and Social Philosophy (June 1993). I thank all those who attended for their valuable comments.

My students at Yale, York University, and the University of Toronto have proved able and skeptical interlocutors over the past few years, and they have improved the clarity of my thinking more than they know. In particular, my thanks are due to those who have also become friends: Brennan Brown, Sayuri Oyama, and David Arnold. Among new colleagues, I would like to thank Wes Cragg, Leslie Green, Margaret Schabas, Sonia Sedivy, Bill Seager, and Catherine Valcke for their support and interest. Among other friends, my thanks for lively discussions to Barry McCartan, Mathew Ingram, David Adams, Charles Blattberg, Todd Ducharme, and, as always, Gail Donaldson. And thanks, finally, to Sandy Thatcher and Peggy Hoover of Penn State Press for their enthusiasm and care.

Some of this material was previously published, in different form, as follows: parts of Chapters 1 and 2 appeared in *Philosophy and Social Criticism* (Fall 1993); part of Chapter 5 appeared in *International Philosophical Quarterly* (March 1994); part of Chapter 6 appeared in the *Journal of Philosophy* (August 1993); and parts of Chapters 6 and 7 appeared in *Philosophical Forum* (Spring 1994).

By Manners, I mean not here, Decency of behaviour; as how one man should salute another, or how a man should wash his mouth, or pick his teeth before company, and such other points of the Small Morals; But those qualities of man-kind, that concern their living together in Peace, and Unity.

—Hobbes, *Leviathan* 1.11

Truth . . . has no such way of prevailing, as when strong Arguments and good Reason, are joined with the softness of Civility and good Usage.

—Locke, *A Letter Concerning Toleration*

PART ONE

1

Interpretation, Dialogue, and the Just Citizen

In a recent series of articles entitled "The State of Philosophy," John Gray contributed an assessment of contemporary political philosophy—that is, the products of the first two decades after John Rawls's *A Theory of Justice*.[1] Gray reiterated a familiar complaint in his survey. "Because recent political philosophy in the Anglo-American mode remains for the most part animated by the hopes of the Enlightenment," he said,

> above all, the hope that human beings will shed their traditional allegiances and local identities and unite in a universal civilization grounded in generic humanity and rational morality, it cannot even begin to grapple with the political dilemmas of an age in which political life is dominated by renascent particularisms, militant religions

---

1. John Gray, "Against the New Liberalism: Rawls, Dworkin, and the Emptying of Political Life," *Times Literary Supplement*, July 3, 1992, pp. 13–15. See John Rawls, *A Theory of Justice* (Cambridge, Mass.: Belknap Press, 1971).

and resurgent ethnicities. As a result, the main current in recent political philosophy has condemned itself to political nullity and intellectual senility.

Gray went on to argue that it is the mainly Kantian legacy of these thinkers, and also their allegiance to what Charles Taylor has called "Locke's punctual self," the self of purely rational moral choosing, that has led them astray.[2] Their searches for justice via "abstract individualism" are rendered irrelevant, and their "new liberalism" is exposed as a "hallucinatory perspective" that turns us from "the real world of human practices and forms of life in families, schools, workplaces, nation states, and so on." In sum, "the thoughts of the new liberals evoke no political echo: the project of securing agreement on principles of justice among metaphysically neutered Kantian selves arouses little interest, inevitably, among the political classes, or the voters, of the Western world, or anywhere else."

Like many other critics of this new liberalism, Gray points to recent "communitarian" responses as decisive: Michael Sandel's nitpicky dismantling of Rawls's rational chooser, Michael Walzer's attempt to write a more eclectic story, Alasdair MacIntyre's plumping for Aristotelian/Thomist tradition.[3] These responses, and the dialogue that has resulted between liberalism and communitarians, has been fruitful for both sides: liberalism has emerged

2. Charles Taylor's magisterial study of the history of influences that create the modern self-consciousness, *Sources of the Self: The Making of the Modern Identity* (Cambridge, Mass.: Harvard University Press, 1989), is especially illuminating on the centrality of "inwardness" in modern conceptions of the self (see part 2, esp. ch. 9). In an interestingly related set of arguments, Barbara Herrnstein Smith claims that certain Enlightenment tendencies of thought, in particular those associated with Hume's "natural standard of taste" and Kant's "pure judgment," have twisted subsequent philosophical reflection concerning judgment. See her *Contingencies of Value: Alternative Perspectives for Critical Theory* (Cambridge, Mass.: Harvard University Press, 1988), esp. ch. 4. This skewing of judgment conceptions leads to, among other things, a debilitating fact/value distinction that ultimately collapses moral judgment into emotivism. (I have more to say about this in Chapter 4 when I discuss MacIntyre.)

3. Michael J. Sandel, *Liberalism and the Limits of Justice* (Cambridge: Cambridge University Press, 1982), and "The Procedural Republic and the Unencumbered Self," *Political Theory* 12 (1984): 81–96; Michael Walzer, *Spheres of Justice* (New York: Basic Books, 1983); Alasdair MacIntyre, *After Virtue: A Study in Moral Theory*, 2d ed. (London: Duckworth, 1985) and *Whose Justice? Which Rationality?* (Notre Dame, Ind.: University of Notre Dame Press, 1988). In addition to these more influential and ambitious works, there is a vast literature of comment directly on Rawls's theory, which I do not attempt to cite in detail here. (The best of these commentaries are arguably the ones included in Norman Daniels, ed., *Reading Rawls* [New York: Basic Books, 1974].) It is fair to say, as Gray does, that "political philosophical during the past two decades has been—at least in the English-speaking world—in very substantial part a commentary on Rawls's work."

improved. But in stating such a spectacular thesis, Gray appears to miss several key developments in recent liberal political theory, all of which serve to render his argument less widely damning. First, there is the work of a younger generation of liberal theorists, such as Will Kymlicka and Nancy Rosenblum, who have been attempting, with some success, to put substance back into liberal models.[4] Second, Gray does not mention that Rawls himself, in well-known and powerful revisions of his original theory, has always been a moving target, running as fast toward some of his critics as they were running away from him.[5] The most important of these revisionist articles— some of which, indeed, merely fought off persistent misunderstandings of the original theory—form the basis of Rawls's recent *Political Liberalism*,[6] his first major work since *A Theory of Justice*. Finally and most important, Gray does not note that two important developments in contemporary political and moral theory, while increasing still further the distance from philosophical commitments of Kantian lineage that determined Rawls's early work, have at the same time given new life to some old liberal aspirations.

These are, speaking with necessary crudity, the revitalization of so-called "virtue ethics"[7] and what Georgia Warnke has called "the hermeneutic turn in

---

4. See, e.g., Will Kymlicka, *Liberalism, Community, and Culture* (New York: Oxford University Press, 1989), which discusses the issue of cultural membership, minority rights, and conflicts between cultural and civic membership; and Nancy Rosenblum, *Another Liberalism: Romanticism and the Reconstruction of Liberal Thought* (Ithaca: Cornell University Press, 1987), a sensitive consideration of the Romantic elements embedded in the liberal tradition.

5. The most prominent of the early revisions is John Rawls's 1979 Dewey Lectures, "Kantian Constructivism in Moral Theory," *Journal of Philosophy* 77 (1980): 515–72. Here, where he emphasizes the "interpretive" aspects of his theory and the status of the (then already much-criticized) original position as "a device of representation," Rawls appears to make his own hermeneutic turn. Indeed, elements of interpretive modesty were present in the otherwise apparently universalistic arguments of the original theory, especially in the discussion of "reflective equilibrium." Richard Rorty, among others, has wanted to save Rawls from foundationalist misreadings of the theory. See his "The Priority of Democracy to Philosophy," in *Objectivity, Relativism, and Truth: Philosophical Papers 1* (Cambridge: Cambridge University Press, 1991), where Rorty confesses to having misread Rawls's use of "rational" as a metaphysical claim about original-position choosers (pp. 182–92; esp. n. 21). Many others have made the same mistake— prominent among them Sandel, who mistook Rawls's model of fairnesss and choice for a substantive account of human nature—but the company of those who have admitted this and revised their critical views is much smaller.

6. New York: Columbia University Press, 1993.

7. This revitalization has been spearheaded by moral theorists, but the implications are frequently political. In general, virtue ethics turns from the assessment of *acts* to the assessment of *character traits* and tends to give priority of place to a thick form of ethical life in which such traits are fostered. See MacIntyre, *After Virtue*; Philippa Foot, *Virtues and Vices* (Berkeley and Los Angeles: University of California Press, 1978); Martha Nussbaum, *The Fragility of Goodness:*

recent political philosophy."[8] In political philosophy, these two themes converge in a strong emphasis on the Aristotelian virtue of *phronesis*, or practical
wisdom, emphasized by both Hans-Georg Gadamer and such avowedly liberal
theorists as Charles Larmore and William Galston.[9] As a result of this convergence, the emphasis in thinking about justice has, arguably, been shifted: away
from the justification of rules of social organization under conditions of ideal
or rational choice, and toward a plausible interpretation of the *character* of a
citizen and of the *discussion* in which he or she struggles to understand other
citizens.[10] It should not be a surprise, given the dialogic commitments embedded in the philosophico-hermeneutic influence on the "turn," that the citizen
emerges clearly in these developments not as a rational chooser but *as a talker*.

But what kind of talker? In this book I explore some implications of the
hermeneutic recasting of the justice question in dialogic terms, implications
that point to the difficulty of giving a firm characterization to the dialogic
citizen.[11] I argue that most versions of the talker presented by contemporary

---

Luck and Ethics in Greek Tragedy and Philosophy (Cambridge: Cambridge University Press,
1986); James D. Wallace, *Virtues and Vices* (Ithaca: Cornell University Press, 1978); the contributions to *Midwest Studies in Philosophy* 13 (1988); and Raimond Gaita, "Virtues, Human Good,
and the Unity of a Life," *Inquiry* 26 (1984): 407–24. A National Endowment for the Humanities
seminar on virtue ethics was held in the summer of 1992.

8. Georgia Warnke, "The Hermeneutic Turn in Recent Political Philosophy," *Yale Journal of
Criticism* 4 (1990): 207–30. See also her "Social Interpretation and Political Theory: Walzer and
His Critics," *Philosophical Forum* 21 (1989–90): 204–26. These papers appear in revised form in
Warnke's *Justice and Interpretation* (Cambridge, Mass.: MIT Press, 1992); see chs. 1 and 2, and
ch. 6, which links the role of interpretation in political theory to the emphasis on what Warnke
calls "hermeneutic conversation."

9. See Charles Larmore, *Patterns of Moral Complexity* (Cambridge: Cambridge University
Press, 1987), esp. ch. 1. See also Richard Bernstein's shrewd reading of Aristotelian sources through
the lens of hermeneutic theory, "From Hermeneutics to Praxis," in *Hermeneutics and Modern Philosophy*, ed. Brice R. Wachterhauser (Albany: SUNY Press, 1986), pp. 87–110. William Galston's
Liberal Purposes: Goods, Virtues, and Diversity in the Liberal State (New York: Cambridge University Press, 1991) is an extended critique of contemporary right-over-good liberal theory combined
with a detailed defense of the substantive goods contained in liberalism. Like Larmore, I view the
challenge for liberal theory as putting interpretive substance back into the priority of right; Galston
sees substance as more effectively recovered by surrendering the notion of right's priority.

10. One difficult question is whether such interpretations will, to borrow Galston's terms,
stand as "deep descriptions" or as "wide justifications" of practices. For reasons that will become
clear later in this work, I favor a theory with the status of a deep description, one that justifies
itself with reference not to an external standpoint but to features within forms of political life. For
an alternative view, see Galston's "Peirce's Cable and Plato's Cave: Objectivity and Community in
Contemporary Political Philosophy," ch. 2 of *Liberal Purposes*.

11. Throughout this discussion I shall be concentrating on the role of citizen. This is by no
means the only role we play, nor indeed always the most important one. It is, however, the most

philosophers are, for different reasons, inadequate. In order to outline the path this critical discussion will take, I shall first say a few words about the notion of "dialogic" theories of justice, and then discuss some of the benefits of hermeneutic or interpretive theories of justice. In the next chapter, I sketch a preliminary version of what I consider a more adequate version of the just dialogic citizen.

I. DIALOGIC JUSTICE

Justice and *dialogue* are two words frequently conjoined in political rhetoric, but the philosophical link between them is less often explored. We might expect to read in a newspaper report, for example, that justice for Palestinians, or African-Americans, or women depends on dialogue. Only through some kind of principled talk, it is implied, will these historically disenfranchised groups obtain what they deserve, need, or want[12]—with what they deserve, need, or want being conceived in terms of money, land, respect, employment opportunity, or any other set of desired social and material goods. And yet, despite the ubiquity of this sort of appeal, there exists no common understanding of just what political dialogue about justice is meant to be, how it is to proceed, or what rules are supposed to govern it. Calls for a dialogue are frequent in disputes about justice; detailed and convincing models of it are far less so.

The topic of this study can be located in the space created between the common political appeals to dialogue and the uncommon philosophical discussion of its political role. My discussion attempts to find, in other words, a

---

important role with respect to questions of political legitimacy, and an ability to take it up—to engage in the dialogue of legitimacy—is something we must all possess in order to raise for ourselves the question of a just society. I am of course aware that many people will consider this role, and any defense of its centrality, as unwarranted inhibition: their other roles (ethnic, cultural, familial) may seem far more important. The point of liberalism's priority of right is to make a response to these cries for subsocial roles and to motivate the role of citizen. What I shall suggest ultimately is that civility gives us a way of characterizing the role that is compelling across a number of expected differences relating to other roles. I have been aided in seeing the issue by way of a struggle with, among others, Susan M. Okin's *Justice, Gender, and the Family* (New York: Basic Books, 1989).

12. We cannot specify any one such principle—say, desert—because even here principles of justice are controversial. I want only to indicate that supporters of political dialogue think it is crucial to obtaining justice, *however* that is finally to be understood.

philosophically plausible model of what I shall call *just talking*, a convincing model of the kind of dialogue relevant to a theory of justice. It does this by critically examining a number of recent theories in political philosophy. These theories address justice as a problem of *social interaction* in a pluralistic society, with the principles or norms of justice acting as an answer to the question of how diverse individuals and groups within a society, who may wish to pursue very different conceptions of the good life, will divide resources, perform exchanges, contract, and reward or punish in a manner justifiable to them all. And each of them hopes, in their quite different ways, to generate, assess, and justify such norms and principles of distribution and reparation, punishment and exchange, from within the practices of interpersonal talk.

These norms and principles are needed, it should be added, as part of the larger social task to which justice theory is habitually oriented, namely that of a defensible social organization conceived more generally. Justifiable norms or principles of justice will ultimately be those that allow citizens to find their society well ordered, that is, made up of a basic structure of institutions genuinely answering to their needs and interests. (How those needs and interests are conceived and determined may also be a part of what dialogue addresses, as we shall see.) Each of the theories under consideration here is therefore concerned with what can be called the problem of legitimation. If it is always a good question to ask of a society "Is it a just society?" then a theory of justice is one that makes this question answerable in a principled way, by exposing to view the principles on which social institutions are organized. And while it is true that justice will always be at bottom a matter of distributing goods (though not always *material* goods), the focus of most theories of justice is not particular distributions but *the norms or principles on whose basis the distributions are performed.*[13]

What we shall find, in dealing with dialogic theories of justice, is that the focus of justice is actually shifted once more: away from particular norms or principles, to the conversational spaces in which they are generated and justified, and so to the talkers who do the generating and justifying. That is,

13. It is frequently remarked, with some justice, that contemporary justice theory is too much concerned with material goods and, more deeply, with justice as a matter of property distribution (that is, even nonmaterial goods like respect may be "commoditized" by distributional theories). One advantage of dialogic theories is that they shift focus from goods distribution to a kind of political conversation in which norms are continually being assessed and justified against the (developing) interests of citizens. It is nevertheless true, here as elsewhere, that distribution of scarce social goods is what makes justice a social issue, and the first virtue of societies; in this respect, we are all children of Hume.

instead of specifying (as Rawls, for example, does) a set of principles that can be set out as ordered propositions, dialogic theorists of justice favor a strategy in which a certain kind of principled and legitimating talk will itself justify a set of norms or principles, without defining those norms or principles in advance. By defining, and philosophically defending, the dialogic forum in which norms or principles can be raised and assessed for their legitimacy, such theories create in this fashion "gates" or "grids" of justification. Whatever passes through a set of (justified) conversational constraints can be expected to be the valid norms or principles of justice. On this view of justice, we need not specify in advance even minimum conditions of what those norms or principles will be, but only the requirements that *any* set of justified norms or principles will have to meet in order to be acceptable in legitimate dialogue.

These requirements vary enormously. A certain sort of liberalism—the main focus of Chapter 3—finds principles of justice in a political dialogue subject to external constraints of *neutrality*. According to this view, exemplified by the work of Bruce Ackerman, citizens of "the liberal state" may have to be banned from uttering any claims that depend on the assertion of their personal superiority, or of the unconditional superiority of their conception of the good. Only in dialogue neutrally constrained will we generate rules of distribution that do not depend on controversial moral commitments, that is, commitments that cannot reasonably be expected to extend to every citizen of a diverse society. By thus drawing a line between the politically relevant and the morally controversial (and therefore politically irrelevant), this defense of neutral dialogue exhibits a trait that may be taken as characteristic of liberal justice theory, one that will play a recurrent role in our examination of justice and dialogue: the so-called priority of the right over the good.

This influential limit claim, original with Kant but today most often associated with Rawls, entails that ideas of right (those that form a political or structural conception of justice) set a limit on the pursuit of ideas of good (deeper philosophical or religious conceptions of the worthy or excellent life).[14] In this way justice provides in the liberal paradigm a *political structure* in which individuals and groups are free to pursue their own goals without interference, while at the same time the structure defines when and how those

14. John Rawls, "Justice as Fairness: Political Not Metaphysical," *Philosophy and Public Affairs* 14 (1985): 223–51; and "The Priority of Right and Ideas of the Good," *Philosophy and Public Affairs* 17 (1988): 251–76. (These papers appear, in revised form, in lectures I and V, respectively, of Rawls's *Political Liberalism*.) One of the most eloquent and influential statements of a contrarian position is Iris Murdoch's *The Sovereignty of the Good* (London: Routledge & Kegan Paul, 1970).

goals may not be pursued. The priority of right over good, says Rawls, therefore "implies that the principles of (political) justice set limits to permissible
ways of life; hence the claims citizens make to pursue ends that transgress
those limits have no weight (as judged by that political conception)."[15] Such a
limit is both positive and negative in that it draws firm boundaries but also
creates opportunities for the free pursuit of goods. "[J]ust institutions and the
political virtues expected of citizens," the claim goes,

> would serve no purpose—would have no point—unless those institu-
> tions and virtues not only permitted *but also sustained* ways of life that
> citizens can affirm as worthy of their full allegiance. A conception of
> political justice must contain within itself sufficient space, as it were,
> for ways of life that can gain devoted support. In a phrase: justice draws
> the limit, the good shows the point.[16]

Ackerman does not, as we shall see, argue at length for this political or
structural view of justice, nor does he specify the exact conditions of forming
or holding a conception of the good.[17] He instead begins with the following
assumptions, defining along Humean lines the "circumstances of liberal justice": that citizens have conceptions of the good; that these are various, and,
moreover, sometimes in conflict (e.g., over scarce goods); that there is a prima
facie political need for adherents of conflicting conceptions to occupy the same
social space; and finally, that principles or norms of justice define the way in
which these conflicts are resolved and the common space is structured. Constrained neutral dialogue is then advanced as a principled way to resolve these
political conflicts by separating claims that can be relevantly addressed at the
level of social organization from those that concern the excellence of individual
or group conceptions of the good life.

The advantage of right-over-good theories is that they take differences of
moral vision seriously and attempt to specify conditions of peaceful coexistence without reference to claims known in advance to be controversial. In this
way they control conflict by abstracting from it, separating the political from
the personal, the public from the private, the citizen from the person. The
strategy is typically advanced by liberal theorists of justice as the only viable

---

15. Rawls, "The Priority of Right," p. 251.
16. Ibid. (emphasis added).
17. Rawls attempts such a specification, with limited success, in ibid. See also the far more
detailed account of what it means to have, and hold, a conception of the good that is provided by
Taylor in part 1 of *Sources of the Self.*

response to the condition of pluralism, the presence of various conceptions of the good life within a single society. The presumed benefits of the strategy are social toleration of differences in moral visions and the continued civil peace that comes with keeping deeply controversial issues off the public agenda. All liberals, whatever their other differences, find some version of this strategy compelling. Moreover, in some configurations of the strategy the emphasis on neutrality in decision-making, the abstraction of contractors (say) from their particular interests and desires, is meant to be rationally foundational and convincing. Nothing substantive needs to be assumed in such theories, beyond the desire of individuals to reach some kind of social modus vivendi. This they do precisely by following neutral procedures of debate or decision designed to generate agreement out of diversity. The procedures are neutral because they are silent on the question of individual commitments; nothing is presumed in advance of the decision-making process. More than this, that very process of reaching agreement is meant to be impartial with regard to the relative moral worth of citizens. And, the argument goes, it is just this impartiality that we require when it comes to the project of social legitimation and the determination of those principles of organization we think of as addressing issues of justice: fair distribution of goods, the treating of like cases alike, the prevention of group domination.

But at least since Kant there have been those who find this political abstraction from particular moral commitments indefensible and possibly dangerous, for it is a strategy that courts atomism, incoherence, and the loss of deep community feeling. The so-called communitarian critics, both left and right, who today attack liberalism with such force are the inheritors of a long tradition (sometimes longer than they know) beginning at least with Hegel and such Romantics as Herder and Novalis, a tradition invigorated by Marx and revived most recently by, among others, Sandel, Taylor, and MacIntyre. Though complex and nuanced in practice, the basic commitment of these communitarian critics can be stated fairly straightforwardly, in the thesis that there is (or ought to be) a single ruling conception of the good life in which each of us operates, and that moreover personal identity and community are always functions of this conception. Such a conception is set out in the now increasingly common defenses of virtue-based ethics, which restore depth to ethics by overturning formal approaches to moral decision-making with appeals to concrete features of ethical life. In the political realm, the communitarian restoration of context is marshaled most often as a refutation of the purely political conception of justice, which sets off such deep commitments as devoid of political relevance. In some cases, the refutation takes the form of finding the separation of public and private spheres ineffective in its own terms; in others, it takes the form of finding the liberal conception of political justice infected with substantive moral commitments and therefore incoherent.

Communitarian conservatism, the focus of Chapter 4, finds both of these tactics of refutation congenial. This view, which I associate mainly with Alasdair MacIntyre, begins with what is considered a factual claim: that moral and political disagreement is endemic and in principle unresolvable under the liberal paradigm. The neutral dialogue imagined by liberals cannot do what it intends, namely resolve conflict in talk. This is so because the neutralist paradigm is not in fact neutral, and narrow commitments masquerade therein as universalizable truths. A wider objection is that neutrality is a false goal in justice theory, a misleading strategy that serves to obscure the fact that liberal theories depend as much as all others on a particular conception of the good life in their framing of justice principles.[18] Stated broadly, that conception involves the primacy of individual autonomy, guarantees on personal property, and social protection of individual rights. It also conceives of the individual not as a locus of concrete ethical virtues but rather as a generator of preferences, a bargainer in the marketplace of interests. *These* substantive commitments can never be overcome by employing right-from-good abstractions, because such abstractions in fact presume them. And to this extent the liberal project of justice is doomed to incoherence, because there can be no truly neutral theory of justice.

Instead of vainly seeking a notion of justice that transcends particular conceptions of the good, communitarian conservatism enjoins us to fall back to defending the integrity of justice as a virtue *within particular traditions of rational inquiry.* Here the richly detailed and identity-fostering substantiveness of deep moral commitments is maintained and nurtured, not denied. Moral discourse is not fractured and endlessly disagreeing precisely because it is no longer conceived as aiming toward universal agreement. Within traditions, context and coherence are restored in a single moment of recognition:

18. For an acerbic version of this criticism, see Allan Bloom, "Justice: John Rawls vs. the Tradition of Political Philosophy," *American Political Science Review* 69 (1975): 648–62. A more considered discussion is provided in George Grant's *English-Speaking Justice* (Sackville, N.B.: Mount Allison University Press, 1974). William Galston finds unsatisfying the use of liberalism as a decision-procedure only and criticizes this tendency while also attempting to defend liberalism as a political conception. See his "Defending Liberalism," *American Political Science Review* 76 (1982): 621–29 (this essay is adapted and included in *Liberal Purposes*). As we shall see, MacIntyre's objection to liberalism is a version of this criticism taken to a logical extreme: if conceptions of justice are always particular, it *makes no sense* to continue looking for a theory of justice in terms of the structural priority-of-right view sketched earlier.

that I am not an entity who can separate his political commitments, his citizenship, from his deeper commitments, his moral vision. I find myself, as both person and citizen, within and only within a concrete tradition of moral and epistemological inquiry. Any abstract conception of the person, say Kant's noumenal self, will always fail to capture some crucial aspects of my rich human identity, my sense of myself as occupying a particular place in a long and continuing story of common moral development. With the restoration of moral context comes the restoration of moral coherence.

But there is more than one tradition of inquiry in this sense. And conflict among these diverse traditions will have to be mediated in some fashion if, as is true today, they must occupy the same limited social space. It might be suggested that this mediation of conflict occurs in a "translation conversation" among traditions. But this conversation, in which the rational superiority of a tradition (with its table of relevant virtues, including justice) can be vindicated, actually appears to commit the communitarian conservative to a version of the transcendent rationality he seemed so anxious to avoid. That is, even while the restoration of substance and context convinces us that its picture of the moral self is more accurate and compelling, the transtradition rational commitments presumed in that restoration are made evident by the pressing issues of social coexistence. When we attempt to work out just how we will talk to one another from within our various traditions, we cannot avoid the need for rational commitments that, however minimal, extend across traditional boundaries. In my reading of communitarian conservatism, the priority of right over good is not defeated, but instead restored in a new, richer, and more deeply convincing form.

Critics of liberalism are not always conservative in this sense, nor do they uniformly marshal their points against structural justice in the form of a revitalization of the virtues. This is nevertheless an influential version of what I shall call the context-restoration project. (I have more to say about this project in a moment.) I do not think some of its most pertinent critical sallies actually hit the mark; in particular, I think a version of neutral political justice can be maintained, even on the basis of the conservative's own commitments. The advantage of such criticisms, however, is that in restoring to view the depth of individual and group moral commitment they show more clearly what is at stake in a well-ordered society. In other words, indicating the incoherence of a purportedly liberal deracinated or unencumbered moral self does not so much defeat liberalism as a *political* theory as it shows once more how necessary it is that we find an adequate defense of political justice if we— thick encumbered moral selves of diverse commitment—are going to live together peacefully and justly.

One influential version of the Kantian limit claim about right and good, the one perhaps closest to Kant himself, works by isolating commitments among all moral actors which transcend the boundaries that arise inevitably between them. Frequently, though not uniformly, these transmoral commitments have been thought to be available in the structure of rationality itself. One such set of responses to criticisms of the conservative communitarian type is explored in Chapter 5, which focuses on the work of Jürgen Habermas. The strategy has been to isolate what are considered universal commitments to rational argument or the fair standards of debate as a basis for political dialogue.[19] On this basis, neo-Kantian theorists attempt to restore the validity of a more far-reaching approach to justice in reformulations of the Kantian strategy of rational justification. These thinkers suggest that only *unconstrained* dialogue is equal to the demands of justifying norms and practices. Presumed here is the notion of an "ideal speech situation," a space in which the force of the better argument alone dominates because it is ruled only by the rational commitments of the concerned speakers: a cooperative search for truth, a performative inability to evade the rational force of arguments, and so on. Norms and practices are justified by agents' unconstrained talk, provided they all have equal access to the podium of argumentation and their locutions are not distorted by force, deceit, or ideological manipulation.

And yet it is not clear that this sort of talk really is unconstrained, or whether the conditions modeled by the ideal situation are the right ones—that is, the ones that could usefully apply to *our* problems in practical political debate and the project of social legitimation associated with justice. Objections of a type associated with "postmodern" theories of right indicate that this neo-Kantian fulfillment of the aspirations of modernity may contain within it an instance of structural injustice: not the tyranny of perfectionism we may fear in the conservative vision of a single moral code, but a closing-off of innovation or plurality in a single project of rational legitimation.[20] And though such

19. See, e.g., Larmore's account in *Patterns of Moral Complexity*, and Stuart Hampshire's in *Innocence and Experience* (Cambridge, Mass.: Harvard University Press, 1989). Hampshire argues that the "cross-frontier and therefore rational standards of fairness in argument" will mediate conflicts among substantive conceptions by keeping the talks going, ensuring that divergent (even hostile) participants in negotiation reach some kind of modus vivendi. Yet standards of fairness in argumentation are not necessarily cross-frontier. See my review of Hampshire in *International Philosophical Quarterly* 31 (1991): 112–14.

20. These criticisms come most pointedly from Jean-François Lyotard, in *The Postmodern Condition: A Report on Knowledge*, trans. Geoff Bennington and Brian Massumi (Minneapolis: University of Minnesota Press, 1984) and (with Jean-Loup Thébaud) *Just Gaming* (Minneapolis: University of Minnesota Press, 1985). As I indicate later, Lyotard defends a dialogic theory of

objections can easily descend into overstatement and hectoring, they neverthe-less indicate that disagreement is a practical problem that will not easily be solved by reference to shared rational commitments. The ideality that arises naturally with the neo-Kantian view, an ideality about discursive structure which inherits from Kantian morality a desire to make these procedures of justification applicable to all rational actors, is open to question. Even if we are prepared to grant that rational agents share some common commitments inso-far as they are rational, are these the commitments that can be thought effective in guiding our talk to the generation of justified political norms, among other things? It will be my concern to show that such commitments, though in some sense unavoidable in the processes of argumentation, are of themselves a base not stable enough to support even the modus vivendi ver-sion of justice I think most feasible given the facts of pluralism. Without the additional impetus provided by political-pragmatic commitments and a more detailed (and therefore less universal) picture of practical judgment—that is, the necessarily not universal commitment of citizens to sharing a single well-ordered society—justice will not issue from the rational commitments isolated in discourse ethics.

So this version of the talker is still too Kantian; it cannot succeed in addressing the deep political differences that motivate the legitimation conversation in the first place. In short, I believe we must somehow join the wide rational commit-ments of communicative competence with narrower pragmatic commitments of determinate citizenship. My conviction is that a contextualized liberalism, a liberalism that takes difference seriously but also emphasizes community self-interpretation, is the best possible answer to the problem of bringing justice and dialogue convincingly together. This combination of the virtues and vices of contemporary political philosophy makes for a dialogic, interpretive version of the liberal priority of right over good. It can, I believe, be modeled in dialogic constraints associated with what I will call civil dialogue, which I describe briefly in the next chapter and defend at great length in the last part of this book. My hope is that these reflections will give us some vocabulary for assessing the character of citizens concretely, and provide a sense of the day-to-day obliga-tions of dialogic citizenship. The necessity of having such a sense is demon-strated in a preliminary way by the fact that calls for a revitalized sphere of public debate—a call common among the thinkers associated with the "herme-

---

justice that is at odds not only with Habermas's reformation of the Enlightenment project but also with MacIntyre's indictment of it.

neutic turn" (Warnke, Walzer, Taylor, Rorty)—will be of little import if we cannot give a positive, concrete account of the kind of debate that is needed. To see this, we must examine more closely the impact of hermeneutic approaches on recent political philosophy.

II. THE HERMENEUTIC TURN

The advantage of hermeneutic political philosophy is that it avoids certain conceptual errors, associated above with Kantian theory, while displaying the positive benefits of political self-interpretation. Instead of hypostatizing a conception of the individual as a locus of rational choice, divorced from his prejudices while choosing among basic-structure options, usually under artificial conditions of epistemological constraint, hermeneutic political philosophy takes seriously the unavoidability of context in human life and action. It is an attempt to acknowledge Charles Taylor's well-known claims in favor of an interpretive social science which would be "unformalizable," lacking "brute data" and a "verification procedure" and therefore "nonarbitrable by further evidence." In cases of conflict, "each side can only make appeal to deeper insight on the part of the other."[21] Taylor goes on to argue that the case for "sciences of man" that admit their own lack of *Wertfreiheit* is based on both negative arguments (current "objectivist" sciences "are founded on intuitions which all do not share") and positive ones (interpretive sciences are "rooted in our own self-definitions, hence in what we are"). In interpretive social science, "a certain measure of insight is indispensable" and so, lacking any algorithm of theoretical proof, we face a kind of conversation among those who disagree, each trying to display the error—or, as it may be in cases of limited insight, the illusion—of their opponents.[22] Since we cannot coherently appeal to some authoritative conception of the ways *things* are, we must appeal to our own set of (possibly conflicting) insights concerning who *we* are. "To say this is not to

21. Charles Taylor, "Interpretation and the Sciences of Man," *Review of Metaphysics* 25 (1971), reprinted in his *Philosophy and the Human Sciences: Philosophical Papers* 2 (Cambridge: Cambridge University Press, 1985), pp. 15–57 (quotations from pp. 52–57); see also, for discussion of concerns raised in the present book, the papers in ibid. entitled "Neutrality in Political Science" and "The Nature and Scope of Distributive Justice."

22. "Interpretation and the Sciences of Man," pp. 53–54. Here Taylor introduces a notion of *Ideologiekritik* into his conception, but it is not pursued very far. In Chapter 5 I give a more explicit and detailed account of how error and illusion differ and how we, as conversational partners, deal with each.

say anything new," says Taylor. "Aristotle makes a similar point in Book I of the *Ethics*. But it is still radically shocking and unassimilable to the mainstream of modern science."[23]

So, while Taylor admits that this may be "a scandalous result according to the authoritative conception of science in our tradition,"[24] hermeneutic investigation displays a positive and deeply important value: it acknowledges what we all know to be the case in our moral and political lives, that the context-eliminative bent of that tradition of science fails to take account of essential things. As moral and political beings, we are always standing somewhere in particular, embedded in language and tradition and determined in innumerable ways by the effects of history,[25] including the effects of prejudice, or forejudgment.[26] These effects cannot be eliminated; moreover, the thought that they can—and the process of rational assessment associated with their elimination—is misleading and perhaps dangerous. According to this view, legitimacy purchased at the price of repudiating particularities of ourselves and our situations (as, prominently, in Rawls's original-position thought experiment) is of false coin. The principles agreed to under conditions of universalizing choice—what Rawls calls a "thin" theory of the good—face a commitment problem when they are imported back to the "thick" contexts in which citizens actually live; at best the importation results in principles under severe "strains of commitment," and at worst it results in principles that are, as Warnke suggests in her lucid survey of the hermeneutic turn in political philosophy, simply irrelevant. In contrast, the aim of hermeneutic political theory is,

23. Ibid., p. 57.
24. Ibid., p. 53.
25. This is one posssible translation of what Hans-Georg Gadamer called *Wirkungsgeschichte*. It is also translated, rather misleadingly, as "tradition" (more about this in Chapter 4). The magnum opus of Gadamer's philosophical hermeneutics, the grounding text of the twentieth-century concern with interpretive theories of meaning, is his *Wahrheit und Methode* (Tübingen: Mohr, 1960), translated into English as *Truth and Method* (New York: Crossroad, 1975). Good book-length expositions of basic Gadamerian theory are provided in Joel Weinsheimer's *Gadamer's Hermeneutics: A Reading of "Truth and Method"* (New Haven: Yale University Press, 1985) and in Georgia Warnke's *Gadamer: Hermeneutics, Tradition, and Reason* (Stanford, Calif.: Stanford University Press, 1989).
26. The presence of forejudgments, and their indispensability in the making of all subsequent judgments, is what creates the (virtuous) "hermeneutic circle." Heidegger's discussion of the hermeneutic circle is at secs. 31–33 of *Being and Time*, trans. John Macquarrie and Edward Robinson (New York: Harper & Row, 1962). The hermeneutic circle—where preunderstanding is confirmed and/or modified by acts of understanding, and thus necessary for beginning the task of understanding—received earlier discussion in nineteenth-century classics of hermeneutic theory, notably in the work of F.D.E. Schleiermacher. See, e.g., ch. 2 of the useful collection by Kurt Müller-Vollmer, *The Hermeneutics Reader* (New York: Continuum, 1990).

according to Warnke, "no longer to construct neutral procedures for a new choice of political principles, but rather to uncover and articulate the principles already embedded in or implied by a community's practices, institutions, and norms of action."[27]

However, difficult issues are raised by such a theory. Warnke—taking seriously and expanding on possibilities opened up by Taylor and Walzer[28]— mentions two, both familiar from general hermeneutic theory. First, *whose* understanding of these shared practices, institutions, and norms of action will count as definitive in an assessment of justice? And second, how are these practices, institutions, and norms of action to be critically assessed, not simply articulated in a manner that leaves everything as it is? I shall call these two issues the *problem of difference* and the *problem of critical purchase*, respectively. It is not difficult to see why they arise as problems for any hermeneutic political philosophy, or its conception of justice. If justice is to be understood as a matter of giving a sensitive and convincing account of our always already existing social norms—bringing what is there into clearer focus, as it were—it will always be relevant to ask who is holding the focusing lens, whether that lens is distorted—indeed, whether it is a lens at all and not simply a piece of flat glass.

Consider the last possibility first. The problem of critical purchase arises in interpretive political theory whenever an interpretation of a given set of practices or institutions is offered, since all such interpretations, insofar as they are hermeneutic, begin only with what is already there and do not allow appeal to external standards of justification or origin. The rejection of foundationalist approaches to political legitimacy allegedly avoids the errors of Kantian political theory, but it appears to court a simple justification of the status quo. If we cannot remove ourselves from our prejudices and traditions and preexisting contexts, how can we ever put them decisively into question? Will we not always end up giving ourselves interpretations that are possibly clearer, but not thoroughly overhauled, articulations of what is already there?

The response to this charge (sometimes marshaled as a charge of conservatism) is familiar to students of hermeneutics,[29] but it is worth mentioning

27. Warnke, "The Hermeneutic Turn," p. 209.

28. Michael Walzer's general defense of the role interpretation plays in certain types of political investigations is found in his *Interpretation and Social Criticism* (Cambridge, Mass.: Harvard University Press, 1987). As mentioned earlier, Walzer's extended discussion of an "interpretive" theory of justice is *Spheres of Justice*.

29. The charge of conservatism is the focus of the celebrated debate between Gadamer and Habermas. Habermas's specific objections began with his review of *Truth and Method* in *Zur*

explicitly in the context of justice theory. The notion of immanent critique, or internal criticism, is what allows us to put *part* of a social cluster of norms, practices, or institutions into question against the background of other parts of the whole cluster, which are granted a provisional firmness for the purposes of assessment.[30] In other words, not being able to stand *outside* our context of social practices does not mean that we cannot stand *aside* from some portion of them as we evaluate their legitimacy on the basis of other practices or principles not under scrutiny now. By implication, any part of our cluster of practices or principles could be put into question in this fashion, including those that, at another moment, we held to be provisionally firm in the interests of assessment in some other quarter. What we cannot do is put the entire cluster into question all at once, for that would involve moving to a standpoint conceptually external to our identity as social actors, a standpoint aptly called (but not aptly defended) as "the view from nowhere."[31] There is no such place, and the desire to stand there and assess everything we do of a piece is akin to the desire to leap over one's shadow: understandable, shared by many of us at one time or other, but in principle incoherent.

Logic der Sozialwissenschaften (Frankfurt: Suhrkamp, 1970). A good English translation of the review is in Wachterhauser, *Hermeneutics and Modern Philosophy*, pp. 243–76, together with Gadamer's reply, "On the Scope and Function of Hermeneutic Reflection," in ibid., pp. 277–99. Habermas replied with several subsequent essays, the best of which is "On Hermeneutics' Claim to Universality," a fusion of two early papers published in the journal *Inquiry* (I discuss these papers in Chapter 5). The combined essay can be found, together with excerpts from *Truth and Method*, in Müller-Vollmer, *The Hermeneutics Reader*. Richard Bernstein's survey article "What Is the Difference That Makes a Difference? Gadamer, Habermas, and Rorty" (in Wachterhauser, *Hermeneutics and Modern Philosophy*, pp. 343–76) provides a good overview of this debate. For its relation to issues of competence and normativity, see esp. Dieter Misgeld, "Discourse and Conversation: The Theory of Communicative Competence and Hermeneutics in Light of the Debate Between Habermas and Gadamer," *Cultural Hermeneutics* 4 (1977): 321–44.

30. For a discussion of the problems and limits of immanent critique, see Charles Larmore, "Tradition, Objectivity, and Hermeneutics," in Wachterhauser, *Hermeneutics and Modern Philosophy*, pp. 147–67. See also, in the same volume, Paul Ricoeur, "Hermeneutics and the Critique of Ideology," pp. 300–339. Ricoeur's interpretive theory, which goes beyond the Gadamer-Habermas debate by, in effect, appropriating elements of each in a highly original way, may represent a position superior to either. See, e.g., Ricoeur's defense of "critical hermeneutics" in his *Interpretation Theory* (Fort Worth: Texas Christian University Press, 1976) and his *The Conflict of Interpretations* (Evanston, Ill.: Northwestern University Press, 1974). Ricoeur attempts to reintegrate "method" with "truth" and thus build in a critical pivot for interpretation in the form he calls "the dialectic of suspicion and recovery."

31. See Thomas Nagel, *The View from Nowhere* (New York: Oxford University Press, 1986), where Nagel argues that our commitment to this view is what allows us to vindicate (some) subjective judgments by matching them to an objective standard.

It may be objected that immanent critique is still not critical enough because it never allows us to employ standards that go beyond what we already have in play. If that is so, the argument that an external standpoint is incoherent is small comfort, since it amounts to little more than saying we are trapped in a cage and cannot get out. We should not, simply because we are trapped, take imprisonment for freedom.[32] But this objection underestimates the critical force of internal assessment. The standards embedded in a tradition or cluster of social practices are not fixed and immutable; they are responsive to challenge. Comparison with other standards is a fruitful process, for new and interesting tensions can create growth in our abilities to judge and criticize. If we were to assess all the parts of our cluster, one after the other, each against a background of a provisionally firm whole, we would not emerge with an exact replica of the cluster with which we began. Conflicting standards would have forced decisions, new and interesting complications would have reinforced other standards, and conviction and principle would have played together a kind of critical fugue resulting in what Rawls, in his own rather reluctant hermeneutical turn, emphasized as "reflective equilibrium."[33] Such equilibrium is never more than provisional, and it is never more than internal, but it is always critical.

Standards of political criticism, then, are found within our social practices,

---

32. This particular instance of making a virtue of necessity is a frequent focus of attack. For the most part, though, the kinds of interpretive theory that are open to this objection—e.g., reader-response theory in literary criticism, and certain versions of the "end-of-philosophy" or "against theory" schools of thought in philosophy—are simply the least developed and least convincing versions of practice-based and/or hermeneutic accounts of justification and legitimacy. Influential examples of such reductive approaches to practice-based thinking include the work of Stanley Fish (for a particularly bold statement, see Fish, "Play of Surfaces: Theory and the Law," in *Legal Hermeneutics: History, Theory, and Practice*, ed. Gregory Leyh [Berkeley and Los Angeles: University of California Press, 1992], pp. 297–316), and the essays collected in W.J.T. Mitchell, ed., *Against Theory: Literary Studies and the New Pragmatism* (Chicago: University of Chicago Press, 1985). But it is a mistake to think that a rejection of external standpoints of criticism means the beginning of "anything-goes" nihilism, or that the rejection of method (as in Gadamer) means the end of all claims to validity in interpretation. I say more about this in the next chapter, where I discuss the work of Richard Rorty, himself sometimes thought to be an exemplar of the reductive and dangerous nihilist, skeptical, or relativist (take your choice) new pragmatism.

33. Rawls's remarks that justification may proceed by seeing whether "the principles which would be chosen [in the original position] match our considered moral convictions of justice" are contained, though not emphasized, in *A Theory of Justice*, pp. 19–21, 47–51, 580–82. Joseph Raz, among others, has criticized Rawls's notion of reflective equilibrium as vague; see Raz, "The Claims of Reflective Equilibrium," *Inquiry* 25 (1982): 307–30. Norman Daniels has attempted to sharpen the justificatory force of reflective equilibrium in his "Reflective Equilibrium and Archimedean Points," *Canadian Journal of Philosophy* 10 (1980): 83–103, and "Wide Reflective Equilibrium and Theory Acceptance in Ethics," *Journal of Philosophy* 76 (1979): 255–82.

institutions, and norms, not outside them in some imagined sphere of pure rational justification. The challenge for hermeneutic political philosophy is to offer interpretations that allow fruitful assessment of parts of these against the background of others. Better interpretations are ones that take more of our (provisionally) shared standards into account when evaluating some particular issue, and that minimize or even eliminate the contradictions that one might expect to arise in a pluralistic political context. Choosing between interpretations will not be easy, for greater or lesser degrees of complexity and sensitivity will not always be obvious, but we can in principle lay claim to the idea that hermeneutic political philosophy possesses enough critical purchase to be worthy of our attention and, more to the point, of our normative approval.

Still, it is not yet clear that there is one and only one "correct" or "best" interpretation of a given section of our social cluster, let alone of the whole.[34] In other words, the problems of politics are not always, or even usually, problems of choosing between two competing interpretations of (say) justice, each of which seems just as good as the other—still less where one of which is, by common consent, better than the other. More often, competing interpretations arise in such a way that no choice between them seems possible because of the depth of reference they make to values or standards that, however contradictory, are nevertheless present in a single society.[35] One common

34. The conflict of interpretations is arguably the central problem of philosophical hermeneutics, and debates about the status and defensibility of decision-procedures or rules for resolving such conflicts are prominent. Gadamer's main concern was to eliminate the temptation of strict "method" in interpretation, restoring cultivation, sensitivity, and (as we shall see) tact to the center of interpretive practice. Brice Wachterhauser's notion, popular with other thinkers, is that hermeneutics provides certain "rules of thumb" concerning valid interpretation: comprehensiveness, semantic depth, inclusivity, and teleological structure (i.e., anticipation of completeness). See Wachterhauser, "Must We Be What We Say? Gadamer on Truth in the Human Sciences," in his *Hermeneutics and Modern Philosophy*, pp. 219–41. These rules of thumb are not strict "disciplining rules," but instead guidelines taken from the subtleties and tacit knowledge of practices themselves and given a kind of theoretical clarity. I say more about this when I come to discuss civility, but see also Warnke's "Habermas and the Conflict of Interpretations" and "Dealing with Interpretive Conflict," chs. 5 and 6 in her *Justice and Interpretation*.

35. This is the basis of Warnke's critique of Ronald Dworkin in "Legal Interpretation and Constraint," ch. 4 in her *Justice and Interpretation*. Dworkin's arguments in favor of the affinity between law and literature heralded an interpretive turn in legal theory (see "How Law Is Like Literature," in Dworkin's *A Matter of Principle* [Cambridge, Mass.: Harvard University Press, 1985]). But in Warnke's analysis, Dworkin turns out to have an odd and decidedly uninterpretive view of interpretation. In deciding cases, his imagined superjudge Hercules (who has infinite patience, time, and resources) simply chooses between a number of rival and incompatible interpretations (see Ronald Dworkin, *Law's Empire* [Cambridge, Mass.: Harvard University Press, 1986]). Warnke's argument is that interpretive conflict is not really like this, and that finding a valid interpretation is never a matter of simple choice between sufficient and equal rivals. I discuss in

example of such a divergence, and one that Warnke and Walzer both employ, is the conflict between justice as provision of basic needs and justice as market freedom. Specifically, the issue is addressed with regard to health-care legislation, where it remains an open, and controversial, question whether the limited resources of care should be distributed in practices, on the basis of norms, of market availability and one's ability to pay; or in practices, backed by norms, of minimum just provision. Or is some combination of these, and perhaps other, visions the answer?

This question can be answered only in the kind of principled legitimation dialogue imagined by the theorists associated with the hermeneutic turn. That is, only the process of just talking itself, not some theoretically constructed decision procedure, can decisively address such a question. Yet as soon as we ask the begged question, namely *what sort* of dialogue this is going to be, the problem of difference shows its true force. For it is not clear that public dialogue of the kind with which most of us are familiar—as exhibited, say, in parliamentary democracy or argument before a supreme court—is equal to such a task. Even if we are inclined, I think rightly, to supplement this kind of public dialogue with a more searching and critical dialogue of intellectual and artistic evaluation, it is not obvious that we possess any standards against which we could judge questions of this tricky kind. Using the programmatic version of the dispute, communitarianism versus libertarianism appears to many people to be just the sort of "philosophical" difference that no amount of talking, however dedicated and well intentioned, will serve to decide. If the route to firm external standards is blocked, as hermeneutic political theory appears to insist, then are we not lost in a sea of confusion, a cacophony of voices each not only claiming impossible amounts of social resources (i.e., more than moderate scarcity allows us to distribute) but also claiming them on the basis of conflicting standards of rational distribution?

Here, in other words, the notion of internal criticism is not yet enough to decide the question, for each of two (or more) imagined interpretations of a cluster of practices, institutions, and norms is apparently able to justify itself against a background of other, provisionally firm norms. It is here that Warnke, and others, make a decisive conversational move. "[T]he task of political theory perhaps should not be to adjudicate between different interpretations of the meaning of our political heritage," she writes. "Perhaps it should

---

more detail the implications of these arguments for legal theory in my "Let's Ask Again: Is Law Like Literature?" *Yale Journal of Law and the Humanities* 6 (1994): 317–52.

rather be trying to discover what each can learn from the other and to encourage a kind of hermeneutic conversation in which different interpretations can become more educated, refined, and sophisticated through their contact with others."[36] The "rational pluralism" underwriting such a conversation is defended best, she thinks, by Habermas's notion of communicative reason, where the idealizing presuppositions of rational discourse (presuppositions modeled in the "ideal speech situation") connect with communicative action in an unconstrained, normative conversation. In the dialogic "space" where only the unforced force of the better argument holds sway, questions of legitimacy and justice (among others) can be assessed for their rational weight, and the constraints associated with force and ideological manipulation can, in principle, be eliminated dialogically. Moreover, this space is defended precisely by recasting Kantian assumptions in dialogic form, saving the aspirations of rational assessment associated with the Enlightenment project, but leaving behind its (dubious) metaphysical foundations.

Yet difficulties persist here. Warnke herself mentions that, though "a communicative conception of rationality allows one to discriminate between those comprehensive interpretations of our social understandings and traditions that are free and rational from those perhaps equally comprehensive interpretations that are constrained by relations of power and ideology,"[37] it may not succeed in resolving all differences of interpretation. This is good, since sometimes, perhaps often, such differences are fruitful and illuminating. In a dynamic public sphere, political interpretation must be fluid—we must be able to learn from as well as challenge one another. To have a hermeneutical conversation of the kind imagined here, we want not a monolithic dialogic crucible of rationality but a rich public debate undistorted by ideology but lively and even fractious, where a variety of voices can be heard and followed. "[W]e need," writes Warnke, "to promote a revitalized public sphere in which we recognize alternative claims about justice as merely alternative interpretations of our experience and traditions."[38] That means, concomitantly, that we need to eliminate barriers to open dialogue and to promote the institutions and mechanisms that will make such dialogue possible.[39]

36. Warnke, "The Hermeneutic Turn," p. 223.
37. Ibid., p. 227.
38. Ibid., p. 228.
39. I have imported a significant change here: like Habermas, Warnke writes consistently of "unconstrained" conversation. I argue later that normative dialogue will have to be constrained by civil commitments; it will nevertheless remain open in the significant sense of being receptive to the possible truth-claim in a rival interpretation.

But how to do it? I dwell on these reflections because I believe they are an eloquent and straightforward account of the best prospects for contemporary political theory. Yet the calls for "a revitalized public sphere," increasingly common in the literature, face a dilemma. Stated abstractly, such a project is not an obvious candidate for any kind of rational objection. (Who could say no to better public debate?) And yet, when details are filled in and the character of the dialogue is sketched more fully, objections proliferate just to the extent that rival interpretations exist. The position is similar to the one regarding "conceptions of the good" that drove some liberals to speak of *neutral* procedures of decision or a *neutral* dialogue of justice.[40] Only a decision unaffected by particular commitments could navigate the shoals of dispute that are characteristic of pluralistic societies. Since, however, it was just these defenses of neutrality that hermeneutic political theory claimed to find incoherent, this is not a valid route of escape here.

The issue may therefore be posed in this fashion. Is there a conception of dialogue (just as there is no conception of the good) thin enough to be immune from particularistic objection? Or is rationality itself, as Habermas suggests, the one and only firm proceduralistic base we require for normative discourse? Even if we accept this latter claim, how are we to assess institutions and mechanisms, to say nothing of citizens, for their degree of rationality? And will such an assessment be enough to decide messy questions of political debate? Or will we need to add other kinds of "thicker" commitment to the pot? I shall now explore one kind of positive answer to the last question, and its important limits. This "first look at civility" will provide the background we need to make sense of the criticisms launched in Part Two of the present study. Then, in Part Three, I strengthen and deepen the account.

---

40. A prominent advocate of the first strategy is Ronald Dworkin (see, among other works by Dworkin, *Law's Empire*). Bruce Ackerman, while agreeing with the dialogic emphasis in focus here, nevertheless argues for a "neutralist" account of the legitimation conversation in his *Social Justice in the Liberal State* (New Haven: Yale University Press, 1980). As I make clear in Chapter 3, in an important revision of *Social Justice*, "Why Dialogue?" (*Journal of Philosophy* 86 [1989]: 5–22), Ackerman defends his version of dialogue in more voluntaristic, contextual terms.

2

A First Look at Civility

In choosing to concentrate on civility in my attempt to save justice theory from the charge of aridity, I am dealing with a notion that already has a long pedigree in liberal theory—and indeed an even longer one in political thinking considered more generally. Rousseau spoke of "the first duties of civility" emerging from the early stages of the social contract, and several thinkers prominent in the Enlightenment made civility a central political notion, drawing on a tradition of civic virtue that stretches back as far as Cicero, if not further.[1] While I shall explore this moral and political background of civility in greater detail in Part Three, it is worth distinguishing immediately the kind of thing I am going to mean by civility.

Rawls claims in *A Theory of Justice* that citizens have "a natural duty of

1. See Rousseau's *Second Discourse*, part 2, par. 33. J. Donald Moon has drawn attention to Rousseau's model of constrained discourse ethics in his "Constrained Discourse and Public Life," *Political Theory* 19 (1991): 202–29, esp. pp. 205–12. For the role of civility in eighteenth-century Britain, see my "Politics and the Polite Society in the Scottish Enlightenment," *Historical Reflections/Réflexions Historiques* 19 (1993): 363–87.

civility not to invoke the fault of social arrangements as a too-ready excuse for not complying with them, nor to exploit loopholes in the rules to advance our interests."[2] This claim is motivated by Rawls's general worries about the doubts we may have concerning state authority once basic structural principles are chosen: do we obey or not? is there any sense of obligation to do so? Civility here demands that imperfection in social institutions cannot provide prima facie justification for disobedience. Leslie Green made this claim a cornerstone of his argument that civility is a basic civic virtue, weaker but more justifiable than the civic virtue of obedience.[3] Imperfection does not justify anarchism; civility is the virtue of citizens that allows the state to have authority, while at the same time allowing us to exercise our faculties of critical judgment about state institutions.

My sense of civility is related but distinct. For these thinkers, civility functions as an element of what Hume called "the circumstances of justice"—those social conditions and conventions that formed the conditions of the possibility of social justice. Under this reading, civility is one of the things that makes citizens capable of being just; it is not justice itself. My reading of justice differs, and largely because the commitment to interpretive political theory means we are no longer in the business, as Hume was, of providing a single determinate answer to the question "What is justice?" We are instead attempting to specify conversational conditions under which citizens can begin to negotiate their political differences. Here it makes sense to speak of justice *as* civility.[4] So, in keeping with the dialogic emphasis of this study, I shall argue that civility is indeed a basic civic virtue, but one primarily focused on political conversation. It is a feature of our talk about justice, not our attitude about the results of that conversation. In that sense, I have in mind the idea of a vibrant and politically engaged set of conversational practices, all of them governed by a commitment to self-restraint and sensitivity.

Some recent liberal thinkers have spoken in these terms of civility, but none has yet given the virtue of civility what I consider its due.[5] At the same time,

---

2. Rawls, *A Theory of Justice*, p. 355.

3. Leslie Green, *The Authority of the State* (Oxford: Clarendon Press, 1988), ch. 9.

4. I thank Leslie Green for helpful discussion on this point.

5. See, e.g., James S. Fishkin, *The Dialogue of Justice* (New Haven: Yale University Press, 1992), part 3. Fishkin underestimates the role of civility in political dialogue because, like Habermas, he *overestimates* the role of reason in his notion of "a self-reflective society." I say more about this theory later. Two multiauthor works, not of political theory but of contemporary sociology, are also worth mentioning here. *Civility and Citizenship in Liberal Democratic Societies* (New York: Paragon House, 1992) is the proceedings of a roundtable discussion of comparative citizenship in the West; *Pushing the Faith: Proselytism and Civility in a Pluralistic World*

some other recent defenses of civility have veered alarmingly toward the all-is-healable rhetoric of self-help literature and do nothing to give civility a more secure place in our political culture.[6] In this chapter I consider one prominent liberal thinker who combines my concerns with conversation, contextualization, and civility—but does so in an unsatisfactory way. I argue that our dissatisfaction with Richard Rorty's version of civil conversation points the way to a more critical, and more emancipatory, version of it. I do not mean, by providing this preliminary sketch, to help myself to conclusions that in fact require argument. I only mean to paint, in broad strokes, an outline of my answer—an answer that can be presented in detail only after dealing at length with available alternatives. The point of this "first look" is to provide necessary background, and to clarify the argumentative stakes, for the critical assessments of Part Two. It also provides an idea of what the interpretive rereading of the priority-of-right claim might plausibly be. Seeing the limits of Rorty's attempt shows, among other things, just how large the task of dialogic justice theory is.

I. CONTEXTUALIZED LIBERALISM

If we accept the charge that political theory ignores social and cultural context only at its peril (see Chapter 1), we must begin to seek viable alternatives. What are the best prospects for restoring context to political theory? It may be, as Charles Larmore suggests in his reformation of Kantian ethics, that we need to rehabilitate a notion of *phronesis* or practical judgment as a supplement to the formal conditions of justification.[7] Without this concrete notion of judg-

---

(New York: Crossroad, 1988) discusses the issue of propagating the Jewish faith in pluralistic societies.

6. M. Scott Peck, the American "psychospiritual" guru, published *A World Waiting To Be Born: Civility Rediscovered* (New York: Bantam Books, 1993) in an avowed attempt to discourage sharp practices and anticommunity feeling. But Peck's book is little more than a series of pedantic excurses and self-serving anecdotes that stitch together elements of a largely unexamined definition of civility. (I offer an examined definition of it in Part Three of the present work.) For a work of a similar mind adorned by more respectable scholarly trappings, see Glenn E. Tinder, *Tolerance: Toward a New Civility* (Amherst: University of Massachusetts Press, 1976). Tinder's arguments in favor of toleration typically quote the Bible or refer hopefully, and rather vaguely, to Buberian notions of dialogue.

7. Larmore, *Patterns of Moral Complexity.* Steven B. Smith makes the same point in a short critical passage on Habermas found in his *Hegel's Critique of Liberalism: Rights in Context* (Chicago: University of Chicago Press, 1989), pp. 244–46.

ment, we have no interpretive measure of success in our actual discursive encounters, and no standard by which to judge the value of continuing the search for agreement on one level or, perhaps, of moving to other spheres of discussion. We talkers need to examine the prospect of our common desire to understand one another's diverse commitments, and to assess the political solutions—or compromises—that will be possible on their basis. And for this we need a kind of sensitivity and openness to diverse claims that I think is at odds with superimposed neutrality or a strict orientation only to the unforced force of the better argument—options for dialogic justice theory explored in Chapters 3 and 5, respectively. My interlocutor and I are members of a real community, with pressing needs of social cooperation. Our disagreement must be mediated, not overcome. Since our real differences are irreconcilable ones, we also exhibit the difference between real community and any ideal speech community anticipated by our rational commitments or created by gag-rules of justification.

The most detailed, if also the most controversial, articulation of this sort of criticism against rational consensus had been provided by Richard Rorty. Rorty's position invites caricature and objection in about equal measure, and he frequently speaks in a brisk, either-you-see-it-or-you-don't manner that philosophers find uncongenial. Still, the position he defends is a powerful one that avoids the idealizing problems of Kantian theory and attempts to give a concrete characterization of legitimation dialogue and the citizen who speaks it.

Rorty's motivations may be stated with only slight exaggeration as a desire to take Gadamer's contextualist view of understanding more seriously than Gadamer did himself. That is, where Gadamer attempted, by a criticism and distancing from method, to preserve a truth-claim in the *Geisteswissenschaften* as much as in the *Naturwissenschaften*, Rorty wants to overturn this distinction inherited from Dilthey and move past the old-style notion of truth-claim in general. He wants, in other words, to be not a "weak textualist" of Gadamer's sort—the kind who, in wanting to retain notions of truth and objectivity, arguably opens himself up to objections of relativism—but a "strong textualist" who plunges headlong into the inescapability of context.[8]

___

8. Rorty himself poses the weak textualist / strong textualist distinction in his "Nineteenth-Century Idealism and Twentieth-Century Textualism," in his *Consequences of Pragmatism* (Minneapolis: University of Minnesota Press, 1982), p. 152. He distinguishes both between the weak Dilthey and Gadamer and the strong Nietzsche and James, and between the weak Lionel Trilling and M. H. Abrams and the strong Harold Bloom and Michel Foucault. In both cases, the former pair fail to see that concentrating "method" on the text to exhibit its "inner workings" or "effects"

By doing so, he grasps one horn of the following dilemma that most philosophers will not touch. If understanding and meaning are context-dependent, it follows that no transcontextual claims, even claims about truth or rationality, can be coherently made. Either we accept the limitations of our conceptual point of view, or we struggle to isolate some features of language or thought that we can put to ourselves as common presuppositions. To do the latter would seem to commit us to a rationalism that is at odds with contextualism; to do the former would seem to lock us into relativistic isolation.

Rorty's reply to this charge of relativism has not varied, in recent papers, from his early claims (1) that it is a superficial objection to his pragmatism and (2) that relativism is not a position anyone really holds.[9] Relativism is the thesis that any set of views (in our case, any set of moral views—but the reply holds too for epistemological issues) is as good as any (at least one) other. "No one holds this view," Rorty has said. "Except for the occasional cooperative freshman, one cannot find anybody who says that two incompatible opinions on an important topic are equally good."[10] To make such a claim would require us—at least one of us—to stand in a position not within either of, or any of, the views under discussion. It would require a God's-eye view—in other words, a view from nowhere. Since there is no such place, for this is just what contextualism tells us, relativism is not a view that can be coherently implied by a hermeneutic move away from Enlightenment-style reason.[11] Rorty's

---

is just another species of what Heidegger called "the metaphysics of presence." Richard Bernstein puts Rorty on the strong side in his "What Is the Difference That Makes a Difference? Gadamer, Habermas, and Rorty," in Wachterhauser, *Hermeneutics and Modern Philosophy*. Bernstein argues correctly that Gadamer and Habermas, appearances to the contrary, share with each other more modern and justificatory traits than either does with the postmodern, contingent Rorty.

9. The foundations of this view were laid in Rorty's *Philosophy and the Mirror of Nature* (Princeton: Princeton University Press, 1979) and expressed concisely in "Pragmatism, Relativism, and Irrationalism," in his *Consequences of Pragmatism*, pp. 160–75. It has been pressed most consistently and most recently in the Rorty collection *Objectivity, Relativism, and Truth, Philosophical Papers 1*, esp. in the introduction, "Texts and Lumps," "Pragmatism Without Method," and "Is Natural Science a Natural Kind?"

10. Rorty, "Pragmatism, Relativism, and Irrationalism," p. 166. There is a vast philosophical literature on the topic of objectivity and relativism, but an illuminating and wide-ranging discussion of recent controversies by a historian is Peter Novick's remarkable *That Noble Dream: The "Objectivity Question" and the American Historical Profession* (New York: Cambridge University Press, 1988). For Novick's helpful—if brisk—survey of philosophical influences, and their relation to developments in literary and legal theory, anthropology, and the social sciences, see ibid., ch. 15, "The Center Does Not Hold."

11. This being so, objections to relativism most often miss the mark; they say more about the objector and his or her worries than anything about a contextualist or anti-essentialist

position is therefore not "relativistic"—he does not believe, nor could anyone believe, that it is *just as good as* some other position—but it is "ethnocentric": it defines, though loosely and provisionally, a group of those for whom the kinds of positions Rorty takes are intelligible and, possibly, defensible.

Characterizing this group will be a serious problem, as I indicate shortly. There is also a difficulty in the linkage Rorty constructs between his critiques of traditional epistemology and metaphysics and his vision of liberal politics. It may, after all, be possible—if rather limited—to remain happily ethnocentric about politics, locked into speaking only to those for whom a conversational justification seems necessary and appropriate. But philosophical claims are not so easily boxed in, and Rorty's work faces the dilemma, frequently noticed by his critics, of appearing to make claims whose status *as claims* actively undermines what they purport to say. That is, unless Rorty can convincingly demonstrate that he is not attempting to get at the truth when he describes to us what goes on in our misguided attempts to get at the truth, it remains systematically unclear what status his work should have for us. The vocabulary of therapy and critique goes only so far in this quarter—certainly we can submit to overhauls of our conceptual language and its temptations, but beneath that are we not always committed to a general project of "getting things right" with respect to our practices, including the practices of rational inquiry? And if not—if, on the contrary, our practices of inquiry are just as specific, historical, and contextualized as our practices of novel-writing or politics or basketball—then what sort of purchase can they have on necessary criteria of judgment, such as truth and falsity?

This dilemma is not quite the dilemma of the relativist, of course, for that dilemma turns on the making of an explicit relativist claim. And Rorty's reply to the bare charge of relativism is convincing. Some philosophers, especially recently, have taken such a reply to indicate that objectivity is once more

---

project. The main reason for this is that the worst consequences of the positions called "relativist" can be generated only by the prior (and unnecessary) commitment to what Barbara Herrnstein Smith calls "objectivist axiology": the strong view of objective truth sometimes associated with naive or common-sense realism. Her version of the relativism specter is a mocking progression of dangers, sketched in her *Contingencies of Value: Alternative Perspectives for Critical Theory*. It begins with charges of self-contradiction and fallacy, moves through "fatuous forbearance" and "Panglossism and status-quoism," and ends with "the breakdown of law and morality" and therefore "the Gulag, the Nazi death camps" (pp. 152–53). Her book's main point, shrewdly argued, is that noting the presence of contingency or variability in judgment—including interpretive judgment—does not lead to this gallery of horrors but to better judgments.

available after all in epistemology *and* morals: to the extent that what Bernard Williams called "the truth in relativism" can be shown to be incoherent, it follows for them that objective truth can once more be vindicated.[12] They too surrender, as it appears they must, the so-called detachment view of objectivity that requires us to stand outside ourselves and judge the truth of propositions or firmness of concepts. Yet, inside a given context or horizon, they suggest, it still makes sense to speak of "true" and "objective" because of what Jonathan Lear has called "the disappearing 'we.' "[13] When we say "true," it follows, if detachment is incoherent, that this really means "true for us"; the view *sub specie aeternitatis* is no more accessible to us than immortality or godhood. Yet the "for us" drops out once we see that detachment is indeed impossible, no longer an option to be entertained and that our always contextualized truth-claims fail to meet. We are left speaking only to those who understand us, true; but then no other situation is, after all, intelligible. Objectivity is vindicated by taking contextualization seriously, not by attempting to overcome it in a project doomed to conceptual failure.

While Rorty sometimes speaks in a manner similar to this, he is more willing than most thinkers simply to jettison the vocabulary of objectivity, along with a number of other "false gods" inherited from the Enlightenment: rationality, a theory of knowledge, certainty, generality, and so on. This throwaway approach to the traditional vocabulary of philosophizing is, for him, immensely liberating. It allows us to reconceptualize our situation, to see it anew in its possibilities and fragilities. For, if Rorty is right, context goes, as he would say, "all the way down": there is nothing firm in the world if "firm" means not subject to linguistic interpretation and determination. He does not want to save a truth-claim for the human and social sciences, seen as still distinct from the (firmer) natural sciences. He wants instead to rid us alto-

---

12. Hilary Putnam's "internal realist" position is similar to this one, and indeed the Quinean view of epistemology as sailing, more or less inevitably, on a "Neurath's ship" is now dominant. See Putnam's *Reason, Truth, and History* (Cambridge, Mass.: Harvard University Press, 1981), where he criticizes the "God's-eye view" misconception—and thereby refutes the relativist label—at pp. 49–50 and 54. Rorty has recently attempted to clarify his relation to Putnam and relativism; see his "Putnam and the Relativist Menace," *Journal of Philosophy* 90 (1993): 443–61. Christopher Dustin makes the objectivist argument for ethics in "Ethics and the Possibility of Objectivity" (Ph.D. diss., Yale University, 1991). Geoffrey Sayre-McCord, ed., *Essays on Moral Realism* (Ithaca: Cornell University Press, 1988), has many illuminating contributions, esp. Sayre-McCord's "Introduction: The Many Moral Realisms."

13. Jonathan Lear, "The Disappearing 'We,' " *Proceedings of the Aristotelean Society,* suppl. vol., 1984. See also Lear's "Ethics, Mathematics, and Relativism," in *Essays on Moral Realism,* pp. 76–94.

gether of what Donald Davidson has called the scheme/content distinction, the distinction that allows us to conceive of a preexisting (unconceptualized) world that is "carved up" in various ways by our conceptual schemes.[14] This notion of the preconceptual world is itself a conceptual creation, a chimera of enormous usefulness in vindicating the claims of natural science. If we can think our way outside of it, remind ourselves that we have created this notion of the world, it would render the claims of the natural sciences no less contingent than those of literary criticism, sociology, or politics.

Contingency, a favorite buzz-word of Rorty's latest work, is here divorced from its metaphysical partner necessity, cut loose in the world as a kind of reminder of just how provisional and flimsy our structures of understanding really are. They all, in other words, could be otherwise than they are. Here fragility and liberation are coexistent possibilities. We have to see just how weak our useful notions and concepts are. They are not woven into the fabric of the universe, or stuck in any other kind of metaphysical glue. And so they could come apart at any moment (the demise of liberal institutions of tolerance into tyranny and authoritarianism is a particular bugbear of Rorty's here). At the same time, this lack of necessity allows us endlessly and creatively to reconceptualize our situation. Rorty's "anti-representational" or "anti-essentialist" position is thus one in which "one does not view knowledge as a matter of getting reality right, but rather as a matter of acquiring habits of action for coping with reality."[15] So stated, the link between Rorty's views on epistemological and metaphysical questions, on the one hand, and his liberal politics, on the other, comes into clearer focus. His position on our ways of thinking entails the possibility that, as well as getting worse, things can always get better—meaning, here, that we can at any moment adopt better or worse ways of coping with reality. "An anti-representationlist view of inquiry leaves one without a skyhook with which to escape from the ethnocentrism produced by acculturation," Rorty says, "but . . . the liberal culture of recent times has found a strategy for avoiding the disadvantages of ethnocentrism."[16] The point is to stop looking for "skyhooks" and start looking for "toeholds"—small fissures of disagreement and dissatisfaction

14. See Donald Davidson, "On the Very Idea of a Conceptual Scheme," in his *Inquiries into Truth and Meaning* (New York: Oxford University Press, 1986); and "A Coherence Theory of Truth and Knowledge," in *Truth and Interpretation: Perspectives on the Philosophy of Donald Davidson*, ed. Ernest LePore (Oxford: Basil Blackwell, 1986).

15. Richard Rorty, "Anti-Representationalism, Ethnocentrism, and Liberalism," introduction to his *Objectivity, Relativism, and Truth*, p. 2.

16. Ibid.

with our fellows that allow us to look beyond where we happen to be standing and talking now. And so, far from being in tension, Rorty's views on philosophy and on politics actually converge: antirepresentationalism is precisely the conceptual precondition for a renewed openness to the project of climbing up toehold by toehold. Because there is no metaphysical distinction between politics and philosophy, there is also no true ethnocentric dilemma. The vocabulary of epistemic inquiry is just as contingent and historically determined—just as practice-specific and community-specific—as the vocabulary of liberalism.[17]

There is, then, a utopian and indeed transcendental element embedded in Rorty's contextualized politics. But this is a utopianism of liberal tolerance and openness, a triumph of persuasion over force. Unlike Habermas, Rorty is not willing to argue that these positive features can be considered rational presuppositions of argument, except as a matter of contingent fact. (Hence his defense of "consensus," but without the adjective "rational" that Habermas is so keen to attach to it.[18]) Yet, at the same time, he does not believe this utopianism and its possibilities of directed reform commit him to what Jean-François Lyotard calls, dismissively, a meta-narrative of emancipation.[19] Indeed, in distinguishing his first-order narrative of cosmopolitanism from any rationalist meta-narrative of emancipation, Rorty believes he has put himself on the side of the postmodern angels, and done so incidentally in such a way as to make Lyotard and other fashionable French thinkers appear frivolous. I will not consider the details of that internecine dispute here, though they make diverting reading. I want to concentrate instead on how Rorty's extreme contextualism fits into the general hermeneutic turn in political philosophy.

Rorty claims, following Judith Shklar, that liberals are people who "put cruelty first"—that is, who see cruelty as the worst of the "ordinary vices,"

17. It may be, however, that in taking up this position Rorty is guilty of bad faith. That is, he does not really believe—could not believe—that "true" and "false" are no more grounded than, e.g., "tasty" and "cute." The bad faith is demonstrated by his willingness to address us with precisely those tools of epistemic inquiry—evidence, argument, consistency—that are taken to be defining features of truth-seeking. The only possible reply to this charge (ironically, a version of the charge he frequently brings against others) is for Rorty to insist that he talks the way he has been acculturated to talk, and to the community for whom his views have some relevance. But this is thin soup indeed. For more on this issue, see Ermanno Bencivenga, "Rorty and I," *Philosophical Forum* 24 (1993): 307–18. (I thank Mark Migotti for this point.)

18. See Rorty's "Habermas and Lyotard on Postmodernity," *Praxis International* 4 (1984): 32–44. This article also appears in Rorty's *Essays on Heidegger and Others: Philosophical Papers 2* (Cambridge: Cambridge University Press, 1991), pp. 164–76.

19. Ibid. Lyotard's definition of postmodernism as "incredulity towards meta-narratives" is defended in his *The Postmodern Condition*.

the worst thing we do.[20] He takes this claim to be self-evident, suggesting (as usual) that he is talking now only to those who see the prima facie force of the claim. On the basis of this commitment, and others already mentioned (persuasion over force, openness), Rorty is able to tell himself a story about the liberal experiment, the attempt to create a social space in which divergent personal visions—sometimes called "conceptions of the good"—can be pursued independently of interference. Liberal states are those in which this pursuit is safeguarded against the intolerant imposition of other views, however majoritarian they may turn out to be. They are committed, in other words, to the priority of right over good, and insofar as that is true they draw a firm public/private distinction: my pursuit of a personal vision of the good life is my business, and mine alone, just as long as it remains true that this pursuit does not impinge on the personal visions being worked out by my neighbors.[21]

It follows in turn that the criteria of personhood and citizenship diverge in a liberal state. As citizens we must be committed to the free and open exchange of views that will allow a well-ordered state to emerge. Here we are equal participants in a general conversation about legitimacy, equal defendants before the law, and equal actors in the polling booth. As persons, by contrast, wide differences and even enmity may be allowed to emerge—indeed, anything else is impossible to imagine. You and I have very different ideas about how to live a good life. Mine involve a nontaxing job, watching football on Sundays, having a beer-fridge in the rec room, and intense devotion to my wife and children. Yours involve a demanding career as an architect, a love of classical music, and an ability to have casual extramarital affairs. Or I am a Roman Catholic and you are a Muslim, both of us coexisting with the witty secular humanist down the hall. In each imaginable case, what is crucial is that personal differences—differences that are sometimes, perhaps often, irreconcilable—are present. For pragmatic reasons, we abstract from these differences when we talk politically—not because they can ever

20. See the papers collected in Rorty's *Contingency, Irony, and Solidarity* (Cambridge: Cambridge University Press, 1989), esp. "The Contingency of a Liberal Community," "Private Irony and Liberal Hope," and "Solidarity." Shklar's claims about "putting cruelty first" are made in her brilliant essay *Ordinary Vices* (Cambridge, Mass.: Harvard University Press, 1984), esp. the chapter so titled.

21. Many critics have found this firm distinction all too firm—Stephen K. White refers to Rorty's public and private spheres as "airtight boxes"—yet if we take other aspects of the argument seriously, they cannot be so conceived: the public/private line itself must always be under dialogic investigation and, crucially, must be so on the public side of it. See White's *Political Theory and Postmodernism* (Cambridge: Cambridge University Press, 1991), p. 93.

be unimportant to us, but because coexistence is the one goal that trumps them all when we come to discuss what Rawls called "basic social structure."

Rorty must, crucially, tell this tale of tolerant liberalism without any reference to neutral principles of justification, and without committing himself to any meta-structures of defense (as in, e.g., the universal commitments of rationality). His cosmopolitan liberalism can be, in principle, extended to universal dimensions—that is one of its crucial traits—but it does not do this on the basis of some already shared universal competence. Not even language ability, as the medium of political discussion, is enough in itself to ensure universal extension. That can only be purchased at the price of long and difficult conversation. As he is fond of saying, the only criterion for success in this conversation is its continuance. The irony in play here, as Rorty reminds us in some recent restatements of the position, is that we sometimes speak and act just as if we (and our close fellows) have access to the one and only moral truth, while at other times we surrender this kind of claim on principle in a conversation governed only by openness, sensitivity, tolerance, persuasion, and the idea that there is nothing worse between people than cruelty.

Of course, irony is not to everyone's taste. Nor, indeed, is it clear that all members of even a liberal state would agree, without further ado, that cruelty is the worst thing we do. Yet I do not think Rorty is open here to a now-aging objection to liberalism—that in defending neutral procedures of governance it has no choice but to adduce nonneutral bases of argument. This is partly because such an objection misses the main point of liberalism, namely that it does not claim to be neutrally defended, but only to issue in (some) neutral procedures of evaluation; partly also it is because Rorty never makes the mistake of invoking a vocabulary of neutrality, explicitly rejecting that line of defense. Rather, the objection that seems to be still alive is one hinted at earlier, one I will call (in another sense now) the problem of the disappearing "we."

Rorty is good at making the claim that his "post-modern bourgeois liberalism" never oversteps the bounds of coherence by seeking quixotically to speak to all the people all the time. We are justified, he says, in seeing some potential interlocutors as, for one reason or another, beyond the pale: mad, or impossibly intolerant, or dogmatic, or domineering. In so seeing them, we do not need to appeal to standards of rationality and find them irrational (Rorty wants to suggest, not surprisingly, that this is one more piece of dichotomous vocabulary we can do without). It also follows, because we can make judgments of this sort, that this liberalism is not the caricatured "wet" liberalism that backs itself into a corner of tolerance where no value judgments are possible. But the consequence of these two advantages is that our community of interlocutors has a limit—some people are inside, and some are outside. In my view, the simple fact of such a limit is not yet a problem, though there are those who would disagree, but what *is* worrying is the placing and control of the limit.

II. THE DISAPPEARING "WE"

Rorty's project—or "mission," as Rebecca Comay calls it[22]—is to save the aspirations of modernity (civil society, technological progress, parliamentary democracy) without the foundations of modernity. So Rorty's attitude to the community of relevant speakers is, as we saw, defiantly ethnocentric: those to whom we should feel compelled to justify our actions, norms, and institutions are just those who feel the force of the kinds of (liberal) argument we give. Rorty's political writings are shot through with "we"-descriptions—"we liberal intellectuals," "we liberal democrats," "we Western liberal intellectuals," "we pragmatists," etc.—that define not only his current sort of self-identification but also his relevant ethnos.[23] "To be ethnocentric," he writes, "is to divide the human race into the people to whom one must justify one's beliefs and the others. The first group—one's *ethnos*—comprises those who share enough of

22. Rebecca Comay, "Interrupting the Conversation: Notes on Rorty," *Telos* 69 (1986): 83–98. I focus on this version of the many criticisms of Rorty from the left because it concerns itself explicitly with the issues of conversation and the imagined participants in it. Rorty classes Comay's objections among these others: Richard Bernstein, "Philosophy in the Conversation of Mankind," *Review of Metaphysics* 33 (1980): 745–76, and "One Step Foward, Two Steps Back: Richard Rorty on Liberal Democracy and Philosophy," *Political Theory* 15 (1987): 538–63; Christopher Norris, "Philosophy as a Kind of Writing: Rorty on Post-Modern Liberal Culture," in his *The Contest of the Faculties* (London: Methuen, 1986); Nancy Fraser, "Solidarity or Singularity: Richard Rorty Between Romanticism and Technocracy," in her *Unruly Practices: Power, Discourse, and Gender in Contemporary Theory* (Minneapolis: University of Minnesota Press, 1989); Frank Lentricchia, "Rorty's Cultural Conversation," *Raritan* 3 (1983): 136–41; Lentricchia, *Criticism and Social Change* (Chicago: University of Chicago Press, 1983); and Milton Fisk, "The Instability of Pragmatism," *New Literary History* 17 (1985): 23–30. Though Rorty is fairly scrupulous about listing objections to his political views, he has only scratched their surface; there are many others of a similar mind.

23. Novick, *That Noble Dream*, notes that Rorty's own father, James—one of the "six liberals" to whom *Contingency, Irony, and Solidarity* is dedicated—finds this "we"-vocabulary highly suspect. Americans, the elder Rorty wrote in *Where Life Is Better* (New York, 1936), would do well to get rid of "the democratic dogma expressed in the phrase 'We, the people.' We have never had in this country any such identity of interest as is implied in that first person plural" (p. 169). See Novick, *That Noble Dream*, p. 572.

one's beliefs to make fruitful conversation possible." Comay sees Rorty's ethnocentric descriptions constricting further and further until, unsurprisingly, Rorty is left talking to himself in a conversation Comay is not certain ever actually began. "It is a 'we' which is defiantly parochial and names itself without flinching," she writes. " 'We' does not proselytize; 'we' is as we are. To claim more than this is sanctimoniousness; to claim less, bad manners."[24] And attempts to overcome the parochial nature of the "we," in teleological adventuring or rationalist posturing (Habermas, Peirce, Putnam), are marks of cowardice—a failure to face the reality of social contingency, a refusal to take history and time seriously, a childish longing for what Nietzsche called "metaphysical comfort."

The result is, according to Comay, a position that puts philosophy both higher and lower than it ought to stand: higher because Rorty makes claims about society's conversational nature that are hopeful (and deluded) reflections of his own gentlemanly proclivities; lower because this conversation, carried on with due decorum, leaves everything as it is, the task of structural assessment surrendered for good and all. "Secure in his privilege, aristocratic in his protests, Rorty only flatters philosophy as he chastizes it, and sets out to elevate its 'tone,' " she writes. "Effete, cloistered, reduced to the innocuous prettiness of l'art pour l'art, philosophy ends up only affirming the tyranny of the consumer society which it can in fact neither negate nor properly engage."[25] And so "[c]ulture is both aggrandized and debilitated here, and philosophy both idealized and belittled."[26]

The cheerfulness of Rorty's anti-essentialism, his simultaneous raising up and casting down of philosophical aspiration, masks the real conflict and repression built into his notion of liberal conversation. The problem with the foundationless project of legitimation is not that it is relativistic but that it is dangerously repressive: a conclusion that has come crashing down on many leftist critics of Rorty's easygoing liberalism.[27] The following quotation from Comay sums up a host of objections to Rorty:

Had Rorty actually worried more about getting the picture to "fit," he would have, of course, had to deal with the discrepancies and contradictions agonizing society as a whole, rendering the whole idea of "conversation" pretty academic, in more than one sense, and bordering on the

24. Comay, "Interrupting the Conversation," pp. 84–85.
25. Ibid., p. 94.
26. Ibid.
27. For a powerful recent critique of this kind, see Bencivenga's "Rorty and I," in which he dissects the two sides—fuzzy and threatening—of Rorty's political theory.

absurd. He would have had to face the fact . . . that the Jeffersonian "tolerance" he cherishes in his Western liberal democracies may be more "repressive" than real; that exhortations to "civility" . . . may, when applied abstractly, serve above all to legitimate the exclusion of marginal or dissident voices from the conversation; that the appearance of open pluralistic debate may, as often as not, more often than not, mask the monolithic interests of the dominant power group; that the virtues of civic tolerance have in any case been rendered pretty theoretical by the ideological distortion endemic to late capitalism; and, finally, that the strictly cultural satisfactions he promotes—and here Rorty's "we" contracts easily and spontaneously— . . . not only remain necessarily restricted and elitist, but may indeed preempt and deflect the drive to fulfil more profane, noncultural satisfactions.[28]

"When Rorty actually participates in the ongoing conversation," adds the political theorist William Connolly, "he constantly wards off dangerous or disturbing possibilities within it."

Rorty's language tranquilizes and comforts his fellow Americans, first, by celebrating the technocratic values, self-conceptions, and economic arrangements operative in (though not exhaustive of) American institutions and, second, by implying that once these endorsements have been offered there is not much more to be said. Rorty's prose inhibits discursive mobilizations of political energies; it closes the conversation before it manages to disturb the sense that all is well with America.

So, Connolly concludes, confessing his frustration with the ultimate philosophical moving target, "Rorty drops out of the conversation just when it should become most intense and demanding."[29]

Insofar, then, as "keeping the conversation going" is the only goal Rorty's dialogical pragmatism can offer us, it is at bottom not merely conservative (it leaves everything as it is) but reactionary (it casts out those who do not agree that everything should be left as it is). "Where jovial appeals to good sportsmanship don't work," Comay says, referring to Rorty's decidedly nonconversational rhetorical style,

28. Comay, "Interrupting the Conversation," p. 91.
29. William Connolly, "Mirror of America," *Raritan* 3 (1983): 129, 131.

there is always the threat of expulsion. "We," unswerving in its solidarity, becomes as stern as an Un-American Activities Committee. You don't cooperate, we see no point in continuing this conversation. This is, of course, the final privilege of the post-modern "we": no longer pretending to be more than we are, we can now be just what we are— "we" *simpliciter*, a tensionless monad, without discomfort or change.[30]

The serious mistake here is Rorty's notion that his rejection of traditional philosophical vocabulary is the royal road to political emancipation. In fact, according to Comay, Rorty's historicism is too partial, in both senses, to underwrite any genuinely critical program of politics. "To give philosophy both less and more than this," she writes, "would require a genuine historicism: it would replace an acquiescent pragmatism with a form of critical praxis; it would replace a yea-saying conversation with a speech that has learned to say no."[31]

Rorty's "we," then, shrinks in the end to a small circle of the like-minded (he once referred to it as a kind of gentleman's club) whose only wish is to keep the disrupters and willful nonparticipants in conversation out of the way. Even congenial anti-essentialist allies of Rorty are likely to balk at *this* exclusive community. "To the extent that the concept of communal solidarity denies or obscures both *difference* and *dynamics*, including *internal* difference and dynamics," notes Barbara Herrnstein Smith, "it can only encourage the illusion, undesirable for political theory and dangerous for political practice, that there is some mode of thought or set of principles that would ultimately eliminate all difficult and disagreeable encounters with other people."[32] The defense of a pragmatic legitimation conversation founders, in this objection, on its inability to characterize a conversation that would be genuinely liberating for most of us, indeed the inability to make conversation itself a compelling model for fruitful social interaction.

I think the objection is overstated—but not because Rorty has succeeded in this task, or because (in his own reply to Comay et al.) it is an objection that

---

30. Comay, "Interrupting the Conversation," p. 96.
31. Ibid., p. 94.
32. Smith, *Contingencies of Value*, p. 168. Smith suggests that Rorty's attempts to distance himself from the relativist label lead him unwittingly into an implied essentialism about "community" or "solidarity." She bases this charge on an unsympathetic reading of a single article, "Solidarity or Objectivity." In all fairness, however, Rorty's most illuminating articles on these issues—especially the ones in which he too adopts Smith's vocabulary of "contingency"—were published later than her study of value language and its pitfalls.

could arise only in just the sort of liberal conversation of the kind he has been defending.[33] The objection is overstated, rather, because it does not allow for the possibility that the most compelling version of social conversation can both include and pass beyond the clubbishness Rorty demonstrates. It is, indeed, a version of the conversation that can be found in Rorty's work, especially of recent vintage, but that remains overshadowed by his aggressive, sometimes sneering remarks about ethnocentricity and the misleading desires of philosophers.

This version of the conversation begins, as it must, with the solidarity and like-mindedness of the club, but it goes beyond that self-enclosure in response to external pressures, in particular demands concerning coexistence with other clubs. Rorty likens the second part of the conversation to a bazaar, a teeming and often chaotic chorus of voices, each clamoring for its own interests to be met. The basic regulator of this second conversation is the pragmatic desire for peaceful coexistence, and a generally shared desire to have one's club do as well as possible. It is essential that we mark this division between clubs and bazaar as intranational, something Rorty is not fond of doing (his romanticism about "Americanness" is what leads him to some of the tendentious remarks skewered so effectively by leftist critics). Coexistence is a national imperative; solidarity cannot be presumed across the board in even a liberal democratic state—on the contrary, that presumption can be, as suggested, a weapon of exclusion. The priority of right over good, the cornerstone of liberal theory, is here maintained only in terms of conversation: when we enter the bazaar, we must put aside or at least temper our genuine feelings for the members of other clubs. We do this not because we think conversation in itself a nice and cultured thing. We do it because that is the only way, short of open group warfare, that we can get (some of) the things we want. The scene of conversation is not peaceful—it is deeply conflict-ridden, driven by disagreement—but it must remain civil *in some sense of the word* for interests to attain expression.

In what sense civil? Comay worried, with good reason, that tolerance and civility were sometimes (in the wrong form? in the wrong hands? always?)

---

33. See Rorty, Introduction to *Objectivity, Relativism, and Truth*, p. 15: "Most of my critics on the left . . . think of themselves as standing outside of the sociopolitical culture of liberalism with which Dewey identified, a culture with which I continue to identify. So when I say ethnocentric things like 'our culture' or 'we liberals,' their reaction is 'who, we?' I, however, find it hard to see them as outsiders to this culture; they look to me like people playing a role—an important role—within it. I do not see them as having developed an alternative culture, nor even as having envisaged one. I see the culture of the liberal democracies as still providing lots of opportunities for self-criticism and reform, and my critics on the left as fellow citizens taking advantage of these opportunities."

repressive. When "applied abstractly," she said, they legitimated exclusion of marginal or dissident voices. What about when applied concretely? In the last section of this chapter I sketch a preliminary version of the civility I hope can meet this objection. This version of civility also contributes to the task with which I began, namely the characterization of the critical, conversational citizen who seems to lie implicit, undiscovered, in the calls for revitalized public dialogue that are characteristic of hermeneutic political philosophy.

III. CIVIL CONSTRAINTS

What are the alternatives to the exclusion and "acquiescent pragmatism" of Rorty's attempt to contextualize liberalism? What, for example, are the prospects for an appeal to universal standards of rational debate, a strategy mentioned briefly in the previous chapter? Faced with the difficulties of a shrinking "we," this strategy can seem compelling; yet the appeal to rational standards, as I argue in detail later, faces severe problems of application and effectiveness. Even when the rationalist proceduralism that is a legacy of Kantian political theory is given a hermeneutic reading, as in Habermas, it becomes obvious that "what reason demands" is not, politically speaking, enough. If this is so, Rorty's balking at the adjective "rational" in front of "consensus" is justified—though perhaps only as a warning not to expect too much of rationality. At the very least, we seem indeed to require, in addition to any universalistic and rational presuppositions of public debate, a commitment to self-interpretation—a commitment understood as basic to the life of citizens. Thus Rorty's conversational liberalism, though tendentious and ultimately inadequate, succeeds in showing that a commitment to the virtue of civility *as it applies to a social conversation of legitimation* could be the missing link in hermeneutic rereadings of liberal political theory. In other words, the constraints of a "civil discourse" of legitimation are, in addition to constraints of rational discourse, necessary for processes of genuine political compromise—the negotiation of moral difference by public means. A concomitant result of this suggestion is that we gain a firmer grip on the sort of citizen required by the interpretive versions of justice now thought, with good reason, to be so compelling.

This is a significant advance in dealing politically with moral difference. If we cannot in some sense abstract from moral disagreement, we can never isolate principles of justice that *both* take moral differences seriously *and* refrain from particular commitments enough to justify themselves across those differences. Most contemporary justice theory fails to meet this challenge, in two opposing directions. On the one hand, the increasing minimalism of some kinds of procedural justice theory, the progressive shying away from substance in all forms, is an indication of justice theory's inability to address our deepest concerns and the substance of our ethical lives. On the other hand, the communitarian urge to plump honestly for one or another tradition or conception of the good appears to give up the project of social legitimation by turning inward to a single community of like-minded individuals, a turning inward that can be viciously exclusive, even genocidal.[34] Both strategies surrender too quickly, for they do not allow the possibility that a theory can be substantive about rules or principles of justice while at the same time maintaining a formal silence about particular conceptions of the good. It is true that this possibility means surrendering one aspect of the contemporary justice project, namely its sweepingly universalistic urge to generate principles justifiable to all rational actors, possibly including extraterrestrials and angels. We will have to reconceive justice, viewing it now as a matter of (1) isolating "*our* considered moral convictions" about basic social structure, whoever we are—the actual and potential citizens of a given society;[35] and, what follows from this, (2) isolating normative principles that are interpretive of our form of ethical life but not foundational in any wider metaphysical or transcendental sense. My conviction is that the priority of right over good does not itself rule out substantive elements in a theory of justice, and the search for defensible substance in such a theory is what drives this discussion forward.

From this perspective, then, the goal of justice should be reconceived as the cultivation of the sensitivity and acumen necessary for the daily *discernment* and *toleration* of varying moral conceptions. This sensitivity—which is what I will mean by civility—is indeed a form of right-over-good abstraction because it suspends judgment of moral differences in the interests of social coexistence. But it does not come to us from nowhere, nor is it something we could argue is coextensive with rationality *tout court*. That is, to adopt civility as the faculty

34. The corrective force of communitarian critiques is important and substantial (see Chapter 4). But the brutally exclusive aspects of community must be kept always in view when we assess the prospects of communitarian justice theory. To put it rather controversially, the problem with communitarianism is the specter of "ethnic cleansing."

35. I use this formulation to forestall objections that my view of justice as civility would automatically exclude all those who are not currently members of the society in question. One of the features of our political life we most cherish is an openness to those whose situations and desires lead them to request entry into our civil conversation. As long as this remains an element of our political culture, no interpetation of our political values could be considered complete without it.

of discernment necessary for social justice is not to recapitulate a Kantian or quasi-Kantian strategy. Civility is not to be understood the way some thinkers understand the sense of fairness, as something that can be found in some form or other in all rational agents. Civility is culturally determined, *sittlich*, present in determinate form in given societies and not others. It is therefore something in need of cultivation and ever-fuller realization of already-existing potential, not articulation by appeal to those philosophical chimeras, the universal rational agent and his or her basic commitments. It follows immediately that justice so understood cannot be conceived universally but must instead be restricted in scope to the citizens of a given society: those social actors who, because they share pragmatic goals of living together, may also aspire to sharing the deeper goals of living together well—that is, justly.

This appeal to civility, which may seem an odd notion in which to locate the hopes of justice theory (or indeed, as for Comay and others, a *dangerous* notion), turns on the existence of dialogic constraints that are explored at some length in the final chapters of this work. I find in the analysis of communicative pragmatics a strong sense of context-dependence in the availability of locutions oriented to particular social tasks. In other words, to the extent that one is cognizant of the particular goals associated with a certain dialogic situation—e.g., having an interview, conducting a seminar, trying a case— one willingly restrains oneself from saying all the things one might conceivably say, given one's commitments and stock of veridical propositions. That is, some things are routinely and unproblematically unsayable under some conditions. Sensitivity to this, which is part of our competence as communicative actors, is one intuition captured by the notion of civility, properly conceived. In society we always operate under voluntary restraints, restraints associated with social role-taking, sensitivity to context, and the perceptions of the pragmatic goals particular to a given situation. In this sense, it may be rational to be civil—and, it follows, irrational not to be.

A second feature that I will associate with the civility view is the sort of interpretive "tact" outlined by Gadamer in *Truth and Method*. Here interpretation, of text or person, is a matter of "having the right touch," the ability to assess claims other than my own with sensitivity and openness. Tactful interpretation is by virtue of this sensitivity a de-centering strategy, an orientation that takes me beyond my own interests and puts me in touch with those of other citizens (or, as it may be, those of a tradition or a text). This interpretive version of civility brings to the fore a virtue with a longer and perhaps more respectable pedigree, *phronesis* or practical wisdom. Larmore suggested, in his criticism of liberalism, that one salutary "pattern of moral complexity" restored by virtue ethics is the place of *phronesis*—practical wisdom or judgment—in the realm of the good. Cultivation of this virtue in moral theories, he argued, marks an advance over strict rule-governed moral systems, systems that as a result of their formal strictness fail to account for how we really reach moral decisions.[36] Still, Larmore adds (echoing Adam Smith), the realm of *right* cannot be inexplicit in this way, if only because predictability is a central virtue of justice.[37] If morality is governed by *phronesis*, justice should still be governed by strict rules of decision. Yet it is just this separation that the civility view challenges. While a set of laws may, at a given time, be strictly codified, their interpretation and, moreover, the ongoing debate over their legitimacy will not be so codified. *Phronesis* is as much a feature of just talking as it is of moral decision-making. I will argue that Gadamer's analysis indicates for us how tact may operate as a garden-variety version of the centrally important virtue of practical wisdom, the virtue debilitatingly absent in abstract procedural conceptions of justice.

The constraints of civility, as I conceive them, are thus two-sided: on the one hand, a willingness not to say all the true, or morally excellent, things one could say; and, on the other hand, an interpretive sensitivity to the legitimacy of claims made by others.[38] These are the two sides of a basic civil orientation to public problem-solving, an orientation that is by definition hermeneutic. On one side, there is a recognition that moral difference will show some of my arguments and claims (say, those from Islamic law, or papal directive, or philosophical commitments) to be publicly irrelevant. I do not say them—but not in the interests of agreement, or impersonal reason; these goals may fail to be normative just as surely as the ideological critics indicated. Instead, I refrain from saying them in the political-pragmatic interests of continuing the conver-

---

36. See Larmore, *Patterns of Moral Complexity*, p. 12: "By overlooking the importance of judgment, modern moral theories have presented a dessicated view of virtue. . . . It fails to capture the way in which exercise of virtue, through imagination and judgment, is an organ of moral discovery."

37. Ibid., p. 17; see also pp. 40–42. Adam Smith, in *The Theory of Moral Sentiments*, averred: "The rules of justice are the only rules of morality which are precise and accurate, . . . [while] those of all virtues are loose, vague, and indeterminate" (7.4.517).

38. "By tact," Gadamer says, "we understand a particular sensitivity and sensitiveness to situations, and how to behave in them, for which we cannot find any knowledge from general principles." "One can say something tactfully," he continues, "but that will always mean that one passes over something tactfully and leaves it unsaid, and it is tactless to express what one can only pass over. But to pass over something does not mean to avert the gaze from something, but to watch it in such a way that rather than knock against it, one slips by it. Thus tact helps one preserve distance, it avoids the offensive, the violation of the intimate sphere of the person" (*Truth and Method*, pp. 12, 16–17). So stated, this "interpretive tact"—the basis of civil dialogue—involves *both* not saying *and* listening to, fostering, the other.

sation. That is, I do this not because the conversation itself is culturally uplifting or edifying, but because the conversation is all we have—politically we are what we say, and social compromises are forged nowhere else than in a vigorous public discourse. So, on the other side, we must also force ourselves to be sensitive to the arguments being publicly offered by others, that we may show the minimal good faith necessary for a society to hold itself together. Social debate must have these two sides. And so the results of such debate are normative just to the extent that we are all participants in it, not—to mention two prominent alternatives—to the extent that it is rational (i.e., gives way to the rational force of the better argument) or to the extent that it issues in agreement (i.e., allows consensus, or hypothetical contract). Our political compromises may, in practice, fail to instantiate a liberal utopia; that is the reality of political debate. The paradox is that to have a truly liberal society we might have to surrender the particular moral goals of the liberal vision. At the very least, these goals are no more prima facie compelling than those of any other particular vision.

Crucially, the constraints of civil dialogue must operate as screens not on issues but on justifications: they are argument-excluders, not issue-excluders. Even more crucial, they must be internal and not external for their exclusionary force to remain legitimate. We must feel them to be virtues of political judgment that we all share to a minimum degree, whatever other virtues we share or disagree about. There might be, in other words, a kind of "overlapping consensus"—not, as Rawls thought, on the principles of justice themselves, but only on the phronetic virtues of just talking. It is not unreasonable to think that such talking would, in its more self-critical moments, prove able to attack the ideological distortions and exclusions that worried Comay and others like her. Indeed, what is her worry except such an attack? *Ideologiekritik* folds itself back into the routine processes of justificatory talk because it does just what that talk is supposed to do: identify interests, point out obscured power relations, heal distortions in communication. These tasks are not *prior* to just talking; they are elements of it. In dialogic theories of justice, we are all legislators. We are likewise all critics and therapists of justice and our fellow citizens.

This view of the citizen—both civil and critical—goes significantly beyond the Rawlsian citizen, who was imagined only to be "rational" and "reasonable," a citizen who, as Michael Sandel correctly argued, was so "thin and unencumbered" that he was not recognizable as relevantly like us. The dialogic citizen has, by contrast, some of the thick, encumbered traits we associate with real people. She has a deep moral vision, which she pursues in common with some like-minded others. She has likewise a place in real society, one that happens to accommodate, however uneasily, other kinds of moral vision. Her civil commitments are virtues she has, in other words, in addition to those "deeper" ones associated with her moral outlook. But, significantly, these civil virtues may often have to trump the moral ones—not because they are from her private point of view more important, but because social coexistence is a good without which she could not even pursue her other shared goods. In short, the picture of civility provides a hermeneutic rereading of the standard liberal priority of right over good, but does it in such a way that communitarian worries about hyper-rationalist (and therefore irrelevant or inaccurate) liberalism can be met. The priority of civil virtues does not mean denying the moral self, or posting the fiction of a punctual moral self in the Lockean style. It means rather that some virtues can be classed as distinctively political, while others are classed as distinctively moral. And as long as citizens share some civil virtues, politics remains possible. The citizen is not being asked to cultivate schizophrenia, only irony—to realize, as a matter of course, that sometimes one cannot say all the things one wishes to say, that the full perfection of a moral vision must be curbed when one ventures into public.

This is the irony Rorty takes to be definitive of the liberal citizen, but now with a more concrete and explicit dialogic-interpretive orientation. It is likewise chastened by the necessity of having political virtues, the thought that on the other side of society lies open, rather than mediated, conflict. The liberal citizen is a talker, and a talker of a particular kind. She knows what she thinks the moral truth is, but she knows just as well that she cannot always make claims about that truth and expect to get very far in public debate—and so that too is part of what she considers important. Barring theocracy or a moral utopia organized around her particular moral vision, society is always going to involve compromise. It is a power struggle, not a genteel chat among gentlemen of the kind apparently imagined by Rorty. Within societies, where claims compete, we are *already* in the cacophonous bazaar. Justice resides not in the particular compromise settled on, a settlement that is temporary and contingent anyway, but in the shared commitment to the conversation about compromise itself. That, and that only, is what can give us a valid self-interpretation.

It may, of course, seem strange to focus attention on irony when one purports to talk of basic civic virtue. Was that not, after all, part of Comay's worry about Rorty that this cultivation of dual roles was too intellectual by half? Yet, as I said earlier, this objection is overstated. The kind of irony sketched here is no more—but of course *no less*—than the distance we open up daily between our homebound selves and the limited, goal-directed agents we carry into the thousand mundane interactions of social life. No public/private distinction is a neutral property, nor are its limits fixed or permanent, nor again is control of its placement a trivial issue. Yet such a distinction does exist, and we make this clear every single day of our social lives: the gap between person and citizen is the gap between the perfection of the moral vision each of us (or each group of us) is committed to pursuing, and the limitations and compromise that result from sharing social space with others of divergent commitment. Difference is the engine of political life, conflict the electricity running through the legitimation conversation.[39] No conversation that purports to eliminate difference can be considered compelling or true, but no political theory that did not plot some strategies of dealing with it would count as worthy of our attention.

Our self-interpretation as a society is the basic political project. That project is, I am arguing, a conversational one, a great flurry of voices and claims, a sometimes heated and always riven dialogue about how we can best see ourselves, best preserve the things that we hold important. Because there is a real "we" here—the "we" of those who find themselves necessarily sharing a society—the pragmatic imperatives of the conversation are obvious. Less obvious is how best to govern the conversation, to channel it productively. No single answer to that task will seem right to every affected group—that is in the nature of the game. The most we can hope for is a set of constraints or, better, an orientation to public debate, that will make possible genuine exchange of views, genuine emergence of difference, and genuine questioning of power imbalances. If citizens are to talk to one another, they must refrain from saying all the things they have it in mind to say; they must likewise open themselves up to the

39. Liberalism has recently been judged unequal to the task of taking difference seriously. As Stephen K. White notes: "Liberal thought has often come in for heavy fire from postmodernists, as well as feminists, for endorsing, explicitly or implicitly, various ways of suppressing or marginalizing difference. Defenders of liberalism counter that perhaps particular formulations are guilty in this regard, but that the liberal tradition in general is best understood precisely as a response to the emergence of moral pluralism as a primary reality of political life in the modern West. This understanding places special emphasis on the principle of toleration" (White, *Political Theory and Postmodernism*, p. 126). So stated, the debate is reminiscent of the Comay-Rorty exchange. White goes on to argue that liberal *tolerance* must expand to include a *fostering* of difference—without, however, threatening normativity in the "anything goes" manner characteristic of some postmodern solutions (e.g., that of Lyotard and Thébaud in *Just Gaming*). Like Walzer, White suggests that some constraints are necessary here, and concludes with a not very helpful suggestion about the community of the nontraditionalist liberal tradition. Like Walzer and White, I am suggesting the same kind of modified constraint, but hoping to find it in our ways of talking themselves.

possibility that a claim made by someone else has merit.[40] That is all that civility means, and it may be all that is necessary for the kind of interpretive legitimation that remains our only possible course of political action.

Still, there will be worries—worries I sometimes share—that even this much detail is too much. There are good reasons that civility has been viewed with distrust by the disenfranchised; for most of human history, conversational restraint has been used as a means of preventing the subordinate from gaining a voice in the conversation, covering them with confusion and putting them down in order to keep them down. More deeply, calls for an ordered public debate may, to some minds, simply mask the real business of society: the power struggles that really determine who gets what. Talk can be a sham, a shadow play that distracts us from those who rob us blind. From this point of view, the bare commitment to keep the conversation going, and to keep it civil, will appear risible.

Yet these critical claims too are public ones. They are arguments made in a forum that extends beyond the limits of the already like-minded. Indeed, in a healthy society there is a plurality of such forums: intellectual journals, newspapers, courts of law, sidewalks, barbershops, classrooms, church basements, television talk-shows. The call for a retreat from debate is itself a debating point, and claims that dialogue is impossible are themselves dialogic claims. Even a society apparently on the verge of falling to pieces, each piece determined by group loyalty or particularistic moral commitment, is going to be abuzz with talk, with claims and objections, with arguments and protests. As I make clear in Part Three, "civil" in the sense I mean does not imply quiet, obedient, or even necessarily well-mannered. It means open and restrained—not in the interests of the ruling class or the dominant power-holders, but rather in the interests of pragmatic social goals we all share and the vibrant social debate necessary to keep them in play. Until we actually cease to share those goals—until we in fact go our own ways—this debate is the only kind of justice we can either desire or defend. It is not perhaps very much—just talking indeed. But I believe it will be enough.

It is not enough, however, to settle with this too-brief account of justice as civility. In Part Two I assess in some detail the impact and shortcomings of three prominent options in the construction of dialogic justice. Then, armed with a keener sense of the available options and why they fail, in their own ways, to be fully convincing, we return in Part Three to the question of civility.

40. Listening is the first responsibility of the civil talker. Argues Sara Ruddick: "If difference is to emerge there must first be silence, a willing suspension of habitual speech" (See her "Remarks on the Sexual Politics of Reason," in *Women and Moral Theory,* ed. Eva Feder Kittay and Diana T. Meyers [Totowa, N.J.: Roman & Littlefield, 1987]).

PART TWO

3

Constrained Liberal Dialogue

This chapter examines the externally constrained dialogue of liberalism, particularly as defended by Bruce Ackerman, and its reliance on a cogent defense of the priority of right. While we may indeed find that such a defense is plausible, and see that there are strong pragmatic motivations for citizens to draw a right/good distinction, Ackerman's solution to the problem of justice and dialogue must be criticized for the degree of abstraction employed in its theoretical devices. As a result, the constraints generated in this model possess only a dubious justifiability.

Ackerman can also be challenged for having succumbed to a tendency, perhaps more marked among liberals than among other theorists of justice, to overdetermine the decision-making of justice. That is, instead of stopping short with a defensible clearing of dialogic space, and letting the citizens themselves decide what rules are just, Ackerman (like Rawls, Nozick, and others) wants to work out, in some detail, a set of justified rules. I suggest that a late revision of his general theory is effective in overcoming some of these shortcomings, in particular by outlining a more voluntaristic view of the moral self, abandoning some of the counterintuitive devices of justification, and contenting itself with a determination of dialogic space concerned with justice and not actual rules of justice.

I. INTRODUCTION: A CIRCLING SPACESHIP

Our consideration of Ackerman's dialogic liberalism must begin with the following piece of science-fiction fantasy.[1] Circling a virgin planet is a giant spaceship filled with people, eager colonizers of new worlds. The collective past of these odd space travelers—how they got here, where they came from, who built their magnificent interplanetary craft—is unknown to us, but their personal pasts are, in varying degrees, clear. There are basketball players and gimps, Nazis and Jews, shouters and wallflowers, people who love to go on adventures, and those who like to stay home and watch television. In short, they have diverse goals and aspirations, varying conceptions of happiness and fulfillment, and different notions of what constitutes a good human life. Around the planet they orbit, sizing up their situation. What they discover is that the planet's surface has available a finite amount of "manna," a strange, malleable substance that can be fashioned into anything the colonizers desire.

But they also discover that there is not enough manna to give everyone as much as he or she wants. Conflicts about the distribution of existing manna are bound to arise. Who will get how much, and on what basis? The abilities and technology of the spacecraft—an all-powerful Commander, perfect computers, protective ray guns, filtering devices known as "transmitter shields"—can all be put to use in resolving these conflicts. The colonizers retreat to their spaceship's Assembly Hall to discuss the situation in a conversation presided over by the Commander and guided by the following enforced rules of dialogic procedure:

1. No person will be allowed to suggest that his or her conception of the good is superior to that of another.
2. No person will be allowed to make an argument based on his or her intrinsic superiority to another person.[2]

---

1. B. Ackerman, *Social Justice*, pp. 31–34.
2. For the definition and statement of the neutrality rules, see ibid., pp. 8–11.

These rules, as we shall see presently, are designed to ensure the smooth justificatory character of their conversation. The central questions exercising the colonizers are: How is the resolution of social conflict to be achieved? And (what is much the same) how are the planet's limited goods to be justly distributed?

Good questions, but perhaps posed within a bad scenario. At first glance this story appears to be an example of just the sort of foundational fantasy, long favored by liberal theorists of justice, that invites attack by critics who do not see how normative force can even proceed from *imagined* scenarios of justification.[3] Such stories, the objection goes, are typically used by theorists to argue justificatory points that could not be made taking people, and the world, as they really are. And this is surely a cogent objection, for what, after all, can science fiction have to do with grounding a just society? There are two related features of Ackerman's theory that show why his unusual tale might be the right one to examine, and it is worth quickly examining those features before moving any further into an evaluation of that theory. The first is what can be called Ackerman's Humean conventionalism; the second is the notion that constrained neutral dialogue is central to the project of legitimation. Emphasis on these features will not lay to rest the immediate objections to Ackerman's strategy of justification, but it will modulate and fine-tune those objections into a form that makes the task of evaluation clearer.

Like many theorists of justice, Ackerman takes from Hume the notion that the "circumstances of justice" must include the fact of a moderate scarcity of desired social goods. (This feature can be expressed as the *external* circumstance of justice.) So he begins with the fact that the space travelers have more demands than the planet's supply of manna can satisfy. But they also have very different notions of the best use for *any* manna, and, in the theoretical vocabulary that has become common, this means they have different conceptions of the good. (This is the *internal* circumstance of justice.) Because this variation in ultimate goals seems to them ineradicable, not merely accidental, the colonizers understand their basic social problem as one of determining how

---

3. For a recent example of this kind of criticism, see (as mentioned) Warnke, "Hermeneutic Turn." For Warnke, normative force is more relevantly derived from ongoing interpretation of our needs and interests than from a foundational procedure, which may presume controversial commitments. In Fishkin's view, Bruce Ackerman's story is, like Rawls's original position, an example of a decision procedure with refined motivations in a hypothetical situation. These will always prove controversial, open to what he calls "the jurisdiction problem" because their grids of neutrality are either too strict to have content or too loose to be uniquely normative. Fishkin argues—as I will—that a refined motivation view will not work unless it addresses our actual situation. See Fishkin, *Dialogue of Justice*, pp. 51, 79–101.

– to live together peacefully, avoiding or resolving the conflicts that will inevitably arise. What the colonizers face is therefore just what Hume presumed in a situation in which "there is not a sufficient quantity of [material possessions] to supply everyone's desires and necessities."[4] For Hume, the conventional institution of private property resulted initially from this common recognition of the scarcity of desired resources. "After this convention, concerning abstinence from the possessions of others, is entered into and everyone has acquired a stability of possessions, there immediately arise the ideas of justice and injustice," he said.[5] Only when we each know what is actually ours can we begin to consider whether or not it is our fair share.

Significantly for Hume, our ways of resolving this question are never forged by reference to a single threatened moment (as in Hobbes) or to a chain of legitimate transfers of original property (as in Locke). We resolve social conflict neither by appealing to an originary social moment nor by claiming the obligations and rights such a moment secures, but instead by holding to actual social conventions like property, whose origin is obscured to our analytical gaze, governed in practice by artificial virtues like justice. It follows that neither the convention of property nor the virtue of justice that governs it can be the result, or the proper subject, of a *contractual* story of justification—for no situation exists in which such a contract can be thought meaningful. What a theorist imagines we *would have done* in such an originary scenario is too weak a basis on which to erect social foundations; indeed, it is an odd place even to look. Hume thus consciously and in principle surrenders the foundational aspirations of contract theory and settles instead for a conventionalism based on institutions that are present and observable in his, and our, society. In order to be considered justified, these institutions must function well—that is, answer to the needs and interests of individuals or groups. We do not assess their degree of health by reference to an original, universal contract that never did, and never could, occur. To believe otherwise is in some sense to miss the point of social justification, namely that it concerns the institutions we must deal with here and now.

Of course "we" must already be a society of some kind when we come to address such issues, for otherwise there would be no basis for our assessment. That is why justice is, for Hume, a virtue of a fairly complex kind, arising only in a social setting of individual interest, moderate scarcity, and conventions of property. Social relations always have a determinate past that provides the

4. David Hume, *A Treatise of Human Nature*, 3.2.2.219.
5. Ibid., 221.

context and the vocabulary of our present talk, and they have an open future, which we must try to shape and control. The questions for justice theory of Humean lineage are these: Are our present conventions of justice legitimate? Can our rules and practices of distribution be justified with reference not to originary scenarios but to our present needs and interests? More important, *in what way* do we think our rules and practices are best justified? On this broadly Humean view, to imagine ourselves, or people supposedly like us, wandering around alone until a moment of social truth forges an initial social contract is irrelevant. No justificatory force can be expected to emanate from a scenario that is so alien to the way we actually live.

Is this not an indictment precisely of the Ackermanian spaceship, just the latest twist in a long liberal tradition of fantastic storytelling? Ackerman thinks not. He claims his story avoids the irrelevant character of some other political fantasies of the liberal tradition by constructing a thought-experiment that, although farfetched in some details, adequately highlights essential aspects of the problem of distributive justice as we now face it.[6] The situation of an initial distribution on a virgin planet is meant not to obscure the reality of current social relations in a foundational tale, but instead to make the task of justice clearer by isolating what is essential to *us:* individuals of divergent interest and a pool of available resources that cannot satisfy them all. As Ackerman notes, the circling spaceship is a way of abstracting a time T_0 from the stream of historically determined social relations—a kind of bracketed temporal slice that isolates, and therefore highlights, the pressing question of how we must deal with issues of just distribution. Because Ackerman's colonizers are conceived as ideal types (Manic and Depressive, Noble and Struggler, Jew and Nazi, Senior and Junior, etc.), the scenario is not one in which our ancestors, or even imagined versions of ourselves, are involved in a foundational contract meant to protect their (predetermined) individual rights.[7] It is instead conceived as an elaborate metaphor for our own real-life situations of social interaction and assessment, abstract in detail the better to isolate what is centrally at issue for us. "Whatever its failings may be," Ackerman has said, "dialogic liberalism does not rely on an image of humans as asocial creatures

---

6. Bruce Ackerman discusses and defends the Humean influence on his theory in his contribution to a symposium on his *Social Justice* entitled "What Is Neutral About Neutrality?" *Ethics* 93 (1983): 372–90.

7. That such rights actually preexist foundation contracts in some versions of the state-of-nature scenario is yet another indication of its incoherence. On what basis are such rights thought to rest? Can they ever be articulated except by appeal to such controversial metaphysical notions as "natural justice" or "the rights of man"?

who gain a sense of themselves and their rights in isolation from one another, and view politics as merely a way of safeguarding their 'natural rights.' . . . We cannot know the rights we have until we figure out what we can say to one another about our basic power position."[8] Ackerman's kind of abstraction, and this rather surprising tale of space colonization, is therefore meant to highlight not the radically individual possession of rights but instead the essentially conversational nature of our ongoing social justification.

This point is clearer in the second feature of Ackerman's theory I want to emphasize immediately, the centrality of constrained dialogue. Just as the general spaceship scenario is meant to emphasize the conventional nature of justice, the constraints on the dialogue of justification are constructed to highlight the *pragmatic* restraint we bring to political forums. Ultimately, Ackerman believes his constraints of "neutral dialogue" will model the *voluntary* self-restraint in play in our talk about the project of living together in a pluralistic society.[9] In the abstract, however, these commitments are rather unhappily modeled in the figure of the all-powerful Commander and her *enforced* restraint on the reason-giving of the colonizers in the Assembly Hall conversation. The spaceship scenario is so constructed that the project of colonizing cannot begin until talk has produced a justifiable distribution rule, and that talk is constrained in the ways Ackerman thinks necessary to get the project started—that is, in the rules of dialogic neutrality that rule out any solution based on claims of intrinsic superiority or superiority in conception of the good life.

So within the thought-experiment the colonizers have no choice about these constraints. If they violate the conventions of neutral dialogue, conventions meant to produce a smooth justificatory conversation, they face the prospect of instant annihilation by ray gun. This is so because the Commander, though generally and outwardly benign, cannot brook any disagreement about the rules of the justification game. (Disagreement inside the game's rules is of course another matter, since that is the very issue constrained dialogue is erected to deal with.) This makes the situation of the space colonizers fairly simple: talk correctly or be killed. Yet that very simplicity seems to put them at odds with us and our difficulties, despite Ackerman's protests about the kind of thought-

8. Bruce Ackerman, "Neutralities," in *Liberalism and the Good*, ed. R. Bruce Douglas, Gerald R. Mara, and Henry S. Richardson (New York: Routledge, 1990), p. 36. The "basic power position" is, as we shall see, one in which I am compelled to justify my possession of goods in response to (usually presumed) challenge from somebody else who wants to know according to what principle I can legitimately have them.

9. That is, in the revision of Ackerman's general theory contained in his "Why Dialogue?"

experiment he is conducting here. It may be that neutrality is an effective means of realizing a goal we can see, without further argument, as being desirable: the generation of justified principles of justice in a condition of moral plurality. But the effectiveness of the neutrality constraints cannot deflect us from a worry that will occupy much of the present discussion. Ackerman believes the spaceship scenario is not misleading because it models (stands in for) real restraint that we, as citizens, bring to justificatory dialogue. In contrast to the colonizers, however, who have no choice about the issue, *we* must decide whether these constraints really do highlight pragmatic commitments we bring to political dialogue. We must also decide whether this highlighting is only a descriptive process or instead involves some kind of prescriptive emphasis we may ultimately find controversial. Any difficulties in accepting the spaceship thought-experiment as valid, and therefore in seeing *this* constrained conversation as justified, will prove to be central problems for Ackerman's view.

The chapter pursues these issues in the following way. In the next section I briefly examine the "just solution" generated by constrained neutral dialogue. I then discuss in detail four aspects of Ackerman's theory, all of them central to a theory of justice that purports to be both liberal and dialogic. Finally, the chapter's fourth section questions, by means of a common example, whether the liberal project of resolving social conflict in tolerant talk will be a plausible response to diversity and scarcity. I dwell on liberalism, and Ackerman's version of it, at some length because liberalism is in many respects still the dominant discourse of justice theory in North America. Only by a close consideration of its points of contention will a way forward prove visible.

II. THE SOLUTION

The denizens of Ackerman's spaceship face a number of problems in their attempt to articulate a general rule (or rules) of justice. Initial arguments in the ship's Assembly Hall are heated and lengthy, and the rules put forward are often inconsistent, beyond the scope of the planet's resources, or fail to specify effects for all citizens. More problematic still is that some colonizers advance rules that depend on reasons that, although uncontroversially true and also neutral in the required senses, prove to be irrelevant. A colonizer named Bruce Ackerman, for example, enters the following rule on the Assembly Hall agenda for consideration: "Bruce Ackerman should get all the manna, while the rest of you should get none."[10] When challenged to provide a reason in favor of this rule, Ackerman responds, "My rule is better because the sky is blue." The colonizers are consternated: this is a true justification in favor of an apparently neutral rule, but one that nevertheless seems clearly wrong. The Commander helps them find a solution to the difficulty which incidentally highlights an important fact about good rules. The factual truth of the character Ackerman's reason is beyond question, but it must be considered *politically irrelevant*. The sky is just as blue for (say) an egalitarian distribution rule as it is for a pro-Ackerman distribution rule; unless the blueness of the sky can be linked up with some *exclusive* feature of the pro-Ackerman rule, it cannot count as a relevant reason in that rule's favor.

These and other failures to find a neutral rule coalesce in a sense among the colonizers that their problem is the following: with all the different conceptions of the good in play (perhaps as many as one for each colonizer), there is no way of evaluating ultimate purposes on a single *relevant* scale. Because final aims and goals are incommensurable, no single principle of justice can *both* adequately take account of their difference *and* generate a justified distribution. This is what Ackerman calls the "common yardstick" problem. Without a common scale of evaluation, there seems to be no way, even given the Commander's impressive technology, to calculate effects for all colonizers on the basis of a single justified rule of distribution. Utilitarian rules purport to provide such a common yardstick in the form of happiness—the thing that everyone wants, regardless of what else we want. Yet the character Depressive proves to have a limited ability (compared with his Type-A buddy Manic) to generate happiness out of resources, and this demonstrates the hidden biases even in utilitarian rules. The Depressives of the world are not treated fairly when efficiency in generating happiness is the criterion of just distribution. This is just one sense in which utilitarianism fails to take the differences between persons seriously enough.

What sort of solution can avoid these difficulties? Ackerman's ultimate answer should not be surprising. Manic and Depressive—who by this stage of the debates are dominating the controversial agenda—begin a decisive dialogue in the spaceship's Assembly Hall. In the course of it, Depressive suggests that he should get some manna not according to any common-yardstick rule but *just because* he has and pursues a version of the good life, because he is "a purposive being." It follows, he says, that all purposive beings should get some manna, and indeed he can think of no better solution than that all such beings should get equal amounts. In the absence of any other criterion of choice, the

10. B. Ackerman, *Social Justice*, p. 39.

Commander agrees that a rule of *equal distribution* passes neutrality's tests. It is neutral to conceptions of the good because it depends on no claims of intrinsic superiority; it specifies effects for all persons on the basis of a consistent reason, and therefore is rational as a decision rule; it appears to take seriously the difference between persons; and it specifies a set of possible social structures while also excluding some others, and so is therefore both conceivable and critical. "So," Ackerman says,

> there *is* a way that you and I can talk about power without claiming the right to judge the merit of each other's conception of the good. While we may disagree about the meaning of a good life, each of us is prepared to say that our own image of self-fulfillment has *some* value. . . . And once we are prepared to affirm the value of fulfilling our life plan, we may use this initial affirmation as the foundation of a public dialogue of right. . . . Our claims to manna can be based on nothing more—and nothing less—a dialogic exchange in which each of us describes himself as a morally autonomous person capable of putting a value on his life plan. Given this self-description, it follows that *something* can be said on behalf of initial material equality.[11]

In other words, neutral dialogue allows us to recognize each other as holders of a conception of the good, and this is thought to be enough to generate a rule of initial equality in distribution. The "something" to be said in favor of this distribution rule becomes the basis of Ackerman's complex picture of egalitarian justice.

Ackerman's egalitarian solution depends on a lowest-common-denominator argument: it is the only solution that has fewest problems (and no debilitating problems) in facing the restrictions of neutrality. As Ackerman says himself, "this is, at one and the same time, a very strong and very weak result."[12] The weakness is clear: an egalitarian starting point seems to create many distribution difficulties. When goods are of many kinds, not just material, what counts as an equal distribution?[13] Should equality in distribution be a function of

---

11. Ibid., p. 57.
12. Ibid., p. 58.
13. "There is no reason," Fishkin says, "to regard equal chunks of manna as a yardstick immune from controversy while every other possible specification of content for equality is regarded as non-neutral" ("Can There Be a Neutral Theory of Justice?" *Ethics* 93 [1983]: 352). Fishkin argues that Ackerman's dialogic neutrality therefore cannot be *both* strict in form *and* "permit any definite answer to the question, 'At least as much as what?' " (ibid., p. 351). These criticisms are recapitulated in Fishkin's *Dialogue of Justice*, pp. 96–101.

opportunities or of outcomes? How are imbalances that may arise over time to be corrected? Is there a difference between formal equality and substantive equality, and how will it be negotiated? The strength of the result is less obvious. As a theoretically justified distribution rule it has a certain elegance, but does it have the amount of critical purchase that we want in a rule of justice? Will it not, despite a certain theoretical attraction, leave many persons deeply unsatisfied with their lot, unable to put into practice the conception of the good that is precisely the reason they have any manna in the first place?

Having raised these important (and vexed) issues, I must declare—consistent with my project's overall focus—that my concern is less with Ackerman's egalitarian *result* than with the talking *procedures* by which the result was generated, and the picture of citizenship implied by them. I now turn to examine in some detail the structure of Ackerman's justification conversation.

III. THE VALUES OF NEUTRAL DIALOGUE

Four aspects of Ackerman's theory may be isolated as necessary to a convincing liberal theory of dialogic justice. All of them have been mentioned or implied already, but I want now to focus detailed critical attention on them. They are (1) the centrality of dialogue, (2) the need for pragmatic constraints on that dialogue, (3) the related need for a neutral theory of justice, understood as one that establishes the priority of right over good, to deal with moral pluralism, and (4) a convincing account of citizenship. Though these features are clearly related in complex ways, and not explicitly separated in Ackerman's treatment, I shall discuss each in turn to highlight relevant points. My contention throughout the following discussion is that Ackerman's theory cannot be convincing unless he can offer plausible accounts of these four features.

1. Dialogue

Why *should* justice begin with talk? Because this is how we must negotiate the distribution of power in our society.[14] We are not concerned here with the kind

14. Though Ackerman's manna, like Rawls's basic social goods, appears to be a stand-in for exclusively material goods, this turns out to be a false view of the liberal project. The legitimation conversation is precisely concerned with how power is spread through a society, and the relations

of talk in which one person clearly has power over another (a military order, for example). Rather, this is talk in which one person challenges the rights of another to this or that limited resource. Ackerman begins with the notion that power claims, and legitimacy claims *about* those power claims, are inevitably carried on in language. "Imagine," he says, "someone stepping forward to claim control over resources you now take for granted. According to her, it is she, not you, who has the better right to claim them. Why, she insists on knowing, do you think otherwise? How can you justify the powers you have so comfortably exercised in the past?"[15] Typically my response will be, or at least entail, reference to a distribution rule, or set of them, that I find legitimate. I will invite my challenger to see whether she does not also find this rule, or rules, legitimate. This is the "game of justification" that lies at the center of Ackerman's dialogic theory of justice. Ackerman furthermore believes that a willingness and ability to play this game is a necessary condition of being rational: "Whenever anybody questions the legitimacy of another's power, the power holder *must* respond not by suppressing the questioner but by *giving a reason* that explains why he is more entitled to the resource than the questioner is."[16]

Ackerman has two versions of this move to the dialogue of justice, both of them fairly weak in justificatory terms. In *Social Justice in the Liberal State*, he considers someone who simply refuses to play the game of justification, responding to dialogic challenges with a blank stare. Such a person is not responding rationally to arguments about common purpose or the need to regulate a political power struggle. He or she has some other agenda, perhaps having to do with irrational or anarchist inclinations, perhaps merely a desire not to be co-opted by any general project of legitimation. In any case, here is a limit-case on dialogic rationality. If such a person will not talk, how are we to deal with his or her place in the social order? After considering some rather extreme tactics to bring about a dialogic response (harangues, talk serums), Ackerman concludes:

> I can use neither force nor reason to impose dialogue on you. All I can do is ask my question and await your reply. If you try to stare me down and impose brute force upon me, I will act in self-defense. If, instead,

---

between power and goods, power and offices, power and leisure, etc., must be conceived as questions subsidiary to the fundamental one, concerning who has what level of power.

15. B. Ackerman, *Social Justice*, p. 3.

16. Ibid., p. 4 (emphasis added).

you answer my questions, I will answer yours, and we will see what we
will see. The choice is yours.[17]

Now Ackerman is, as a matter of fact, confident that most people will see the
usefulness, indeed the necessity, of dialogue in the generation of legitimate
rules of justice. But that confidence cannot be backed by argument. And if
violence is in the cards, that cannot be resolved by argument.

To be more precise, there is an argument here, but it is one of only pragmatic range. We engage in political dialogue because we find ourselves in a
situation (limited resources, diversity of goals) that demands a common response. But if someone does not already see that regulating the political power
struggle is worthwhile, these pragmatic considerations about political situation
will not be convincing. To the extent that we see those considerations as
having weight, they amount to an argument in dialogue's favor—but that
extent may be small, and so the argument may be tentative and tied to other
commitments.

This conditional flavor of the justification of dialogue is even more apparent
in a second version of it, found in Ackerman's essay "Why Dialogue?" There
Ackerman ties the move to dialogue to an acceptance of "the liberal problematic," i.e., the problem of "how people who disagree about the moral truth
might nonetheless reasonably solve their ongoing problem of living together."[18] I shall consider shortly the issue of whether this liberal way of
conceiving the problem of justice is the correct one. Important now is the
notion that dialogue can be justified only in this limited way, and only *political*
dialogue at that. "I do not propose," Ackerman says, "to base my case for
public dialogue on some assertedly general feature of the moral life, but upon
the distinctive ways liberals conceive the problem of public order."[19] This line
of argument rules out, as we shall see, any general, truth-oriented dialogue
designed to generate moral certainty. As a liberal in this wide sense, Ackerman
thinks agreement is impossible on the level of moral certainty. We must
instead concentrate on the less general but more tractable political project of
defining our common social space. And we must do it by talking together.

Once again, this is more hope than argument. "I can use neither force nor
reason to impose dialogue on you," says Ackerman. "All I can do is ask my
question and await your reply." In other words, if public order is not *already*

17. Ibid., p. 374.
18. B. Ackerman, "Why Dialogue?" p. 8.
19. Ibid.

conceived as a matter of right over good, pragmatic defenses of dialogue will not do. I think, however, that we have good reasons for so conceiving the political project in a pluralistic society, and these will be addresed presently.

So the positive arguments for putting dialogue at the center of political legitimation are, by their nature, conditional. But motivation for a dialogic approach can also be generated from negative arguments, by asking in effect "Why not monologue?" I believe there are three levels at which justice can be one-sidedly conceived as monological: the level of models of justice (the picture or procedure a theory uses to justify norms and principles of justice); the level of theories of justice (the way such models are themselves justified rationally), and the level of results of the theory (how the principles generated by a model will play out in practice). Negative arguments combine to show that justice can be fruitfully dialogic in several different ways. It could be a matter of determining social goods and interests together in talk (a conversation of interest). It could likewise be a matter of applying principles to the distribution of goods in a discursive fashion (a conversation of distribution). Or it could be—our central concern—a matter of assessing and justifying norms and principles of justice in a certain kind of talk (a conversation of justification).

Consider a prominent monological *model* of justice. Under a negative conception of political freedom, social coexistence (whether conceived as the result of a fearful contract or a rational compromise) is largely, if not exclusively, a matter of not being allowed to impinge on the rights of others. Here the individual is the primary locus of determining legitimation, for curtailment of rights is the only criterion of freedom. Under such conditions, I will not need to understand or even communicate with fellow citizens as long I do not try to take what is "justly" theirs—and vice versa. And what is justly theirs will mean, most frequently, material goods that have been obtained according to legitimate rules of acquisition and transfer.[20] Such rules are, in the influential Lockean version of this model, derived from intuitions about how we first came to possess anything at all. Locke's state-of-nature thought-experiments are meant to show that acquisition is just if it results from "mixing my labor" with generally available resources, exercising what Marx in another context called "effective control" over them. On this model, what is mine comes to me as a result of work I perform; I make resources my property by exploiting

20. A more recent (and more systematic) example of this influential negative-freedom model of justice is found in the theory advanced by Robert Nozick, *Anarchy, State, and Utopia* (New York: Basic Books, 1974), pp. 149–53.

them, or I am rewarded with other goods for performing exploitation of resources at the behest of another. Transfer is just if done according to procedures generated to protect justly acquired goods and to allow contracts between individuals, each of them doing as much as possible just what they wish with their justly acquired goods.

Here, then, the rules of justice amount to no more than a well-armed police force that protects basic property and contract rights between individuals who already know what they want, namely a greater share of material goods. On this sort of view, when it comes to determining interests I am left talking only to the other members of my group. Indeed, in the strong individualism that is to be found in some theories of liberalism, I am left talking only to myself. This radically individual, propertarian view of justice leaves no room for a common project of determining goals together, no sense in which the achievement of coming to understand and possibly agree with another person has any political bearing. Here, then, is the sense in which the model of justice is detrimentally monological. Citizens are here never engaged in the discernment and cultivation of common goods; instead they pursue their goals in isolation from one another, blind to the ambitions and desires of the persons with whom they happen to share a society. The principles of justice they will find legitimate are limited by the limitations on their conception of themselves and their society.

But, regardless of the sort of model justified in it, a *theory* of justice can also itself be monological, in the way it conceives the decision procedures for principles of justice. In Rawls, for example, the social contractors are blind to the interests of others at the same time they are blind to their own interests. The veil of ignorance is a kind of enforced monologue: in the hypothetical decision taken in the original position, a contractor merely refers to his or her own intuitions regarding fairness, free of particular interests. Presupposed here is a picture of the decision-maker as a bundle of predetermined interests, desires, and assets that have little or no reference to other persons. There is no negotiation or discussion in the original position; the device works on a different pivot, namely that the problem of agreement in justice is not one of actual persons reaching an agreement, but of persons separating themselves from their particular interests in order to give a vote of assent to a preferred set of principles. With the right sort of separation from interests, that vote can be expected to be unanimous, since what is left after such separation is just what is common to all. Justice as fairness may, as a model, turn out to involve social relations; the procedure by which we are supposed to choose it does not.

Yet, finally, the *results* generated by such a theory will be monological unless there is constant revision of principles. Lost in a picture such as this is what we might call "the social construction of meaning." Even if justice is always at base a matter or distributing various kinds of *goods* according to a norm or principle, it is not clear that these goods will always be self-evident or uncontroversial. For example, without extensive public debate we may simply not know what are the goods in education or church offices or arts funding or dozens of other realms of power and influence. Nor it is clear that we will know what our *interests* in fact are, without extensive discussion of a critical kind. We may, for example, be self-deceived about interests, laboring under misconceptions or ideological constraints; or we may simply be ignorant of possible options, not cognizant of talents we possess, tastes we will come to prize. In an obvious sense, we can never at a given time have more than a partial picture of what our interests are. Therefore, matching goods to interests, even if we mean by this general interests and not particular ones, is a larger task than can be performed by a simple individual choice of principles. Monologue at the level of results will prevent the sort of conversation we need to address questions of this type.

Why, indeed, conceive of the assessment and choice of norms of justice as a one-time-only proposition, as the original-position model and other contract models seem to suggest? Social criticism is not merely a matter of asking whether, say, the extant code of laws conforms to the principles of fairness already chosen once and for all. We will also want to ask whether this or that principle is one we think is justified. And that is an ongoing question, one that shifts with changes in population, circumstance, modes of production, economic structure, and social attitudes. It is a question, moreover, to which each citizen must feel the right and duty to contribute. It is a *discussion*, an ongoing interpretive achievement, performed by all members of a society, whatever their other commitments.

I said that our main concern was with dialogic models of justice, i.e., the sort of decision procedures in which norms and principles of justice are determined and assessed in some kind of social talk. But it may remain unclear just how dialogue could be equal to the project of legitimation. *What kind* of talk will do for this task of justifying norms and principles?

2. Constraints

Ackerman's contention is that when the right *constraints* are placed on conversation, the constraints that guarantee the "neutral dialogue" of liberalism, the legitimacy language-game can be carried on in a fashion that produces justifiable rules and practices of distribution. It will proceed, moreover, in a way that serves to test *existing* rules and practices of distribution with regard to their legitimacy. As already mentioned, these constraints are built into the spaceship scenario. The space travelers, controlled by the power of the Commander and her ray guns, can only make certain kinds of arguments in their attempts to articulate a rule (or set of rules) that will allow them to get as much manna as they can for themselves. So, as we saw earlier, arguments must be "neutral," according to the Commander's preprogrammed rule, in the sense that no advanced rule can depend on claims of intrinsic superiority or claims of superiority in a conception of the good.[21] The two goals of neutrality and constrainedness are obviously entwined in this theoretical move, but for our purposes they will be considered apart, at least for the moment. I therefore postpone to the next section the discussion of neutrality as a defensible goal of justice theory, and concentrate here on the notion of dialogic *constraints* in general.

What concerns can motivate the erection of dialogic barriers that screen out certain locutions, arguments, appeals, or justifications in a political conversation of legitimacy? Is it not the case that some project of *full disclosure* promises the best—perhaps the only—route to genuine legitimation? If we are prevented from saying all the things we want to say, the political conversation cannot possibly do that for which it was ostensibly begun. The metaphor of the Commander and her rules of talk is misleading.[22] The space colonizers are not like us in the important respect that they do not have to worry about how the political conversation is set up. The costless implementation of a perfect technology of justice and the image of a Commander already armed with rules of dialogue deny the colonizers any *moment of insight* about what they are doing. "Maybe a better sense of the Hobbesian fragility of liberal dialogue would emerge," Jeremy Waldron suggests, "had the imagery involved the colonists having to come to terms with the fact that it was them-

---

21. Ackerman does not specify it as a rule, but he also thinks power claims must be governed by *consistency:* "The reason advanced by a power wielder on one occasion must not be inconsistent with the reasons he advances to justify his other claims to power" (*Social Justice,* p. 7). Advanced rules must also be *complete,* that is, they must specify effects for all citizens.

22. Ackerman actually admits that his characterization of the Commander "all in all is a very misleading story" (ibid., p. 32) and says that "[e]ven if a single person could successfully impose liberalism on the rest of us, it would be wrong for her to do so without engaging us in a metaconversation that tries to convince us that [liberal] principles constitute the best form of political culture." It is a weakness in the theory that this metaconversation is only briefly outlined.

selves alone who were to agree [on] the terms, not only of their co-operation, but also of the basis on which those terms were to be discussed."[23]

The constraints may also seem compromised in their degree of control. The dialogue imagined is not in relevant respects "real" enough to be considered convincingly *what we do*. It is not, in the language of Part One of this study, contextualized.[24] Designed talk is a kind of theoretical fiction, a strictly (if not always openly) constrained construction of philosophers who are seeking to justify principles on its basis. Because such talk is not "real"—i.e., does not actually occur in our lives, but depends on the control of a theorist's imagination—it cannot, contrary to intention, perform the justificatory work it is constructed to do. Agreement in actual talk is usually impossible (and may be philosophically suspect anyway); at the same time, agreement secured in imagined talk is irrelevant. Any theory of justice that can work only by assuming agreement, actual or especially imagined, stretches the willing suspension of political disbelief too far.[25] No dialogue of this degree of ideality can secure results.

Or can it? True, this sort of critique provides a useful check. If justificatory conversation is always designed so as to produce the theorist's desired end, with no reference to how you and I actually carry on conversationally, its conclusions can be expected to carry little foundational weight with us. But perhaps the view of justificatory or normative conversation as *foundational* is itself in need of reform.[26] (I have more to say on this point in section IV,

23. Jeremy Waldron, "A Perfect Technology of Justice" (paper presented at the Yale Legal Theory Workshop, February 1989), p. 51.

24. See Michael Walzer, "A Critique of Philosophical Conversation," *Philosophical Forum* 21 (1989–90): 182–96. Walzer also targets Habermas for criticism (see below, Chapter 5). The position is similar to Fishkin's point that refined-motivation/hypothetical-situation accounts (Type 3 accounts) always fail to be normative because they are open to jurisdiction problems. Another theorist can always challenge the normativity of my results by offering a different hypothetical account. See Fishkin, *Dialogue of Justice*, p. 51.

25. "If the speakers start by disagreeing about the social and economic parameters within which the meaning of justice, say, is to be worked out, they are unlikely to reach an agreement, later on, about what justice means" (Walzer, "Critique," p. 193).

26. Warnke makes an effective reply to Walzer's critique by accepting the force of his limit arguments but suggesting that neither Rawls nor Habermas is as concerned with foundational social theory as Walzer would like to think. In the recent work of Rawls, Warnke finds the more interpretive reading of his theory of justice sketched earlier, which emphasizes the role of "our considered moral convictions" in the justification of principles of justice. Likewise, in the recent work of Habermas she indicates the universal-pragmatic strain of the theory of communicative action, which cuts against idealization by emphasizing the constraints we in fact presume in any conversation oriented toward understanding and agreement. Both readings show that justificatory talk need not be as abstract, and therefore as dubious, in relation to something called "real" talk, as

below.) To be sure, conversational models must take close account of disagree-ment among social actors, and of the many problematic features of interper-sonal talk: coercion, cajolery, variance in rhetorical skill, disingenuousness, and so on. They must take people as they really are—but not in complete detail, whatever that means.[27] To be normative, our talk must be real, but it must be real only in relevant respects. Does Ackerman's theory succeed in those terms?

I said earlier that commitment to political conversation was pragmatic, moti-vated by a desire to avoid debilitating conflict. These pragmatic commitments are present in Ackerman's spaceship thought-experiment, but in a manner that obscures their force for us. Because the Commander and her ray guns appear as agents external to the interlocutors in the Assembly Hall, because indeed those interlocutors have no say in the way their dialogue is carried on, it is initially difficult to see why they would view the constraints of neutral dia-logue as anything but alien and hostile. This difficulty sheds some light on the issue of talk and constraints: the useful distinction to be drawn is not between "real" talk and "designed" talk, but between talk that is constrained in defensi-ble and relevant ways and talk that is constrained in indefensible or irrelevant ways. Without constraints on human conversation, we may be unable to decide anything; but without *defensible* constraints, our decisions will be of no possible justificatory interest. The enforced neutrality of Ackerman's space-ship presents a hard pill to swallow in these terms, but I believe Ackerman provides a better picture of liberal dialogue, and a better defense of dialogic constraints in general, in "Why Dialogue?"

Ackerman begins that essay by acknowledging the relevance to his inquiry of a Socratic commitment: to finding the truth about the good life by question-ing anyone and everyone who might have an answer. By putting everything in question and opening up all beliefs to rational scrutiny, we might hope, like Socrates, to reach moral truth dialogically. In this respect Ackerman repeats a sentiment expressed in *Social Justice in the Liberal State*, that Socrates is the appropriate figure to fly on the banner of liberalism, someone who tirelessly

---

Walzer imagines. See Georgia Warnke, "Rawls, Habermas, and Real Talk: A Reply to Walzer," *Philosophical Forum* 21 (1989–90): 197–203.

27. The notion of "complete detail" is incoherent here anyway. Calls for "realness" are always conditioned by a hidden criterion of relevance. Otherwise they would court irrationality, perhaps reminding us of Lewis Carroll's mad cartographer, who in a desire to secure complete accuracy succeeded in drawing up a county map on a 1:1 scale. It draped over the entire county.

embodies the will to ask and answer questions about how things stand in the world.

But if that early rhetorical flourish seemed a little simplistic, it was with good reason. On reflection, Ackerman is not satisfied with a simple flag. "I cannot allow Socrates to monopolize my moral vision," he says in the later work. "His fixation on a single question threatens to distort the shape of human life—when will I get on with life itself if I am forever hung up on the question of how I ought to live?"[28] For those concerned with the real-world politics of pluralism, this argument is a convincing one. The meditative figure too caught up in reflection to act is a familiar figure of fun in what is often called "the real world"; when it comes to actually living a moral life, sometimes we simply have to suspend meditation and act, even though we may have incomplete information and only partly thought-out theories. But there is another reason that Socrates does not tell the whole story about liberalism, and that is that people have incompatible notions of the moral truth. It is not impossible that, with enough talk of the right kind, we will all come to agree on a single set of moral nostrums, but the prospect is at the very least unlikely. In any case, it would take a great deal of time, during which we might have to suspend all activity but moral talk. This clearly cannot be done without the sacrifice of many goals we can agree are centrally important. The solution Ackerman offers to this problem is a familiar notion introduced with the unfamiliar name of the "supreme pragmatic imperative." This imperative states that, in order to live together, "citizens of a liberal state must learn to talk to one another in a way that enables each of them to avoid condemning their own personal morality as evil or false."[29] Conversation about the (political) conditions of coexistence must be restrained in such a way that the (personal) commitments of morality do not render that coexistence impossible.

Ackerman believes his conversational constraints are the right ones because they maintain this imperative but do so without screening out the crucial political demand that one justify one's personal possessions. Indeed, the question "Why do you have more than I do?" is still the cornerstone of his conception of justice, the moment of political truth. With this and other late revisions of his basic theory, Ackerman also seeks to protect the integrity of persons "as they really are," laying to rest objections that the space colonizers

---

28. B. Ackerman, "Why Dialogue?" p. 1.
29. Ibid., p. 12.

were not relevantly like us. He does this by avoiding three false moves of justification identified with other, competing versions of liberal theory: trumping, translating, and transcending.

The reason these strategies of justification fail to convince is that, in their different ways, they all ask us to be other than ourselves in some respect. *Trumping* is the strategy of identifying a commitment that overarches individual differences in moral vision. But such commitments—say, the fear of death, and the desire to avoid it, central in the Hobbesian theory of right—will at some point force me to utter things I do not really believe. Such fear, and the commitment to avoiding violent death at the hands of another, is not my supreme moral commitment. It follows that my compliance on the basis of such fear proceeds not from moral assent but from force of circumstance. *Translating* individual interests into a common language will seem beneficial only until (as we saw earlier) the results produced by, for example, the felicific calculus begin to strike me as unfair, not sufficiently respectful of my (or someone else's) particularity. And *transcendence* of my individual interests in the service of justification—for example, in an original position of impartial choice—seems promising only until it requires that I leave behind too much that is deeply important to me, producing the strains of commitment inevitable when transcendent solutions are brought back to practices. All three strategies will force me, in short, to say things I do not really believe to be the case. According to Ackerman, the advantage of neutral dialogue over these rival liberal strategies for solving the public/private problem is that, though it does prevent me from saying all the things I believe to be true, it never requires me to say things I consider false.

For this reason, then, conversational restraint is an advance over previous versions of liberalism. Ackerman wants to maintain two theses: (1) that there is a necessary and defensible division between political and personal-moral, and (2) that political order is a pragmatic good self-evident to all persons *insofar as they are citizens*. The two assumptions are obviously linked, for only by agreeing to set aside one's deep (private) convictions can one, as a (public) citizen, realize that order must be preserved if anything else is to work. Indeed, it is precisely because I have deep personal commitments that I should want to renounce them in the public sphere and there defend the minimal order needed to realize my deep interests in the private sphere or spheres. Or, seen from the other side, this is what Ackerman calls "the asymmetry thesis": "it is precisely because the liberal state does not aim for moral truth that its citizens must recognize themselves under such peremptory dialogic obligations" as embodied in neutrality.[30] The obligation to abide by neutral constraints then becomes the one and only moral obligation a liberal state can impose on its citizens, an obligation that overrides any personal search for moral fulfillment.

Ackerman's revised theory is thus that the supreme pragmatic imperative is not so much "imposed" (who or what, after all, could *legitimately* impose anything like it?) as it is arrived at by the collective dialogic agreement of the liberal state's members. Seen this way, it may begin to appear, for our purposes, as a *shared value* rather than a compromise arrived at through force of circumstance. To the extent that we recognize shared pragmatic commitments in the project of social justice, constraints on our *political* dialogue appear to be justified. A recognition of moral difference in a single society is the beginning of a project of postponing all the true things I (or my group) might say in favor of the pressing need to talk about how we will get along.

Is this argument plausible? Many critics think not. Seyla Benhabib, for example, has suggested that Ackerman fails his own tests here: the offered pragmatic justification (1) does not remain morally neutral (it "trumps") and (2) takes participants in dialogue beyond themselves (it "transcends").[31] The argument trumps because it posits a supreme good, namely *public order*, that is to be valued above all others in deciding how to proceed. "If 'peace' is not the supreme moral good," she says, "then there is no reason to engage in such a public conversation [as outlined by neutrality]: one's vision of the good may in effect dictate that the disruption of seeming tranquillity and civility of this order is the supreme good."[32] The argument transcends because of the abstraction from personal conviction it demands of talkers. In asking participants in dialogue not to make certain arguments, not to talk about the parts of their lives that may be most important to them, the neutrality argument asks for a deep kind of personal abstraction. "It is not clear," says Benhabib, "why this agreement not to talk about fundamental disagreements is any less loaded or controversial an assumption than the idea of a 'veil of ignorance' which asks us to feign ignorance about our conception of the good."[33] She thinks participants

30. Ibid., p. 10.
31. Seyla Benhabib, "Liberal Dialogue vs. a Critical Theory of Discursive Legitimation," in *Liberalism and the Moral Life*, ed. Nancy Rosenblum (Cambridge, Mass.: Harvard University Press, 1989). See also Benhabib, *Critique, Norm, and Utopia: A Study of the Foundations of Critical Theory* (New York: Columbia University Press, 1986), chap. 8, esp. pp. 313–11.
32. Benhabib, "Liberal Dialogue," pp. 146–47. See also Henry S. Richardson, "The Problem of Liberalism and the Good," in *Liberalism and the Good*, pp. 1–28; and Robert Paul Wolff, *In Defense of Anarchism* (New York: Harper & Row, 1970).
33. Benhabib, "Liberal Dialogue," p. 147.

must be allowed to enter into the dialogue with their deepest moral convictions in full play, in an unconstrained "moral-transformative dialogue" whose goal is "self-transparency."[34] Otherwise there is no reason to suppose that the dialogue of politics will be anything more than a series of unjust power plays overdetermined by preexisting (and unassailable) rules of dialogic interaction. These rules of the game must be, at some level, up for grabs just as much as the various goals defined by the game. If they are not—if the neutralist public/private split is ossified and inflexible—we must begin to doubt even its pragmatic legitimacy. Because the neutrality constraints allow into the political dialogue only those issues on which agreement can be expected, they constrain the social conversation too much. Benhabib is right that the line dividing private and public is neither clear at all times nor a neutral property. The certainty of theorists who draw such lines obscures political interests, and the line itself may also serve to remove central concerns (e.g., domestic violence, sexual relations, child-rearing) from the discussion and relegate them to the important but somehow not discussable "private sphere."

To be legitimate, dialogic constraints cannot be features of a dominant ideology, nor can they be imposed externally or arbitrarily. Even if we agree with Ackerman's general defense of dialogic constraints, we should have doubts about the particular constraints he is concerned to defend. The tension between the external picture provided in the basic theory and the voluntaristic picture developed later makes for a degree of incoherence in Ackerman's view of the citizen. And the constraints appear to be justified with a strategy that, despite some concessions to our political realities, still distorts in its level of theoretical ideality. I turn to the latter issue now.

3. Neutrality

The constraints defended in Ackerman's theory are meant to model real pragmatic commitments we bring to the "game of justification." But they are also intended to act efficiently in clearing a space for that game to carry on in a

---

34. J. Donald Moon persuasively argues, in "Constrained Discourse and Public Life," 202–29, that Benhabib's model of unconstrained dialogue may itself be open to charges that it silences some voices, namely those in favor of what Moon calls "privacy and integrity" (pp. 220–22). Though he agrees (as most commentators do) that Ackerman's constraints are too rigid, he believes—as I do—that some constraints, and some version of a public/private distinction, must be available in political dialogue of legitimation (for more on this, see Chapter 5 below). Moon has expanded and deepened his account of the liberal problematic in his *Constructing Community: Moral Pluralism and Tragic Conflicts* (Princeton: Princeton University Press, 1993).

principled way. Ackerman believes we need constraints not only to make our justification conversation a real reflection of shared political commitments, but also to allow only *relevant* kinds of justification in that conversation. Irrelevant in his view, then, are those deeply controversial reasons that depend on comparison among conceptions of the good or among persons' intrinsic worth. It is in this sense that Ackermanian constraints on political dialogue are *neutral*.

Ackerman has five arguments in favor of neutrality so conceived, a neutrality of political conversation in which political power claims are justified. Four of these are explored in *Social Justice in the Liberal State* in what amounts to a defense of complex moral pluralism. They are: the danger of repression in sectarianism or perfectionism (pp. 361–65), skepticism or uncertainty about the good (pp. 11, 365–67), the positive instrumental value of experimentation in ways of living (p. 11),[35] and the intrinsic good of "autonomous deliberation" (pp. 11, 367–68). In "Why Dialogue?" a fifth ground of defense for neutral dialogue is suggested, that of mutual intelligibility, expressed in "the pragmatic imperative to talk to strangers as well as soul-mates."[36]

I say these grounds amount to a defense of pluralism because they share a set of background assumptions, taken to be factual, that characterize the political situation as Ackerman believes we encounter it. That situation has the following features: persons or groups have and pursue conceptions of the good life; these conceptions are varied and, moreover, sometimes conflict; there is nevertheless a prima facie political need for adherents of conflicting conceptions to occupy the same social space; there is, however, no commonly accepted manner in which their disputes can be resolved; and, therefore, principles or norms of *justice* must define the way in which these conflicts are resolved and the common space is structured. Ackerman's defense of neutrality may be taken as an attempt to solve the classical liberal problematic of meeting different and incompatible claims about the good with a structure of conflict resolution that is *in some sense* impartial to those claims, and therefore able to mediate them.

The debate both within liberalism and between liberalism and its theoretical opponents is often a matter of asking whether a given decision procedure is impartial in the *right* sense. Thus neutral liberalism has been extensively criticized in recent years for its "perverse" failure to admit that it actually

---

35. This is probably the weakest link in the defense, since experimentation is too controversial a value to be presumed across the social board. See Fishkin, *Dialogue of Justice*, p. 100. See also Charles Larmore's criticisms, detailed below.

36. B. Ackerman, "Why Dialogue?" p. 22.

pursues a conception of the good just as much as any of the theories among which it purports to adjudicate.[37] Such a failure, it is argued, disguises the status of liberalism as a moral theory and puts into question the impartial conflict-resolution it is designed to produce. Neutrality is therefore a misleading strategy that obscures the fact that liberal theories depend as much as all others on a particular conception of the good life in their framing of justice principles. The desire for neutrality among some liberals therefore has the ironic result of making it less tolerant than a sensitive and detailed defense of the substantive goods—central among them civic and personal virtues—contained in the liberal tradition.

This charge has some weight, but the triumphal attitude displayed by some critics of neutrality often proves to be overplayed. As Ronald Dworkin has noted, the charge against neutral justice is often made on the basis of a category mistake that confuses neutral *government* (or sometimes, *outcome*) with neutrality in reference to *decisions* about principles of justice. Liberalism demands the former, but can do so only by *not* attempting the latter. The anti-neutralists' "picture of liberalism," he says, "confuses *that* principle, about the neutrality of government towards conceptions of the good, with an alleged neutrality about principles of justice, which of course liberalism, because it is a theory of justice, must reject."[38] Ackerman likewise wants to deflate the triumphant anti-neutralist by pointing out several critiques of neutral liberalism he takes to be genuinely effective, but *not* when directed against his neutral conversation, which is a decision-procedure in the sense Dworkin means.

These critiques may be summarized in this fashion: (1) neutrality is used to champion one conception of the good by declaring all others invisible, off the neutral agenda—it is no more than an ideology of dominance; (2) neutrality obscures real injustice by skewing the *terms* of power, not merely the results—it makes important things systematically unavailable for assessment; (3) neutrality is a way of assessing consequences and, insofar as it is, overdetermines the political realm with substantive commitments not open to question; (4) neutrality is particularistic, in that it addresses only partial aspects of the political realm and denies the relevance of, say, historical injustice, cultural determination, or other factors thought to influence the political realm.[39]

37. This criticism has been most assiduously and most convincingly pursued by Galston, *Liberal Purposes*, chs. 4 and 5, esp. pp. 103–6. See also John Mackie's review of B. Ackerman's *Social Justice*, "Competitors in Conversation," *Times Literary Supplement*, April 17, 1981.

38. Dworkin, *Law's Empire*, p. 441.

39. Here I have followed B. Ackerman's discussion of these particulars in "Neutralities," pp. 33–41.

These critiques frequently overlap; moreover, their proponents can and do come from different regions of the political spectrum—for instance, as Ackerman notes, both neoconservative and postmodernist versions of (3) and (4) are common.[40]

Ackerman believes that, however compelling each of these critical points might be, they still fail to touch the heart of *conversational* neutrality. His reasons for so believing concern what is constrained in that version of neutrality, what kind of thing is kept off the agenda.[41] Neutral coversation is a conversational filter, a grid of interpretation that makes some things sayable and others not. "But this simple picture need not be understood in a purely negative spirit," Ackerman says. "We may think of the liberal's conversational filter as a kind of cultural tool by which citizens carve out a discursive public space which has been self-consciously structured so as to express certain fundamental normative commitments."[42] Those commitments concern, as we have seen, the need for public order and a well-structured set of social institutions. That is why, for an Ackermanian liberal, the unsayable concerns only certain kinds of *justification* for distribution rules (i.e., rules to mediate a power struggle). We may think what we like, even say what we like, but only certain reasons will count as *good* reasons when we come to discuss, as citizens, the continuing problem of apportioning scarce resources. Here, and only here, our talk will be shaped so as to label irrelevant the reasons that assert unconditional individual superiority or superiority of certain controversial life-goals. For this reason, Ackerman's conversational neutrality does not operate with "principles of preclusion," those dubious principles otherwise known as "gag rules"[43] that actively preclude certain issues felt to be uncomfortable. Neutral constraints operate on kinds of legitimation, not on the issues or substance of talk.

So stated, does conversational neutrality avoid the criticisms offered by those who find neutrality too restrictive or ideologically loaded? Ackerman does not appear guilty here of bad faith, pretending that neutrality is a way of trancending value: "it *is* a value, which can only be defended by locating its

40. This is what he calls, in ibid., the Michel/Michael objection—as in, that is, Foucault and Oakeshott respectively.

41. Galston, *Liberal Purposes*, p. 100, notes that neutrality can concern any and all of *opportunity, outcome, aim* or *procedure* in liberal theory. He rightly focuses on the last as the locus of current neutralist hopes. Ackerman's point is that even here there are variations concerning just what neutral procedures will be neutral *about*—claims or justifications.

42. B. Ackerman, "Neutralities," p. 37.

43. See Stephen Holmes, "Gag Rules, or the Politics of Omission," in *Constitutionalism and Democracy*, ed. Jon Elster and Rune Slagstad (Cambridge: Cambridge University Press, 1988).

relationship to other values."[44] Dialogic neutrality is a version of the general liberal project examined in Chapter 1 as the establishment of right's priority over good. It will prove a plausible version of that project if it can convincingly link up with commitments we all feel as citizens—if, in other words, it offers a satisfying and usefully prescriptive interpretation of our public discourse of legitimation. I indicated there that the priority-of-right claim that ideas of justice are logically prior to, and set a political limit on, ideas of good is an influential one in liberal political theory, perhaps liberalism's defining feature. On this view, as I noted, justice provides a *political structure* in which individuals and groups are free to pursue their own goals without interference, while at the same time the structure defines when and how those goals may not be pursued. Many liberals, whatever their previous commitments, have come to view this political conception of liberalism as most convincing (contrasting it unfavorably with, on the one hand, perfectionistic liberalism of pure moral development and, on the other, pragmatic liberalism of the pure modus vivendi).[45] Ackerman's conversational version of the conception has the signal advantage, which I have been exploring, of focusing on the central fact of political life: the conversation between citizens with unequal amounts of social power.

Yet, according to William Galston, the most effective version of political liberalism is not one that continues to accept the priority of right, but instead one that honestly and wholeheartedly defends the goods that are intrinsic to the liberal conception. By borrowing some of the fire of communitarian and otherwise disaffected critics of liberalism—critics who, in the main, he thinks are unduly extreme—Galston plots a persuasive middle course between caricatured neutralist liberalism on one flank and caricatured communitarianism on the other. "A leitmotif of my critique has been what I see as a subtle irony," he says near the end of his *Liberal Purposes.*

Neutralist liberalism, whose guiding intention is the widest possible inclusiveness for differing ways of life subject only to the require-

---

44. B. Ackerman, "Neutralities," p. 29.

45. For this formulation of the liberal spectrum, see Charles Larmore, "Political Liberalism," *Political Theory* 18 (1990): 339–60. Larmore suggests that liberal perfectionism is demonstrated by Joseph Raz's Kantian politics, in *The Morality of Freedom* (New York: Oxford University Press, 1986). A few decades ago, pragmatic liberalism of the modus vivendi type was more popular than it is now, especially as a reaction against putatively perfectionistic theories. Early Rawls— i.e., before the Dewey Lectures revisions—is arguably a paradigm case.

ments of social justice, turns out to be far more partisan and exclusionary than its proponents are readily willing to admit. The substantive liberalism I advocate, by contrast, is actually less biased
against many ways of life than is the thesis I reject. In this respect,
among others, it is more political than is the self-styled "political
liberalism."[46]

This is particularly true of the problem posed by diverging religious belief—
the problem that prompted Locke to make the initial defense of liberal tolerance. It is a defense Galston believes subsequent liberals have misunderstood:
tolerance for diverging paths of salvation is not, or not yet, tolerance for
different moral ways of life. A full consideration of the substantive liberalism
Galston defends would take many pages, and I cannot undertake it here; I have
already had occasion to notice that his desire to contextualize liberalism, and
his defense of virtue as relevant to political life, are in sympathy with my own
project. For now I want simply to emphasize one aspect of the critical moment
in Galston's theory.

Galston's critiques of neutralist liberalism are extensive, but the one that
most attends to the present set of concerns has to do with the character of
public debate. After chiding Ackerman for adopting a preclusionary version of
procedural neutrality—a charge Ackerman has elsewhere fended off, as we
saw above—Galston notes that silence on controversial issues is not in keeping
with the goal of vigorous public debate. He thinks the bare possibility of
agreement on moral norms is slim, and therefore that enjoining silence on
controversy will prove an excessive constraint. It is also one that is made to
appear too early in the conversation. Ackerman, Galston says,

> insists that when confronted with moral disagreement, members of
> conflicting groups should not even try to convince each other to change
> their minds. We should rather assume that the disagreement will be
> "ongoing" and accordingly sidestep it altogether. The motivation for
> imposing restraints at the threshold of public discussion rather than at
> its conclusion seems arbitrary, at least to me.[47]

46. Galston, *Liberal Purposes*, p. 290.
47. Ibid., p. 104. Galston brings related criticisms to bear against Larmore's revision of conversational restraint, which is meant to restore "moral complexity" to Ackerman's rather blunt and
hard-edged conception of political dialogue.

This criticism is echoed by J. Donald Moon, who clarifies the stakes by noting that Ackerman's conversational constraints, by excluding questions of moral belief, seem to rule out in turn questions of transformative truth. "Thus to be barred from discussing the truth of contested beliefs," says Moon, "may prevent us from discovering common ones. Indeed, one of the most important ways by which we actually discover beliefs held in common with others is by challenging the beliefs that seem wrong and coming to see the grounds on which they are held."[48]

I am not convinced that these conclusions are in fact warranted by the claims of "Why Dialogue?" where, to my mind, Ackerman does not specify *when* restraints are to be put into play. The notion of "being faced with disagreement" is not given a detailed characterization, and we can imagine it meaning, instead of "immediately on sight," something like "only after protracted and fruitless attempts to convince." (This, after all, would better reflect the process of justification as attempted in the Assembly Hall.) Still, Galston is right to remind us that dialogic justification is not going to be smooth, and the ease of suggesting that we simply remain silent on controversial issues is in many ways a false victory. He correctly notes,

> The point of much dialogue is to invite one's interlocutor to see the world the way you do, or at least to understand what it is like to see the world the way you do. One way of doing that is the reverse of "prescinding" from disputed issues: namely, bearing witness to one's stance at the precise point of difference. This process is more analogous to art criticism than to mathematical reasoning.[49]

Since "good criticism is capable of changing minds on very fundamental points," this sort of debate may be precisely what we desire in the public realm: vigorous, lively, ongoing, and potentially normative. Yet it will still require some form of procedural guidance: even art criticism, with its plurality of voices and claims, is governed by practice-specific discursive norms and ends. Specifying these, as always, forms the core of the interpretive task, and in later stages of this work I provide an account of what I regard as the central features of a public debate that is both pluralistic and normative.

48. Moon, "Constrained Discourse and Public Life," p. 213. Yet, as mentioned earlier, Moon does not favor a model of totally unconstrained conversation. He defends instead a "generalized discourse" of tolerance and respect.
49. Galston, *Liberal Purposes*, p. 106.

So Galston's criticisms, perhaps the most cogent of those leveled against Ackerman's neutralist dialogue, place an effective limit on constraint as a dialogic norm. But by failing to emphasize the voluntaristic aspects of "Why Dialogue?" Galston has overstated the preclusionary tendencies of Ackerman's dialogic theory. As a result, he does not grant this version of liberal conversation its true political merits. It is true that Ackerman generally presumes rather than argues for this political or structural view of justice, at least partly because he simply assumes its relevance to the task of defending any coherent liberal theory of justice. Nor does he specify the conditions of forming or holding a conception of the good. In general, I think it is true that Ackerman is less concerned than, say, Rawls to import right-over-good notions into the institutional structure defended by his theory of justice.[50] But he does want to establish the priority of right over good in the sense that questions of common destiny, goods distribution, and power justification must be addressed free of undue and, more important, politically irrelevant influence by moral and personal commitments related to a particular notion of the good life. As Galston has it at another stage of his critique, it may be that the traditional "priority of right" thesis is often really a "priority of the public" thesis. This means, for him, that teleological or goods-based commitments are in fact to be found there; if so, they should be honestly admitted, and defended on their merits.[51]

It is possible—indeed, it is my considered conviction—that Galston's project of defending substantive liberalism and the interpretive attempt to contextualize the priority of right converge on a shared goal, namely the detailed characterization of a defensible liberal conversation. But for my purposes Galston's defense of substantive liberalism is too detailed, and consequently too controversial, to accept. From the thesis that liberals, no more than other political theorists, cannot avoid substantive commitments, he moves quickly to a full-blown theory of the good that many citizens will find unacceptable.[52]

50. But see, as mentioned, the important qualifications and revisions of that theory in Rawls, *Political Liberalism*.

51. This charge is specifically brought against Rawls's revision of his basic theory. See Galston, *Liberal Purposes*, chaps. 7 and 8. Galston's extended treatment of Rawls is in effect a charge of bad faith: Rawls, like Galston, ought to surrender the rhetoric of impartiality and embrace the liberal good he in fact holds.

52. When we ask what status Galston's substantive commitments have, we begin to see that he is a frustrated particularist. Though many liberals have persisted in denying their substantive commitments—even while importing them through the theoretical back door—we cannot grant those commitments more than minimal status. In general, liberal commitments—to life, or freedom, or pursuit of diverging visions—are precisely those that are designed to hold off particu-

(For example, he is in my view far too accommodating of religious belief as a ground of political argument.[53]) The point of focusing on procedural goods and virtues—the goods and virtues of, say, political conversation; that is, defending the substance of procedure—is not to sail free and clear above moral controversy (as some liberals indeed wanted to have it). It is instead to find values of orientation and discussion that, whatever else we believe, we all can share.

Of course it may still be the case that neutral dialogue is not the only, or even the best, way to accomplish a conversational regulation of the social power struggle. Henry Richardson suggests in a recent survey of liberal debates that, although conversational neutrality is markedly different from other (more dubious) sorts of neutrality, it may still be cause for disquiet.[54] Ackerman's liberalism, Richardson notes, is either a kind of overlapping consensus or a constrained modus vivendi organized around a single good, namely public order.[55] He says,

> What may be particularly troubling about neutrality as a way of implementing either of these justificatory ideals is that in seeking a fair suspense among competing conceptions it both muzzles them and yields principles that will in practice inevitably favor the pursuit of some of them over the pursuit of others. This conjunction invariably

---

larism of the kind Galston ends up defending. No such defense can be free of controversy if it purports to extend beyond a small group. Galston has some harsh words for Rorty's particularism, but his own attempt to be (in his words) both moral and minimal begins to look as limited as Rorty's—and with the added disadvantage, in my view, of being metaphysical.

53. However, Galston is not alone in thus singling out religious belief for an intellectual defense. There appears to be a growing sense among American intellectuals that the main currents of cultural life in the society have systematically devalued religious commitment. Galston's views on this are not fully worked out in *Liberal Purposes*, but see, e.g., Stephen Carter's already influential *The Culture of Disbelief: How American Law and Politics Trivialize Religious Devotion* (New York: Basic Books, 1993).

54. Richardson, "The Problem of Liberalism and the Good," pp. 17–20.

55. The notion of overlapping consensus has been popularized mainly by Rawls, "The Idea of Overlapping Consensus," *Oxford Journal of Legal Studies* 7 (1987): 1–25. See also Lecture IV of Rawls's *Political Liberalism*. In overlapping consensus, there is normative agreement on political principles, but not on the grounds that justify them. Citizens may agree on one set of principles of justice by appealing to different kinds of argument in favor of that set. Richardson suggests that Ackerman gives up this idea (found at, e.g., *Social Justice*, p. 8) in favor of a more minimal and less moral modus vivendi. Richardson's schematic of liberal responses to pluralism is helpful; see his "Problem of Liberalism," pp. 10–11. The criticism that Ackerman's theory of justice presumes a (controversial) commitment to public order as a supreme value is recapitulated by Benhabib.

raises the question whether it makes sense, in constructing the edifice of political theory, to ask citizens to check their deepest convictions at the door.

So it does. We have already seen that a more plausible interpretation of Ackerman's theory is that citizens *willingly* check these convictions, but this interpretation is muted and, moreover, in tension with other theoretical commitments prominent in the theory. The alternatives sketched by Richardson do not have this problem, while sharing with Ackerman a focus on the conditions of ideal political dialogue. Amy Gutmann and Dennis Thompson suggest, for example, that a strong moral value like *mutual respect* can ground the legitimation conversation in such a way that no external conversational constraints will prove necessary.[56] Conversation will thus remain formally unconstrained, and all issues will be allowed to appear on the agenda of public debate; but mutual respect for the moral commitments of others will demand that interlocutors try to understand an opponent's position as a moral one, remain open-minded about it, and minimize rejection of it. Thus a conversation will carry on in a way that *rejects* any formal right-before-good limitation to the political. At the same time, by appealing to a strong shared notion of respect, the view aspires to genuine consensus. "By permitting, under certain conditions, disagreement on aspects of the basic structure itself," this view aims at less than overlapping consensus; it does not formally rule out any kind of appeal or justification. That is considered an advance over theories in which certain kinds of commitment cannot come into play. But by continuing "to seek agreement on substantive moral principles—even comprehensive ones" it aims at more than liberalism typically permits itself to seek.

This project seems overly optimistic, however, when we remember the facts of pluralism with which the consideration of justice began. Moral disagreement runs deep, and the value of mutual respect may not be enough to regulate a conversation unless the scope of that conversation is itself regulated. Valuable in the Guttmann-Thompson view is an insistence that conversation must be governed by real values, values that arise naturally from the ethical life of a society and not from an externally imposed story of abstract justification. At the same time, we can expect genuine shared commitment to such

---

56. See Amy Gutmann and Dennis Thompson, "Moral Conflict and Political Consensus," in Douglas et al., *Liberalism and the Good*, ch. 7 (published in slightly different form in *Ethics* 101 (1990): 64–88). See also Amy Gutmann, *Liberal Equality* (Cambridge: Cambridge University Press, 1980).

values to be at worst unlikely, at best fragile, tenuous, and open to constant challenge. If we instead join ethical commitments that may admit of some kind of society-wide acceptance (respect or, as I shall argue, civility) together with a formal right-over-good silence on *deeper* (and therefore more controversial) moral convictions, we procure the advantage of a political conversation that can carry on in a way such that success—agreement about principles of justice—is not a chimera. In other words, we should not ask for less than overlapping consensus in the way Gutmann and Thompson suggest, by asking for ethical agreement that goes all the way down. Instead, combining silence on issues we know to be deeply controversial with some sense of shared ethical commitment may allow us to talk about social coexistence in the best possible way. The point in just talking may not be to have unconstrained conversation, as these various criticisms suggest, but to have a specifically political conversation constrained in justifiable ways.

Ackerman's model may not answer in these newly revised terms, despite the success of its broad outlines. Charles Larmore has suggested that Ackerman's arguments for neutrality, with the exception of the "mutual intelligibility" line explored in "Why Dialogue?" fail to be themselves neutral, and so the advantages of his dialogic version of neutrality are threatened.[57] Larmore agrees with Ackerman that neutrality must be the goal of a political theory facing a plurality of conceptions of the good, but he finds that Ackerman's appeals to autonomy, experimentation, and skepticism are an inadequate defense of neutrality because they unjustifiably assume controversial commitments among citizens. Not everyone, for example, should be expected to agree that experimentation constitutes a value when it comes to the good. Nor does every rational agent who becomes aware of difference in conceptions think that skepticism or noncognitivism concerning the good is indicated—on the contrary. So Larmore proposes instead that "a universal norm of rational dialogue" be used as the single neutral defense of neutrality. He says:

> In the face of disagreement, those who wish to continue the conversation should retreat to neutral ground, with the hope either of resolving the dispute or bypassing it. . . . In this way the norm of rational conversation would serve to shape a political culture in which the public could continue to discuss disputed views about the good life with the hope of expanding the scope of agreement, but in which it would also

57. Larmore, *Patterns of Moral Complexity*, esp. ch. 3.

argue that the state's decisions cannot be justified by an appeal to the intrinsic superiority of any such view that remains disputed.[58]

The view, with its commitment to retreating to neutral conversational space, clearly owes a good deal to Ackerman. Larmore also claims that his argument in favor of the universal norm of rational dialogue—that is, the commitment to keeping the conversation going by dealing with disagreement according to the better argument—is derived from a reading of Habermas and the idea that stalls in the routine achievement of consensus can be deflected to spheres of discursive norm assessment. (I shall say more about the latter argument in Chapter 5.)

It is worth noting that Larmore does not believe neutrality can be derived from the structures of rationality itself, something Ackerman despite his generally pragmatic justification at times appears committed to saying. (That is, Ackerman appears to think that it would make no sense to be both rational and unwilling to undertake a political dialogue.) "Even if [neutrality] constrains how a conversation should develop," Larmore says, "it cannot alone justify *that* the conversation be undertaken."[59] Larmore indicates the values of sympathy, civil peace, and equal respect as the motivations for the political conversation. And it is the conceptual limitations of sympathy and the pragmatic limitations of civil peace that drive him, like Gutmann and Thompson, to an idea of respect. Also like them, his motivation appears to be a distrust of *external* constraints, though he does not explicitly challenge Ackerman on this point. While civil peace is certainly a motivating force in Ackerman's constrained dialogue, the role of respect is not clear. The "mutual intelligibility" commitment in "Why Dialogue?" may indicate something of what Larmore is calling for here: "To show another equal respect is to treat his demand for justification as part of a rational discussion one must have with him."[60] My own view is that this respect cannot be expected to operate in universal extension, as Larmore seems to suggest. In other words, we have no reason to think that a commitment to equal respect will extend *past* a commitment to civil peace. Sympathy, as a function of moral imagination, may so extend, but it is an unreliable basis for ordering social structure. Respect, if it is a genuine motivating value in civil conversation, will be limited by our shared commit-

---

58. Ibid., pp. 53–54.
59. Ibid., p. 60 (emphasis added).
60. Ibid., p. 65.

ments to living together with other citizens. What I shall later call civility is the version of this respect I believe is most compelling here.

To conclude this lengthy discussion of neutrality: these criticisms make clear that it is not yet proven that the constraints modeled in Ackerman's neutral dialogue can be justified simply by reference to our pragmatic commitments. The tension between the forced and voluntary versions of the neutral interlocutor may prove ineradicable. To examine, and possibly resolve, that tension, I turn now to a closer consideration of the liberal dialogic citizen.

4. Citizenship

Many of the preceding objections, while initially seeming powerful, miss the point of a distinction Ackerman was careful to draw between neutrality constraints more generally and the dialogic ones found in his theory. Crucially, neutral dialogue works to rule out *kinds of argument or reason,* and not deep concerns or wide challenges to legitimacy. Indeed, it was such deep challenges to legitimacy that for Ackerman began the conversation of legitimation—that is, when I demand to know why you have more than I do. The public/private language in late revisions of the theory may obscure this point slightly, since Ackerman appears at times to be saying that neutrality means some things are simply not discussable. But even here neutral dialogue is not meant to rule out *issues,* only *justifications.*[61] And that means, *pace* Benhabib, Galston, and Moon, that issues thought of as part of the private sphere, and therefore potentially barred from discursive scrutiny, could well arise in neutral dialogue—indeed, in some cases (such as Benhabib's examples of domestic violence and child abuse) would have to. What may not happen is that resolution of them will depend on assertions of personal superiority or superiority in life-plans (say, those of *either* feminists *or* Catholics). The deep concerns of disenfranchised groups are not out of bounds; what is marked out of bounds is only the kind of argument that sometimes comes with such concerns—an argument that, because it depends on insistence of special group-limited authority, cannot pass through the grid of neutral dialogue.

Benhabib's discernment of a supreme value in Ackerman's argument is also a conclusion whose force, while first seeming considerable, largely disappears

61. Compare Larmore on this point (ibid., chs. 3 and 4). He appears to employ an unreconstructed and controversial version of the public/private split. The point, however, is not to exclude topics of discussion or groups of interlocutors, but to rule out nonneutral appeals to intrinsic superiority based on commitment to particular conceptions of the good life.

under analysis. Since Ackerman has consciously limited the scope of his theory to citizens, and been careful to phrase the arguments for neutral dialogue in conditional pragmatic terms, there is little room for an objection that finds public order an indefensible basic value. This is simply the starting point of public discourse in a pluralistic society; it is the value that all participants in the imagined dialogue must begin with. Whether, indeed, such order could be considered a supreme value in any deeper sense—any metaphysical, as opposed to merely pragmatic sense—is another question. Ackerman has not claimed that peace is all that we could (or should) want; he has claimed only that it is what we all must want, in addition to anything else we want, in order for a pluralistic society to be possible and, possibly, just. To the extent that someone—an anarchist, an irrationalist, a criminal—is not willing to accept this value as the implicit goal of political dialogue, certainly that dialogue will hold no interest. This is not to show the dialogue suffering from a general ineffectiveness. Ackerman's reliance on the goal of civil peace will not sit well with certain kinds of political actors, of course, revolutionaries and radicals prominent among them, but this reliance does not amount to a defense of quiescence or imply any particular commitment to the status quo. Political dialogue leaves a great deal of room for spontaneity, political revision, and vigorous dissent. True, the conceptions of the good that involve rejection of the political structure cannot be considered in that structure's determination. That, however, is not yet a criticism of the liberal political project itself.

To be sure, these points do not yet address the troubling issue of *force* in Ackerman's constraints of neutral dialogue. The strain on commitments and lack of insight noted in Ackerman's colonizers coalesce in a sense, never fully resolved, that the liberal-state interlocutors are incoherently *both* voluntary *and* forced participants in neutral dialogue. They are, on the one hand, seething cauldrons of desire who want nothing more than to get as much as they can of the available material goods, short of endangering their own lives. The Commander and her ray guns, however we imagine the metaphors in our own terms, are simply conceived as checks on the natural and limitless cupidity of humans who, if left unsupervised, would quickly begin maiming each other in their quest for more and more manna. On the other hand, Ackerman appears to think that an ability and willingness to engage in a legitimation conversation is also a basic feature of these persons, since this was the first principle he identified as a condition of rationality. The legitimation conversation requires that citizens leave aside certain deeply felt convictions and restrain themselves from saying all the morally excellent things they want to communicate. And yet this "willingness" is strictly enforced by threat of death, and there is no way for someone to avoid this conversation and still remain a member of the liberal state. There is no opt-out clause; objectors immediately suffer the fatal effects of the Commander's ray guns.

There is confusion of two different kinds in this view of the citizen. A first and more obvious kind of confusion concerns moral psychology. It seems unreasonable, at least on the surface, to characterize humans as *both* wildly (and incurably) greedy in their own self-interest *and* genuinely willing to participate in a restrained conversation about how that self-interest is to be met together with the self-interests of many others. It may be that these greedy individualists can be shown that a collective legitimation dialogue is in all their self-interests, but that is not what Ackerman has argued. Nor does he want to suggest, in Hobbesian fashion, that fear of the Commander is what makes the citizens "willing" to submit to constraints. And yet, without deeper commitments than those offered by the supreme pragmatic imperative, the degree of cooperation likely in a dialogue situation may be negligible. For that imperative does not rule out, say, deception of the slow-witted by wily fast talkers (or, at least, does not do so without a further specification, which has not been provided). It must be remembered that Ackerman's citizens are people who not only want as much as they can get for themselves but also have very different ideas about how resources should be used in general. Many of them can be expected to be, by inclination, activist in preaching their own conception of the good and hindering those of others. The situation is therefore not simply every person for himself or herself; there will be some persons whose vision of the good life involves active suppression of other persons. The scenario Ackerman offers therefore begins to appear incoherent, his imagined citizens deeply and fatally conflicted. His theory must assume both radical, seething self-interest and a genuine willingness to participate in a legitimation conversation that will almost certainly inhibit one's ability to get as much as one desires.

This incoherence has led some commentators to mistake the intellectual genealogy of Ackerman's conception. It appears, on one kind of reading, significantly Hobbesian.[62] Ackermanian persons, especially before they begin talking, look just like state-of-nature figures who simply want to get as much

62. For this reading, see Richard Flathman, "Egalitarian Blood and Skeptical Turnips," and Bernard Williams, "Space Talk: The Conversation Continued," both in the symposium on *Social Justice* in *Ethics* 93 (1983): 357–66 and 367–71, respectively. Flathman's engagement with Ackerman continues in a new form in Flathman's recent *Willful Liberalism: Voluntarism and Individuality in Political Theory and Practice* (Ithaca: Cornell University Press, 1992), which takes up and critically evaluates the promising story of a voluntaristic liberal theory sketched in Ackerman's "Why Dialogue?" and elsewhere in the liberal tradition.

as they can without getting killed, and so, on this view, the supreme pragmatic imperative and neutral dialogue appear as a new Leviathan, a greater power to which individuals submit because their lives are forfeit under all other options. By contrast, the situation has appeared to other readers more like Kant's "republic of devils": a collection of intelligent, self-interested individuals banding together in a pragmatic association that depends on, and supports, no common moral tenets.[63] Both views are accurate in some respects, but the *voluntary* aspect of neutral dialogue weighs against any simple Hobbesian characterization, while the common valuation of the political project itself may save citizens of the liberal state from being thought devilish.[64] The citizens of Ackerman's world, he has said, *agree* to restrain themselves, and it is explicitly stated that they do not do so simply because death looms in every other option. How do we make sense of this?

The attempt to do so indicates a second, less obvious kind of confusion in Ackerman's view of the citizen. Under the circumstances of the science-fiction story, persons had no choice but to accept the constraints of neutral dialogue and the results generated by it. The Commander and her ray guns were always in evidence, and the compliance of the space travelers demonstrated that they were aware of their power. The space travelers constrained their dialogue because they knew that refusal would mean death at the hands of the Commander. This created, as I noted earlier, a serious problem of commitment.[65] The rules and distributions agreed to in neutral dialogue may easily fail to express anyone's idea of how things should be, being merely the one and only solution-set that walked the tricky path between the Commander's rules of dialogic neutrality. Yet compliance is guaranteed anyway because of the costless police force on the planet. So the choice of principles is not only unfree but also illusory. Unless the space travelers also put into question the Commander and the rules of neutrality themselves, any dialogue of distribution will be no more than a kind of mechanical algorithm of forced compliance. As they stand, they are not persons like us in the very relevant regard that, though they appear to talk and act freely, their situation limits them with powerful effectiveness. They are not even psychologi-

---

63. This is Benhabib's reading.

64. Still, this commitment is not defended by Ackerman as moral, only as pragmatic. One advantage we can discern in revising Ackerman's view via MacIntyre's criticism of liberalism is that the liberal modus vivendi can be made stronger if some features of our common commitments to political organization are considered morally compelling. (Larmore's revitalization of "moral complexity" is something like this sort of project.)

65. See Waldron, "Perfect Technology of Justice," and Williams's critique in *Ethics* 93 (see note 62 above).

cally conflicted humans; they are merely binary functions in a predetermined program. The second type of confusion is thus manifest in their dilemma: they seem free but are unfree, they seem like us but are utterly unlike us. And, given these confusions, why should the results generated by the colonizers' extensive dialogues be of any interest to us? More seriously, how could they ever be normative with respect to the justice issues we face?

As I noted, Ackerman abandons the language of the spaceship thought-experiment in "Why Dialogue?" and emphasizes a more voluntaristic view of the legitimation conversation. This begins to suggest a possible solution to the difficulties raised here, but, because the solution is not pursued in detail, the questions of psychological accuracy are left hanging. Dialogic restraint, Ackerman says, is part of our competency as social actors, something we do with apparent ease every day of the week by assuming different roles within the general sphere of our social interactions. Thus, when I am with my family and performing the role of son or brother, I do not generally begin lecturing them on Kant's *Critique of Pure Reason*. By the same token, I would not typically spend a lecture hour telling my students stories from a terrific vacation in Bali. At least part of what it means to perform a social role effectively is a selective screening-out of information and impulses deemed irrelevant to the practice at hand, whether that is dinner with the family or a lecture or some other contextualized practice. We are familiar, then, with the notion that certain locutions are available within one social practice and not within another; these locutions may even separate off into easily recognizable spheres or patterns of talking. The discourse of the lecture is in general a familiar thing to those who have been in one; it is a language-game of a pretty definite type that they can easily set off from the quite different game called "having a family dinner."

"To be a competent social actor," Ackerman therefore says, "I must constantly engage in a process of selective repression—restraining the impulse to speak the truth on a vast number of role-irrelevant matters so as to get on with the particular form of life in which I am presently engaged."[66] Ackerman's

---

66. B. Ackerman, "Why Dialogue?" p. 20. Ackerman uses the language of social psychology when introducing the notions of role-playing and voluntary restraint into his theory, but philosophers will be more familiar with allied notions from Wittgenstein's analysis of language-games and language competency. Here, as in his basic conception of what "private spheres" look like, Ackerman is relying on that analysis. See Ludwig Wittgenstein, *Philosophical Investigations*, trans. G.E.M. Anscombe (New York: Macmillan, 1953), esp. secs. 1–50 (approx.) and secs. 99–128. For applications of Wittgensteinian ideas to the questions of social and political theory, see Hannah Pitkin's now-classic *Wittgenstein and Justice: On the Significance of Ludwig Wittgenstein for Social and Political Theory* (Berkeley and Los Angeles: University of California Press,

view of neutral political dialogue, then, is that it is simply another instance of this general social competency we all possess to one or another degree. When I am playing the role of citizen, which I do when discussing questions of legitimation and distribution, for example, I voluntarily screen off a host of (perhaps true) locutions I might utter in various other contexts. This is what it means to be a citizen: the exercise of voluntary restraint on my part so that the language-game of politics can carry on free of situation-irrelevant interruptions, however *true* (and ethically wonderful) those interruptions might certainly be. (I shall have more to say about this notion of pragmatic not-saying as a basis for justice in Chapters 6 and 7.)

Here, then, the restraint that makes social cooperation possible is entirely voluntary, but yet depends on a high degree of existing socialization. It is part of a more general human ability to perform a selection of roles with practiced ease and no loss of overall coherence. Only here does Ackerman's theory fulfill the promise to take us as we really are, not goods-grubbers who need to be policed but socialized members of a community who, because of the kind of education they have received and the kind of social context they inhabit, *already* balance individual desire with collective welfare and concern themselves with how best to fulfill various social roles. But this view, though perhaps more accurate to a kind of social psychology we can find convincing, may still be controversial. For example, while not objecting to voluntary restraint in some social roles, we may have difficulty with the notion of "citizenship" as just another role we play. If it is the basic or supreme role, the restraints called for by Ackerman need a deeper justification than the tentative pragmatic arguments he has provided. What if, for example, we incline to the view that playing the role of citizen, though certainly diverting, is far less important than playing the role of Jew or African-American or woman or father? What if we find the entire idea of social role-playing inhibiting and routinizing, and therefore incline instead to a call for radical spontaneity and creative disorder?[67] Can dialogic liberalism deal convincingly with these possibilities?

1972) and the lesser-known but arguably more persuasive account by Elizabeth Wolgast, *The Grammar of Justice* (Ithaca: Cornell University Press, 1987).

67. As Ackerman notes, the most prominent articulation of this view comes from Roberto Unger and his followers in the critical legal studies movement. For a relatively brief and accessible treatment of these ideas, see Unger's primer *The Critical Legal Studies Movement* (Cambridge, Mass.: Harvard University Press, 1983). Despite its occasionally obscure postmodern presentation, the view is in outline similar to anarchist manifestos of earlier decades. For its relation to Habermasian notions of legitimacy, see David Rasmussen, "Communication Theory and the Critique of the Law: Habermas and Unger on the Law," *Praxis International* 8 (1988): 155–70.

IV. THE HOPES OF LIBERALISM

One important concession that liberalism must make in dealing with criticisms of the preceding kind is the failure of agreement as a reasonable goal of political theory. I do not mean by this that the basic structure of the society will extend beyond agreement, especially to the extent that this basic structure—represented by the principles of justice—is understood as a kind of conversational space. In order to be citizens together, there must be a minimal agreement as to what binds us together. But that agreement cannot plausibly be expected to extend very far. Indeed, as I argue in more detail later, it will likely involve only the most basic pragmatic considerations of peaceful coexistence (including those considerations about how best to talk together), conjoined with some moral commitments to civility or respect. Attempting to argue for more than this—attempting to show, for example, that we all possess common rational commitments with strong foundational force—seems to be a project unlikely to bring success. This is true, rather paradoxically, for the same reasons that made liberalism look attractive in the first instance: moral pluralism and disagreement. The liberal hope cannot be to eliminate disagreement about the good, only to control it. What does this mean, and how does it relate to the concerns raised above?

Consider a conversation that takes place every day in a structurally liberal political community. One participant in the conversation argues that human life begins at the moment of conception. She thinks any other line drawn to delineate the beginning of life is arbitrary: brain-wave activity, heartbeat, and viability are, in her opinion, all cold medical notions that cannot in themselves define life. Furthermore, she believes that all life is sacred and must be protected, especially the forms of life that cannot protect themselves. An unborn fetus is an example of such a helpless life. In her view it is therefore morally wrong to end a pregnancy out of choice and by means of human technology. Such an action deprives the fetus of its existence, thereby violating the moral tenet concerning life's sacredness and the entailed fundamental right to life. Because the society's government claims to have an interest in such rights, and indeed (in its more high-flown rhetoric) claims a dedication to life's sacredness, she thinks the state should intervene, by force if necessary, to ensure that the fetus is not terminated.

Her interlocutor argues, contrarily, that the fetus is not a person. This is so, he says, because, until sixteen weeks of the pregnancy have passed, the fetus is not an organism complex enough to be, even potentially, a human being. Since in his view only human beings are persons, and only persons have rights, so long as the fetus is not a viable human being it can have no right to life. It cannot, indeed, have rights of any kind, for (in his view) rights are an ethical and legal category constructed by humans to deal with their complex interactions. As a consequence of these premises, he believes that any attempt to *prevent* the voluntary termination of the pregnancy actually infringes a different right, namely that of a woman to choose how her body is treated. He does not believe that government should have the power to control persons' bodies, for this violates his society's constitutional protection of privacy (or some similarly enshrined right of self-determination or freedom of choice). He hastens to point out that his position is not a matter of a right to life being countered with a right to private control; in such a contest, the right to life would possibly trump. Rather, the only right in play in this version of the situation is the woman's right to decide what should happen to her body, including whether she will continue a pregnancy. He answers his interlocutor's call for government protection of the fetus with a call for government protection of the woman's freedom of choice.

Very few actual confrontations between advocates of these positions will be so calmly rational as this. Nor will coherent arguments usually arise from the talk about this issue in such an orderly fashion. Instead, interlocutors will more likely meet each other on a sidewalk, bearing placards, and they will shout recriminations and insults at each other for as long as they are able. To this extent, the conversation I have sketched is already highly idealized. That, however, is not material to the present problem, which is rather that conversation, even when carried on rationally and under perhaps severe dialogic constraints,[68] is unlikely to produce results that are acceptable to both participants. Once their positions are stated, they may search long and hard for common ground and, with the best intentions in the world, still fail to find it. Although they must agree on a good deal in order to disagree in this fashion—sharing, for instance, concepts of rights and the individual while disagreeing on what extension these concepts have—there is no reason to suppose that dialogue of this constrained kind will ever produce *agreement*.[69] When they reach a cer-

---

68. Those provided, e.g., in the conventions of legal argument.

69. Donald Davidson argued in his well-known paper ("On the Very Idea of a Conceptual Scheme") that substantive disagreement depends on an extensive level of conceptual agreement, exhibited, e.g., in common understanding of locutions in the argument. When you and I disagree substantively, it does not indicate, in other words, that we are members of different forms of life. On the contrary, we could not disagree at all if we did not share a conceptual space. For an effective discussion of how this insight about substantive disagreement and forms of life affects the current debate on moral realism and the possibility of convergence in moral judgments, see S. L. Hurley,

tain level of their talk, when they get down to assumptions and premises (life begins at conception; the fetus is not a person) for which no further mutually convincing arguments can be offered, the conversation will be *blocked*. This is not to say that the talk will then definitely cease. On the contrary, it is likely to continue for many hours, but in a way that gets the interlocutors no closer to a solution.

In the view of some, blocked conversations of this kind are the basic feature of contemporary moral and political debate.[70] Two persons come together with good intentions to debate a moral issue; for a time they outline their positions in a way that seems rational and sane, yet finally they discover that they do not share certain fundamental assumptions, and the debate can go no further. Person A is not willing—how could he be?—to surrender assumption x. At the same time, Person B's commitment to assumption y is equally unquestioning, a pillar of her moral edifice. They can travel no further together. They are then reduced to an emotivist stalemate, with each interlocutor uttering sentences that appear to be arguments and rational value judgments but that in fact are no more than expressions of wish or visceral taste. Prospects for rational agreement are so limited that there seems to be no point in a dialogue that, though it does not always actually descend into acrimony, often simply stalls at the level of first principles. Lacking the resources to circumvent conversational blocks, contemporary moral and political debate founders as a practice. It can no longer perform the role we think it ought to perform, namely the examination and validation of principles, norms, and practices. Instead, groups and individuals within the community carry on a cacophony of rational-sounding moral talk that either preaches to the converted or runs quickly into enemies. On this view, talk gets us nowhere.

Liberals like Ackerman could object immediately to this picture that the dialogue depicted is *not* neutral liberal dialogue, despite the degree of restraint being exercised by our imagined rational interlocutors. Indeed, the very fact that the conversation was blocked is prima facie evidence that particular concep-

---

"Objectivity and Disagreement," in *Moral and Objectivity*, ed. Ted Honderich (London: Routledge & Kegan Paul, 1984), pp. 54–97.

70. Theorists of the so-called difference school are of this mind. Their objections to liberalism are usually that it fails to take difference seriously enough, attempting to flatten out moral disagreement with neutralist procedures or appeals to common commitment. It should be clear that my view of liberalism is more positive and begins with an assumption that difference is precisely the problem liberalism hopes to solve. That hope may be small in scope, but my conviction is that it is a more fruitful path to follow than the potential Balkanization of society apparently entailed by difference thinkers.

tions of the good life are seeping into the conversational space, and the conversation is therefore not relevantly neutral. Justifications are being employed that could not pass the Commander's test of neutrality among conceptions of the good. So unless and until the interlocutors give up their religious and/or feminist roles, say, and assume neutralist conversational rules, *of course* nothing but a block will result in the conversation. We cannot expect dialogue to do the work of justice unless we are willing to abide by the conventions of neutral constraint. Indeed, even if some kind of results were generated, it would not be clear that they were *justified* results unless the arguments employed were relevantly silent on the relative merits of different life-plans. Bare agreement is not normative just by virtue of being real, for it could be the product of ideological deception or majoritarian fear-mongering, or simply monolithic sharing of values.

But here we return to the question posed at the end of the last section. Are the role modifications called for in neutral dialogue possible for us? The interlocutors seem unable to surrender their basic commitments, the ones that gave rise to the blocked conversation, without serious loss of self-coherence. In the context of such deep disagreements, it appears that they cannot straightforwardly assume different roles in order to carry on the debate, for that asks them to be radically other than they are, not simply that they leave some kinds of commitment at home. Even if one of them points to an *agency* of neutral dialogue (perhaps the Supreme Court or, less likely, the methods of moral philosophy) as a forum in which the conversation block can be circumvented, the original disagreement may merely be deflected and not solved. In the end the interlocutors might easily fail to see the decision of the Court as binding—not because they find the Court in general a bankrupt agency, but because *this* decision contravenes commitments that are not up for grabs with them. The commitment to the sanctity of life, for example, may by some be judged *higher* than any general commitment to abide by legal decisions or maintain civil peace. Possibly the otherwise rational arguments of the philosophers will appear to them to miss the real point, that lives are being lost or rights ruthlessly infringed; even more damning, a show of philosophical equanimity when discussing charged moral issues may appear motivated by hidden commitments and moral biases that prejudge the issue. No forum of neutral dialogue seems available; and so strict abstraction from controversial moral commitments seems impossible, even in the interests of political structure. The disagreeing interlocutors stop their conversation and escalate their disagreement into violence. Unless a forum can be found to deal with such fundamental disagreement, equipped with resources that will allow these diverse and contradictory commitments to be worked out, the conversational block will persist forever and violence will never be resolved, only deflected with a show of greater (usually state-sponsored) force. The Court's decision, the philosophers' arguments, may give the appearance of neutral dialogue, but many persons will nevertheless fail to see the verdict or conclusion as just.

Of course, in the case of the Court—and because of aspects of the political project that preexist this particular exchange—these persons may indeed be forced to abide by the verdict anyway. And it is this instance of force that shows the limits of agreement even under ideal conditions of neutral dialogue. This scenario may not be a damaging objection to liberalism if its adherents are willing to admit that force may be necessary whenever disagreement runs deeper than agreement—that sometimes we will have to enforce compliance when it cannot be coaxed out of discussion. This is not to suggest a kind of liberal fascism, the intolerance of tolerance. More positively, a liberal culture can be (and often is) one of vigorous dissent, in which principles are not allowed to ossify but must instead face constant reassessment in light of changing needs and interests among citizens. Still, it is a serious limitation of liberal views that, in search of political agreement, they may play down the depth of moral commitments and the disagreement they bring. Making right prior to good, while perhaps the only feasible strategy in a society of plural conceptions, cannot mean that all moral commitments remain completely off the public agenda. The demanded role-modifications of citizenship cannot be so severe. Yet Ackerman's theory does not provide a fully convincing account of those modifications, and its enforced constraints and excessive ideality once more invite the criticism that these interlocutors "in the liberal state" are not us. Unless the constraints on dialogue can be seen to proceed more organically from real commitments you and I actually share, the result of interpretations and commitments that can form part of a conception of the good life and not remain violently at odds with it, this version of liberal dialogue will not ultimately convince.

That said, I am not advocating a surrender of the right-over-good structural commitment that is most convincing in liberalism, or even of the notion of constraint in political dialogue. What this failure shows is the significance and depth of the problems we face in trying to contextualize that structural commitment and its attendant constraints on public discourse. In now turning to consider a deep critique of liberalism, I am concerned to restore some of the ineliminable richness and *sittlich* character of our moral *and* political commitments. The next chapter focuses on Alasdair MacIntyre's powerful communitarian-conservative indictment of liberalism. My hope is that two mutually reinforcing goals will be achieved by this next step in the overall discussion: (1) the liberal vision of neutral dialogue will be enriched by notions of tradition and virtue otherwise marked out of bounds; and (2) the conservative denunciation of liberalism found in MacIntyre will be modified by indicating commitments to structural justice he cannot avoid. The result, I believe, is a stronger picture still of just talking, a picture that begins to satisfy the demand for context with which this study began.

4

Tradition and Translation

We cannot expect that a liberal solution to justice will be accepted without
further ado, or indeed that it requires no further modification. Though it
begins with an explicit awareness of difference in moral commitment, liberalism does not always seem, as a simple result of that, able to mediate that
difference effectively. Difference sometimes appears to cut too deeply to be
solved by any simple right-over-good model. This chapter discusses the
tradition-based conservatism of Alasdair MacIntyre as one of the most cogent,
and influential, criticisms of the liberal model. MacIntyre's alternative model
of the translation conversation among diverse traditions of rational inquiry is
examined as itself a dialogic theory of justice—that is, as a principled process
by which persons of diverse commitment must relate one to another.

On the basis of this reading, MacIntyre's view is criticized for its hidden
commitments to a kind of universalistic rationality that cuts against his stated
intentions of thoroughgoing context-recovery. It is likewise true, partly as a
result of these commitments being so hidden, that MacIntyre's model of conversation cannot deal with built-in difficulties of deception and force in

justificatory talk. By presuming a rational outcome in the intertradition conversation, he leaves his transtradition rational commitments unexamined, and
therefore critically ineffective. MacIntyre's revitalization of moral context is
valuable, but if and only if it can be combined in some fashion with a solution
to the problem of social coexistence toward which justice is ever directed.
MacIntyre cannot avoid this problem; in acting almost as though he could, he
fails convincingly to solve it.

MacIntyre's rich criticism of the liberal tradition can be approached only by
examining his narratives of intellectual development in some detail. In sections I
and II of this chapter I discuss, in turn, his indictments of Enlightenment
morality and of liberal justice. Section III sketches his alternative model, the
translation conversation, while sections IV and V indicate its limits—limits that
suggest the need for a firmer characterization of the rational presuppositions of
just talking. This need leads us back to a Kantian strategy of justification, now
much revised and deepened, in the work of Jürgen Habermas.

I. THE INCOHERENCE OF MORAL DISCOURSE

1. After Virtue

The criticisms advanced against Ackerman in the last chapter are only particular instances of a wider concern of recent social and political philosophy, the
desire to move away from the allegedly pallid structures of formal liberalism
and back to a "thicker" or more substantive moral and political frame of
reference. We may, as suggested in Chapter 1, think of this concern as one of
"context recovery." As noted there, recent criticisms of liberalism, from both
the left and the right, often turn on the charge that its features are in relevant
respects empty of particular and meaningful content. The charge has perhaps
most frequently been directed against the liberal picture of the moral self,
which is thought to be inadequate in several ways.

We have recently been told, for example, that the liberal conception of the
self is "deracinated" and that its decision-procedures are dependent on self-
imposed ignorance or bizarre separation from personal interests[1]—or that a

---

1. The model of liberalism being criticized here is Rawls's. Perhaps the most powerful statement of this sort of attack on Rawls can be found, as noted earlier, in Sandel's *Liberalism and the
Limits of Justice*.

coherent self must be more than a "bearer of preferences" to which it is strategically related, that is, must be instead connected to purposes and projects in a "strong sense" unknown to liberalism's "thin" picture of the self.[2] We are more than the maximizers of the liberal "performance model" because we are tied to *things that matter to us*, in a variety of ways: self-interpretation, self-understanding, the complexes of desire, aversion, aspiration, and emotional attachment. If this is so—and it is—then the model of a disengaged chooser assessing instrumental goods by way of strictly calculative reasons sells us short. "The center is no longer the power to plan, but rather openness to certain matters of significance," according to one critic. "This is now what is essential to personal agency."[3]

In a closely related argument, it has further been suggested that the very dependence of liberal models of decision on rules or formal procedures serves to obscure the role of moral judgment and moral imagination in ethical decision and action.[4] In sum, then, the generally *instrumental* views of the moral and rational self employed by liberal theorists, though sometimes theoretically elegant, too often fail to take account of deep commitments and the myriad particular details of life that are crucial to moral and political identity. To the extent that liberalism can only operate by ignoring or bracketing this context, its justificatory worth is thought to be in question. The results liberal theories generate face not simply strains of commitment, as Rawls put it, when imported into "the real world"; much more damaging, they begin to appear simply irrelevant, as having nothing to do with us.

Alasdair MacIntyre's *After Virtue* is perhaps the most influential of the many conservative contributions to the recent context-recovery project.[5] The context MacIntyre seeks to recover with his extended criticism of "the Enlightenment project" is of a degree of richness unknown to many other critics of that project, and not to be understood merely as achieving a better depiction of the moral self—though this will prove one area of benefit. More generally, MacIntyre is concerned to rehabilitate the notion of a human *telos*, or ultimate

2. Charles Taylor, "Self-Interpreting Animals," in *Human Agency and Language: Philosophical Papers 1* (New York: Cambridge University Press, 1985), pp. 97–114.

3. Ibid., p. 105.

4. This criticism appears in many forms, but for a clear statement see Charles Larmore, *Patterns of Moral Complexity,* ch. 1. Larmore wants to rehabilitate the notion of Aristotelian *phronesis* in moral theory, but he goes on to criticize MacIntyre's use of another feature of Aristotle's moral theory, namely its monism or generation of a single conception of the good life.

5. Alasdair MacIntyre, *After Virtue.* Early formulations of many of the critical moral points developed in this work can also be found in MacIntyre's *A Short History of Ethics* (New York: Macmillan, 1966), esp. chs. 1, 17, and 18.

end, which gives point and direction to moral practices—a grounding ethical notion that right-over good liberalism by definition cannot address. To this end he seeks, with a growing number of contemporary moral theorists, a greater appreciation for *virtues* as the relevant feature of moral investigation. In MacIntyre's view, the poverty of the Enlightenment project of rationally grounding morality is that it leaves no room for a rich table of desirable traits, features of character that arise organically from human conduct, the cultivation of which secures the conditions necessary for a truly ethical life.

On the neo-Aristotelian model advanced and defended in *After Virtue*,[6] these virtues turn one toward the proper ends of humankind. They do so by generating and fostering just those aspects of the self and the community necessary for the truly good life, which is to say, an ethical life in a just community. And this "turning toward" cannot be accomplished without a vigorous understanding of our moral ends or the personal traits most able to bring us to their realization. According to MacIntyre, then, the three essential factors in virtue ethics are "untutored human nature as it happens to be, human nature as it could be if it realized its *telos*, and the precepts of rational ethics as the means for the transition from one to the other."[7] The only way to recover ethical coherence is to find and cultivate that *telos*, and that is just what contemporary discourse about morality cannot do, for it has renounced all such descriptions of ultimate ends.

The claim about ultimate ends has been renounced for a reason, of course. We saw in previous sections of this work that liberalism's refusal to accept a single vision of the good life as the one and only right one is usually heralded as an advance over the tyranny of a moral perfectionism, where diversity on questions of the good is stifled. Indeed, it is often heralded as an advance over actual political tyranny, where a single conception of the good is expanded to society-wide dimensions. This refusal to endorse a single human *telos* therefore proceeds from a recognition, like Ackerman's, that there are in fact many answers to Socrates' question and that therefore the values of *pluralism* and *toleration* are of utmost importance in the political sphere.[8] But MacIntyre

---

6. The Aristotelianism is no longer in the forefront of MacIntyre's thinking by the time he comes to publish later statements of his position, where a Thomistic strain absent in the earlier works assumes a much greater, indeed central, importance. See MacIntyre, *Whose Justice? Which Rationality?* esp. ch. 11.

7. *After Virtue*, p. 51.

8. I am following Larmore's usage here: pluralism is the recognition that there is more than one conception of the good life; toleration is the recognition that reasonable people may disagree about which one is the best. See Larmore, *Patterns of Moral Complexity*, preface and ch. 1.

sees in this trumpeted advance only the growing *incoherence* of moral discourse (and, by extension, of liberalism) because it closes off the possibility of genuine achievement of moral ends.[9] "Since the whole point of ethics—both as a theoretical and a practical discipline—is to enable man to pass from his present state to his true end, the elimination of any notion of essential human nature and with it the abandonment of any notion of a *telos* leaves behind a moral scheme composed of two remaining elements whose relationship is quite unclear."[10] Those "two remaining elements" are, first, a substantive sense and vocabulary of morality and, second, a sense of what a moral law is supposed rationally to be.

According to MacIntyre's diagnosis, these elements persist in our moral discourse, but without a *telos* to complete the triangle of moral justification. And so, divorced from their genuine roots, the inherited elements are at odds with each other. Theoretically, moral laws are understood to have universal extension in the project of rationally grounding morality, but practically, moral utterances depend on a vocabulary that implicitly invokes the good. Because the context to ground such invocations is lacking, these utterances can refer to the good only in confused ways. Appeals are fractured and partial. Without a teleology that would effectively restore context to moral utterances and give proper range to them, MacIntyre suggests, the bottom falls out of contemporary moral discourse. It cannot generate universal, law-like justifications for morality because it is fragmented; and it is just such universal, law-like justifications that it has set itself the task of seeking. The result is discursive incoherence, in which what are in fact historically particular versions of "human nature" and "rational justification" masquerade as timeless metaphysical entities.

MacIntyre likewise charges, as Sandel did of Rawls, that the Enlightenment notion of "the unencumbered moral self," a self free of determinate nature and defined solely by its ability to act in an instrumental-rational fashion, is a theoretical fiction. Selves, he argues, are always embedded in historical and social particulars that govern what sort of moral agents they are. Particular

---

9. I may seem to be eliding liberalism and modernism a little unfairly here, but it is an elision MacIntyre himself is not especially careful about, for he believes modern moral theory's dominant mode is liberal. Generally, MacIntyre wants to argue that the incoherence of modern moral discourse is not solved by liberal political strategies of abstracting from endemic moral disagreement. "Modern" and "liberal" are therefore conjoined in this critique in a complex way. In the next chapter, on Habermas, we shall encounter both a radical version of modernism (i.e., the Enlightenment project) that is *not* liberal, and versions of antimodern criticism that are postmodern rather than (like MacIntyre) premodern in orientation.

10. *After Virtue*, pp. 54–55.

stories, ends, roles, and virtues "are not characteristics that belong to human beings accidentally, to be stripped away in order to discover 'the real me.' They are part of my substance, defining partially at least and sometimes wholly my obligations and my duties. Individuals inherit a particular space within an interlocking set of social relationships."[11] Without a coherent model of what MacIntyre thinks of as "the narrative self," moral discourse cannot address the concerns that are relevantly mine.

Our inheritance from the Enlightenment is thus indicted as self-delusion. The concealing and self-concealing of contemporary theory issues in incoherent discursive practices. These lead routinely to the conversational blocks discussed in the previous chapter. Says MacIntyre:

> It is precisely because there is in our society no established way of deciding between [competing moral] claims that moral argument appears to be necessarily interminable. From our rival conclusions we can argue back to our rival premises; but when we do arrive at our premises argument ceases and the invocation of one premise against another becomes a matter of pure assertion and counter-assertion.[12]

This fragmentation, the failure of conceptual grounding within coherence-granting context, gives contemporary moral discourse its peculiar and pervasive *emotivist* character, according to MacIntyre. The fact that competing and diametrically opposite claims can be made by someone other than me, without his or her appearing merely misguided or insane, amounts to *prima facie* evidence that morality is never more than an expression of personal taste. Without a shared moral context, we can all express ourselves just as we like and, though our expressions may retain the *form* of moral statements (that is, statements intended to demand agreement), cognitively they will in fact be no different from such preferential (and rationally trivial) exclamations as "Ugh!" or "Yummy!"[13]

MacIntyre's view has been extensively criticized for employing a tendentious caricature of Kantian morality in marshaling this set of sweeping criticisms. MacIntyre's Kant, understood as the paradigm of an Enlightenment moral thinker, leaves absolutely no room for ideas of happiness or human

11. Ibid., p. 33.
12. Ibid., p. 8.
13. Or, as the emotivist charge of moral statements is usually expressed, "I like this. Do so as well." The point here is that the imperative "Do so as well" has no rationally compelling force if the only reason supporting it is my liking this, however true it might be that I like it.

flourishing and any idea of an ultimate end is completely excised from moral reasoning.[14] In common with many commentators, I believe this is an exaggeration of Kant's view—though perhaps not of (MacIntyre's true target) the sort of thinned-out Kantianism to be found in some contemporary moral philosophy. But more seriously, MacIntyre may be guilty of misreading the thinker with whom he wishes to align himself most closely here, Aristotle. For though Aristotle was clearly an advocate of what is today generally known as virtue-based ethics, he did not employ a progressive notion of the virtues and their efficacy in moving humankind from an untutored stage of development to an ethical one.[15] This progressivist tendency in MacIntyre is imported from elsewhere, perhaps from the Benedictine-Trotskyite amalgam that gets a short defense at the end of *After Virtue*, perhaps from the Thomism lately more evident in his work. However, I am concerned not so much with these textual and influential disputes as with the general tendency of MacIntyre's argument at this stage: that the recovery of a *telos* is what we require to reinvigorate morality, a *telos* that will, like Aristotle's, leave little room (and no substantive room) for disagreement about ultimate ends.

It is of course truistic to say that this project is at odds with liberalism, but that is not in itself an argument against MacIntyre's view. The more pressing difficulty—the difficulty that does not depend on any previous commitment to liberalism—is that MacIntyre's view does not appear to take sufficient account of *genuine* and ineradicable differences on the questions of the good human life. The intellectual and moral choice posed at the end of *After Virtue* is a stark and provocative one: Nietzsche or Aristotle. We must choose either manic, mocking irrationalism and a perspectivist skepticism about good and evil, or the rich cognitivism of an ethical life functioning seamlessly in realization of a rich and unassailable human *telos*. Unless we are prepared to court nihilism by continuing a moral discourse in which we can say anything we like, in which nothing is good or bad in anything like the sense things are considered true or false, then we have no choice but to throw our lot in with a strong naturalist like Aristotle and his very concrete (and therefore limiting) picture of the good life.

14. For various versions of this criticism of MacIntyre, and its implications for the rest of his theory circa *After Virtue*, see Onora O'Neill, "Kant After Virtue," *Inquiry* 26 (1983): 387–405; Marx Wartofsky, "Virtue Lost, or Understanding MacIntyre," *Inquiry* 27 (1983): 235–50; and J. B. Schneewind, "Moral Crisis and the History of Ethics," *Midwest Studies in Philosophy* 8 (1983): 525–39, and "Virtue, Narrative, and Community: MacIntyre and Morality," *Journal of Philosophy* 79 (1982): 653–63.

15. Larmore, *Patterns of Moral Complexity*, ch. 2.

2. After *After Virtue*

I do not believe the choice need be so stark—nor indeed is it clear that MacIntyre himself does, especially in the work that has followed *After Virtue*. Even there his answer to Socrates' question ("The good life for man is the life spent seeking the good life for man")[16] appears to open the door to moral pluralism even as MacIntyre is insisting on how firmly closed that door must remain.[17] Moreover, in the promised sequel to *After Virtue—Whose Justice? Which Rationality?*— a model of moral interaction is indicated that is deeply affected by the ineliminability of moral difference. This is most obvious in MacIntyre's notion of a *tradition* of moral inquiry, an idea whose defense grows naturally out of *After Virtue*'s insistence on a recovery of the virtues and of the importance of narrative continuity for a coherent moral self. The essential factors of moral life are only to be found, MacIntyre suggests, in the rich, concrete, shared context of a tradition of moral inquiry. The insistence on tradition as the only relevant ethical scene is likewise meant as a self-conscious reply to the Enlightenment's elimination of tradition as a relevant, or even admissible, factor in rational inquiry.[18]

At first glance, the insistence on tradition would seem to keep MacIntyre deeply at odds with the liberal paradigm of neutral political choice. And MacIntyre may be seen to begin his investigation of traditions just where our discussion of Ackerman left off, namely at the prospect of generating agreement among individuals of diverse commitment under rules of *dialogic* neutrality. Like Michael Walzer, MacIntyre doubts that moral agreement can ever be coaxed out of the contingent and unpredictable nature of real moral talk; he also doubts, again like Walzer, that ideally generated agreement can ever have the foundational force that some theorists want to claim for it. MacIntyre's argument cuts even more deeply than Walzer's, however, for it has to do with a more general loss of moral context than Walzer wanted to claim. Walzer argued that ideal talk was a limited strategy of justification; MacIntyre wants to argue that liberalism itself is incoherent because it cannot generate moral agreement out of difference by retreating, as it wishes, to neutral ground.

Because the diagnosis of moral discourse undertaken in *After Virtue* has these wider political implications, blocked moral conversation and the role of

---

16. *After Virtue*, p. 219.

17. Ibid., pp. 19–22, 35–37.

18. These anti-Enlightenment arguments are not always as new as MacIntyre seems to suggest. Larmore notes how much MacIntyre owes for his critical stance to Horkheimer and Adorno's *Dialectic of Enlightenment*, trans. John Cumming (New York: Continuum, 1993). He might also have mentioned Gadamer's rejection of the Enlightenment "prejudice against prejudice" in *Truth and Method*.

tradition can be considered the starting points of MacIntyre's examination of *justice*. It is perhaps surprising that someone for whom contemporary talk seems to offer so little should be characterized here as defending a "dialogic conception of justice." Yet MacIntyre's insistence on the difficulties of liberal dialogue opens up an analysis of justice that, while it does not seek to generate particular results in justified rules or practices, serves to clarify what is at stake in our thinking, and talking, about justice. MacIntyre's historical investigation places the notion of "justice" squarely within discrete intellectual and ethical traditions, mediated by linguistic practices. It also demonstrates how every notion of "justice-in-a-tradition" is always in conversation with justice-in-other-traditions. MacIntyre clearly has no dialogic conception of justice in the sense of Ackerman's, where dialogue of a certain kind produces decisions that will then be considered (by definition) just; he has instead a conception that shows how particular conceptions of justice arise in traditions—traditions that are now, as always, *unavoidably* in conversation with their rivals. In the context of recent North American debate about justice theory, where sets of results (in the form of principles of justice) are evaluated one to another on their effectiveness, rational plausibility, and so on, this sort of meta-theory about justice will naturally seem unfamiliar in scope.

It may also be unfamiliar in method. MacIntyre is no longer concerned merely to criticize a dominant moral and political paradigm. He wants also to provide a detailed set of historical illustrations that themselves serve to rehabilitate the traditional context lost in the Enlightenment's project of grounding universal reason and morality. For only when we see that moral notions, especially notions of justice, arise in substantive traditions of inquiry, thick forms of intellectual and moral life, will we be able to return to the coherence our rational aspiration has so glibly thrown away. That is, only by self-consciously surrendering the universalist aspirations of liberalism, the hopes of rational agreement on principles, will moral meaning once more be accessible to us—but now always understood as tradition-bound meaning. The general argument therefore presumes what Barbara Herrnstein Smith has called a "lapsarian theology." It is MacIntyre's belief that we were formerly, in some distant but real prehistorical past, morally coherent. That we are no longer coherent is owing to the hubris of rational critique of tradition. But we need not despair at our own folly, for this latter-day fall from grace can be overcome, by a return to the Edenic fold of tradition.[19]

---

19. Barbara Herrnstein Smith, "Judgment After the Fall," in *Contingencies of Value*, pp. 85–107. Smith also notes the implicit "tyranny of normalcy" in this sort of theology, where "incoher-

MacIntyre's historicist thesis is defended for the most part by historical arguments, and these are precisely the sort of arguments that might be expected to count least with the members of the post-Enlightenment world who are likely to assess its rational merits.[20] In examining MacIntyre's conception of justice, I will be, like many of the commentators, less concerned with the particularities of his historical arguments than with his view of how traditions relate one to another, conversationally. What is of concern, therefore, is not justice-in-this-tradition or justice-in-that-tradition, and the historical accuracy of MacIntyre's specific reconstructions, but rather the background structure of rational debate that is meant to regulate relations among the various traditions. We can note immediately that social space is, on this view no less than on Ackerman's, mediated by some kind of dialogue. It is important, indeed crucial, for MacIntyre's view of tradition-based justice and practical rationality that questions of moral import are always carried out in some kind of principled talk.

After examining the structure of rational debate under this conception, which I shall call the intertradition or translation conversation, we will ultimately be justified in saying that MacIntyre's view is less a *destruction* of the liberal project of justice than it is a context-sensitive *reformation* of that project. In other words, if we make bold to translate "tradition" as "conception of the good"—and thereby restore some of the richness of ethical background presumed lost in structural conceptions of justice—the conversation between MacIntyre's examples becomes something very much like the sort of justice conversation we have been seeking to isolate. It is a dialogic crucible in which

---

ent" discourse is split off from "normal" varieties. The same tendency is effectively criticized by Jacques Derrida in his engagement with John Searle and speech-act theory, *Limited Inc.* (Evanston, Ill.: Northwestern University Press, 1988).

20. The reviewers of *Whose Justice?* are quick to disclaim any historical expertise, and thus equally quick to set upon MacIntyre with nonhistorical philosophical criticisms. A frequent comment is that MacIntyre's work may be good intellectual history but is bad philosophy; others—for instance, Jeffery Stout—want to say it is also bad intellectual history. See Stout's review, "Homeward Bound: MacIntyre on Liberal Society and the History of Ethics," *Journal of Religion* 1 (1989): 220–32. See also the following reviews of MacIntyre: Thomas Nagel, "Agreeing in Principle," *Times Literary Supplement*, July 8–14, 1988, pp. 747–48; Charles Larmore, "Alasdair MacIntyre: *Whose Justice? Which Rationality?*" *Journal of Philosophy* 86 (1989): 437–41; and Bernard Williams, "Modernity," *London Review of Books*, January 5, 1989, p. 5. The last contains a slip in the first sentence: Williams inadvertently calls MacIntyre's previous book "After Justice." One point even the most hostile reviewers tend to miss is that MacIntyre's historicism—a kind of genealogy of traditions—ought to be seen as conflicting with his grounds for dismissing Nietzsche in *After Virtue*. MacIntyre addresses this issue to some extent in his 1988 Gifford Lectures, *Some Rival Versions of Moral Enquiry: Encyclopaedias, Genealogies, and Traditions* (Notre Dame: University of Notre Dame Press, 1990).

adherents of rival and diverse groups together forge principles of social and political coexistence. On this un-MacIntyrean view of MacIntyre, traditions still represent loci of ethical agreement, including agreement about the concrete virtue of justice; but the conversation between traditions is now understood as issuing in a kind of moral interaction—"justice" in a less exclusive, and therefore thinner, sense—that ensures social cooperation. To get a closer sense of how the translation conversation arises, we need first to investigate more closely how liberal justice fares in MacIntyre's diagnosis of traditions.

II. LIBERAL JUSTICE

1. Justice Out of Tradition

Traditions of moral inquiry have, for MacIntyre, three basic features. There is (1) a strong sense of *narrative continuity* that governs the members of the tradition, telling the story of who they are and how they got where they are. There is also (2) a list of relevant *virtues*, justice prominent among them, to which appeal can be made when questions of morality arise. And there is, finally, (3) a shared sense of *practical rationality* which provides the concrete daily ability to decide what constitutes a good moral argument, and to reach moral conclusions that issue in action.

Liberal justice, with its denial of the particular contextual self and its search for universal principles of interaction, coupled with silence on questions of the good life, seems at first glance to seek *transcendence* of these tradition-based features.[21] Liberal justice does not deny the fundamental disagreement among moralities pointed out so eloquently in *After Virtue*. But by attempting to reach beyond the bounds of particular, contextualized morality, the liberal justice project still seeks the goal of universal, rationally defensible principles. Moral disagreement, however fundamental, is dealt with in the manner now familiar from the first chapter, by giving issues of right priority over issues of good in some thin and formal fashion. Thus, modern (which is to say, broadly liberal) theories of justice attempt to deal with fundamental moral disagreement among rival theories of the good by abstacting from them in some way— by invoking spaces of neutral dialogue, shared rational commitments, or stan-

21. This language will recall the three strategies of justification rejected by Ackerman—a rejection in turn rejected by some of his critics—in the previous chapter.

dards of fair argument.[22] Here some formal or procedural factors are defended with the intent of generating the minimum consensus necessary for coexistence and the peaceful social management of rival teleologies.

Yet, as we saw in the previous section on moral disagreement, what may lie hidden here is a no less fundamental disagreement among such theorists as to what counts as a good argument, what human nature really is, and what principles or practices of justice are in fact justifiable. Consequently, for MacIntyre "[t]hose who disagree with each other radically about justice will not be able to look to some neutral conception of rationality, by appeal to which they will be able to decide which of them is in the right. For the same or similar disagreements can generally be expected to appear on questions about the nature of practical rationality."[23] This point echoes one made earlier in *After Virtue* about morality and its derivation from rational commitments: "It is very much to the point," we are told there, "that such writers [as Rawls, Gewirth, and Donegan] cannot agree among themselves either on what the character of moral rationality is or on the substance of the morality which is to be founded on that rationality."[24] In other words, if there were such a thing as the character of human rationality, and a minimal morality that could be founded on its basis, disagreement would not be so persistent among the theorists of that rationality. Instead of a chorus of competing claims, each one describing the character of moral rationality in a different fashion, there *should* be a convergence of views on the fact of the matter, namely that moral rationality is of *this* character. Unless this convergence can be demonstrated, the foundational nature of these attempts must fail, for they show no more than that each theorist has a version of moral rationality that arises from his or her own particular commitments and influences. The lack of agreement about the nature of human moral rationality (that is, among those who even suppose there is such a thing) provides, according to MacIntyre, "*prima facie* evidence that their project has failed."[25]

Given this disagreement, "there emerges no uncontested and incontestable account of what tradition-independent morality consists in and consequently

22. I am leaving aside here the many differences among such conceptions. Ackerman believes his version of "abstracting from" disagreement doesn't involve any problematic transcendence from moral values. But as we saw in the preceding chapter, neutral dialogue may serve, in the end, to both trump and transcend disagreement, despite assertions to the contrary. I also argued, however, that this trumping or transcending is not damaging to the theory, given the preexisting pragmatic commitments to which it alone needs to appeal.

23. *Whose Justice?* p. 321.

24. *After Virtue*, p. 21.

25. Ibid.

no neutral set of criteria by means of which the claims of rival and contending traditions could be adjudicated."[26] MacIntyre continues:

> Initially the liberal claim was to provide a political, legal, and economic framework in which assent to one and the same set of rationally justifiable principles would enable those who espouse widely different and incompatible conceptions of the good life for human beings to live together peaceably within the same society, enjoying the same political status and engaging in the same economic relationships.[27]

Yet, put into practice, the neutralist strategy works itself out in decidedly nonneutral ways. The self conceived as a preference generator, public arenas as loci of bargaining, and justice as a matter of maximizing happiness, though all taken to be uncontroversial, actively fail to do justice to other conceptions of the good. This was the problem that afflicted the poor character Depressive in Ackerman's thought-experiment: no common yardstick is uncontroversial enough to be straightforwardly acceptable to everyone. Every imaginable common yardstick will leave off the public agenda some metaphysical, religious, or cultural concerns, those that cannot be phrased in terms of preferences, bargaining moves, utiles, or whatever the yardstick's units happen to be.[28]

Despite the best efforts of neutralist liberals, then, disagreement about conceptions of the good cannot be trumped or translated. It can merely be disguised by apparently universal claims that, because they remain hidden, fail to be convincingly universal. At the same time, the language of *consensus* initiated by these liberal conceptions of the person and of the public sphere serves only to obscure the fact that deep disagreement continues. The apparently value-free liberal conceptions of self and society are actually substantive, and not universal.[29] Moreover, because the version of reason allowed into this conception is limited, particularly in its only instrumental character, liberalism opens the door to a degree of bureaucratic control unknown to earlier eras: only in extensive bureaucracies can the preferences

---

26. *Whose Justice?* p. 334.

27. Ibid., pp. 335–36.

28. This is therefore another version of the "no-common-yardstick" argument introduced by Ackerman and, against Ackerman, by Fishkin.

29. The argument against consensus rhetoric, to the effect that it obscures power imbalances and particular interests with apparently neutral arguments, is common in feminist political theory. See, e.g., Nancy Fraser, *Unruly Practices*, chs. 1, 7, and 8. The last two chapters contain an illuminating discussion of how "needs" are constructed within this rhetoric.

and interests of separate individuals be summed and divided, assessed and treated.[30]

The move to liberal justice must now be reconceived, not as the salutary first conceptual step in taking moral difference seriously, but instead as a last-ditch attempt to *overcome* the issue of moral difference. Liberals, ever inventive, continually adopt new tactics in their effort to realize the end of a context-free set of ethical rules. They turn to new but in fact imaginary teleologies (utilitarianism, for example), or they seek to draw conclusions from the very structure of rationality itself. But the final results of these new tactics are never the same. Disagreement reigns as much among the theorists of contemporary justice as it does among such "street-level" participants in moral debate as the abortion advocates found in the previous chapter's example. Though the conversation is more restrained at the philosophical level, the justice-theory conversation seems to reach blocks just as inevitably as routine moral discourse. Premises about rights, rules, and human nature are as little up for grabs here as they were in heated moral debate; there simply is no principled way for conflicts between premises to be adjudicated.

The unique problem faced by contemporary justice theory is not the simple fact of conflict about moral ideas. The problem is rather the fact of *fragmentation* coupled with such disagreement. Moral conflicts, which may arise in any milieu, in the modern milieu cannot in principle be resolved. And the move from moral disagreement to a purportedly neutral sphere of justice does not solve the problem of disagreement because the neutral spaces of decision are not, and in principle cannot be, neutral enough. Theorists faced with this situation may begin to seek only the commitments shared by all rational agents, but the thinner the notion of rationality appealed to and available on the basis of those commitments, the more it fails to represent anything we can recognize as our rational and moral selves. Disagreement can always be expected to arise again, either about the characterization of rationality itself or about whether such a characterization has anything to say to us. Consider, MacIntyre suggests, "the intimidating range of questions about what justice requires and permits, to which *alternative and incompatible answers* are offered by contending individuals and groups within contem-

---

30. MacIntyre's indictment of modern bureaucracy is one of the most rhetorically effective parts of *After Virtue*; see esp. his chs. 6 and 7. Larmore makes an interesting but only partially convincing reply by suggesting that bureaucratic *predictability* is a genuine good of political neutrality, allowing us always to know where we stand with, e.g., the Supreme Court. The argument appears to overlook the fact that bureaucracy may still be predictably dehumanizing, inefficient, or unhelpful.

porary societies. . . . [U]nderlying this wide diversity of judgments upon particular types of issue are a set of *conflicting conceptions of justice.*"[31]

As long as these conflicting conceptions persist, then, the universalist, transtraditional liberal justice project cannot succeed, even on its own terms. We saw that, for MacIntyre, a moral discourse divorced from ethical context was doomed to descend into incoherence. By the same token, conceptions of justice, once divorced from the life-giving richness of traditions, cannot generate the principles of interaction they set out to find. Success cannot be purchased at the price of abstracting from the good.

2. Justice in Tradition

It may be objected immediately that these criticisms merely (and perhaps deliberately) misunderstand the priority-of-right commitments of liberalism as a *political* theory, not a theory of the good or of human ends. We can recall Dworkin's indication of the category mistake, and Ackerman's insistence that critiques of neutrality miss the mark when applied to constrained dialogue. Liberalism as a political theory does not court incoherence by employing value, as long as it does not commit the error of defending itself as a moral theory. Charles Larmore makes this point effectively within a more general defense of neutrality: "The 'individualism' associated with liberalism is not understood by MacIntyre as a political doctrine, according to which government should treat persons as individuals (i.e., apart from status and ascription)," he says, "but rather as a general theory of human nature that denies the importance of shared commitments."[32] If MacIntyre had understood liberalism aright, in other words, he would have seen that the critical missiles launched in this vigorous salvo mostly fly past the target. Yet such a defense states the case a little too glibly: if MacIntyre will not countenance liberal neutrality, it may be because he thinks it is incoherent in its very claims to be merely political, not simply because he has misunderstood those claims. And more to the point, because liberalism has been so disappointing in advancing truly neutral arguments in favor of neutrality—that is, arguments that do not depend on some previously held (and possibly controversial) political or moral commitment— we may be inclined, like him, to doubt whether such arguments actually exist, or could.

MacIntyre's way out of the impasse of liberal justice is, not surprisingly, the

---

31. *Whose Justice?* p. 1 (emphasis added).
32. Larmore, *Patterns of Moral Complexity,* p. 25.

way back to tradition-based justice. Only in particular traditions, he thinks, can we recover the sense of teleology, and therefore the coherence, that was lost when moral justification made its wrongheaded attempt to break out of context. Traditions are shown to work with lists of virtues, including justice, that direct moral conduct. For MacIntyre, our current disagreement about justice is really the result of our *hidden* commitments to particular traditions, commitments that provide substantive answers to what justice is. Until these commitments are recognized, made explicit, and accepted, interlocutors in moral and political debate can expect to continue disagreeing forever. Instead of continuing their misguided efforts to rise above the fray, then, liberals should accept their limitations and admit (as MacIntyre does) that the particularities of the liberal conception of the good show liberalism to be, no less than Aristotelianism or Thomism, a concrete tradition. Only then will a fruitful round of talk among interlocutors begin.

What constitutes a tradition? For MacIntyre it is essentially *a particular way of talking*, a way of going on with the discussion about an issue or concern, seeing certain argumentative moves as good ones and working with a list of desiderata, the tradition's virtues, that command rational assent. A tradition is also the cumulative story of how its adherents got where they are, with continuity and narrative coherence essential components of their self-understanding. MacIntyre says:

> A tradition is an *argument extended through time* in which certain fundamental agreements are defined and redefined in terms of two kinds of conflict: those with critics and enemies external to the tradition who reject all or at least key parts of those fundamental agreements, and those internal, interpretive debates through which the meaning and rationale of the fundamental agreements come to be expressed and by whose progress a tradition is constituted.[33]

It is important for the success of MacIntyre's critique of liberal justice that the theoretical debates characteristic of modernity be in fact of the first kind, *though they present themselves as debates of the second kind*. In other words, liberalism advances itself as a single grand project of self-interpretation and criticism that continues a history of internal reform. It wants to embrace everything in the hope of ever-greater moral and political self-transparency and therefore ever-greater adequacy. But this project is doomed to failure

---

33. *Whose Justice?* p. 12 (emphasis added).

because the adherents of liberalism are themselves limited by traditional commitments they cannot outstrip.

The moment liberalism accepts its transformation into a tradition, and the concomitant recognition by its adherents that this is so, it achieves an emancipation from the routine conversational blocks and conceptual incoherence that feature in this extensive critique. The disagreement MacIntyre identifies among contemporary interlocutors is intractable just as long as, and to the extent that, we fail to recognize that it is the result of posttraditional fragmentation. The disagreement suddenly becomes manageable, even salutary, once we see that traditional commitments are what block easy convergence of judgments, for this is where a fruitful intertraditional conversation begins.

3. Two Replies

We saw that the prima facie portion of MacIntyre's argument in support of tradition-based justice was the fact of disagreement among theorists who denied the force of traditional commitments. Is this fact enough to support the view that answers to the question "What is justice" make sense only within a particular tradition? There are at least two ways to answer this question in the negative that nevertheless take some account of the richness of ethical background MacIntyre thinks is lost in liberal justice. The first is what we might consider the modernist's considered rejoinder to MacIntyre. The second argues, in a related way, for the transcontextual coherence of the virtue of justice.[34] Both responses work by retaining, in quite different ways, a reformed version of the priority of right over good.

A certain kind of modernist can reply to MacIntyre that he has failed to understand just what the modern project of framing justice wants to accomplish.[35] No one, least of all a sensitive liberal, denies that conceptions of the good arise from, and are always embedded in, traditions of moral inquiry. This is precisely what gives those traditions whatever coherence they possess, and

34. These rejoinders to MacIntyre have been given in various forms by a number of commentators. For what I am calling the modernist reply, see Nagel's review of MacIntyre (note 20 above). The transrelative reply is suggested by Bernard Williams in his discussion of "the truth in relativism," but not pursued at any length. See Williams's *Ethics and the Limits of Philosophy* (London: Fontana, 1985), ch. 9. The possibility suggested here is that a universal form of justice will be given different content in different societies. As Williams has noted, Walzer's defense of complex pluralism in *Spheres of Justice* also follows something like this line.

35. Larmore's concerns to reinvigorate constitutive ties within shared forms of life, the virtues, and the values of context—while at the same time holding to the priority of right in the political sphere ("stopping short of Aristotle")—make him this kind of modernist.

the issue of moral disagreement its persistent character. A shared set of notions about what constitutes the good life, argued about and refined over time,
now commands the assent of a certain loyal portion of a society's population.
All the same, a well-ordered society may easily be composed of elements
deriving from several discrete traditions of this good-supporting type. We may
expect, as a result, that some form of disagreement here is inevitable, since the
individuals and groups within this complex society will have divergent histories and community commitments that bring them into conflict over resources
and social goods. In this society there are various genuine answers to Socrates'
question, and each has an integrity that is fostered and maintained in just the
way MacIntyre suggests, by an ongoing process of discussion and argument,
both with those inside the tradition and with those outside. Disagreement
among adherents of these various answers is simply to be expected; more than
this, it is the basic fact of social life and therefore poses a central challenge to all
members of the society.

Our modernist wants to say at this juncture that such disagreement about
what constitutes the good life cannot, and should not, be eradicated. It can
only be controlled.[36] And this issue of control is precisely what modern justice
theory seeks to address. It may be that in earlier eras, and within certain
traditions still, justice meant something richly substantive and compelling.
Fortunately or not, no *single* such answer to the question "What is just?" can
today be taken to social and political dimensions without risk of tyranny.
Nevertheless we have a society, and that society requires minimum conditions
of coexistence. It requires, most obviously, a principled way in which adherents of diverse traditions can talk to one another without rancor. Possibly they
will have little to talk about, possibly all too much. But the conflict that might
be expected to dominate their interactions must be set aside, or at least man-
aged, in the interests of getting along together.

The apparently transcendent character of modern justice theory therefore
always involves a lowering of expectations: "justice" can no longer mean what
it did within traditions; it can no longer speak to all concerns that an individual
can be expected to have. "Justice" now represents only the minimum conditions of political coexistence. That may mean something like rules of property
distribution, principles of punishment and reparation, or guidelines for neutral

---

36. The force of this "cannot" and "should not" are not equal, of course. Some liberals will
want to stop short at a purely descriptive claim and defend neutrality in justice as the solution to a
certain kind of nagging problem; others, more comfortable with prescriptive claims, will argue
that the more conceptions of the good in play, the better. For our purposes, it does not matter
which claim is preferred, for both take the fact of pluralism as the crucial starting point.

dialogue. It may mean something quite different, yet to be determined. We cannot plausibly ask for justice to provide more than this level of answer, but in so lowering our gaze we avoid the problem MacIntyre identified. Modern justice theory seeks not *the* principles of justice, true for everyone always, but rather whatever principles of justice we can all agree on *given our other substantive commitments*.[37]

Of course, disagreement among theorists who take this modus vivendi view does not cease, but that fact does not in itself provide prima facie evidence that the project is misconceived. It shows only that deciding what minimum principles we can all agree to, in this or any other society, is a more difficult project than is sometimes imagined. In the absence of actual agreement, mechanisms of hypothetical agreement may have to be constructed. Suggested principles will have to be passed through such mechanisms to test them for acceptance and adequacy.[38] Disagreement about the details of these procedures, and the results they produce, is only to be expected.

The stronger portion of MacIntyre's case can perhaps be marshaled here, in the rejoinder that it is not the fact of disagreement itself that is convincing, but what the fact indicates—namely that notions of justice are always tied to other commitments, however minimalist in intention. Neutral mechanisms of generating minimum consensus are simply less honest versions of substantive justice, with a particular and limited history, and they have no privileged status vis-à-vis the general disagreement than any other set of views on justice. In other words, expectation-lowering is not an effective strategy when it comes to solving the problem of disagreement, because expectations are always lowered in controversial ways. A different though perhaps no less serious problem is that the modus

37. MacIntyre might easily rejoin at this juncture that the forces of liberal justice theory cannot articulate and defend even a modus vivendi. I believe that this is true only to the extent that liberals refuse to surrender the most extravagant of their universalist claims. In some cases, of course—e.g., that of Rawls—universalism has been surrendered, or at least modified in some way, but the goal of a modus vivendi is not satisfactory. This illustrates the inevitable dilemma of a theory of justice defended in a pluralistic world: on the one hand, increasing substance will only convince increasingly narrow bands of the population; on the other hand, thin procedural notions may not give us much beyond mere formalism. The challenge is to articulate a theory of justice that is minimalist enough to produce agreement, and substantive enough to produce allegiance.

38. The hope, of course, is that the right kind of mechanisms will isolate for our consideration the principles of "justice" we can all agree on. It is this hope that drives Rawls's construction of the original position, and indeed his use of the mechanism of reflective equilibrium to match "our considered moral convictions" with defensible principles of justice (see Rawls, *A Theory of Justice*, esp. chs. 3, 7, and 8). The problem with these attempts is that there may be no set of considered moral judgments that all of us would be willing to call "ours." See also Lecture I of Rawls's *Political Liberalism*.

vivendi justified under such a strategy simply leaves out of the picture many important things that people care deeply about. Minimum consensus is not enough, even on the strictly political level; we crave coherence, a sense of belonging, and substantive commitments of which we can be proud and approve ourselves having. If, in the interests of neutrality, justice theory stops short of providing such commitments, it may undermine its own ability to demand loyalty and allegiance from the citizens whose interests it is meant to vouchsafe.

But consider the second response to MacIntyre. Let us say that justice is indeed a virtue in the thick sense MacIntyre desires, for it is always manifested within the richness of a particular tradition, within strong constitutive ties and narrative continuity. Yet justice is also a moral value that can in principle extend beyond the fact of disagreement among rival and incompatible views of values. It is, however, the only such value—reflecting the fact that notions of fairness and respect are universally applicable whatever other moral commitments groups may have, and disagree about. So by reflecting on our substantive disagreements, we come to realize that some commitments are actually common across traditions or views: the notion that each person should get his or her due, say, and that respect for divergent claims is essential to ethical life. (The grounds for finding this moral value compelling may vary from context to context without threatening the degree of commonality argued for here.) This articulation of a transtradition virtue of justice is not transcendence from substantial ethical commitments, but the discernment and cultivation of overlap in a certain limited portion of them.[39]

The notion of justice can, when conceived in this fashion, extend beyond what is commonly called the "relativism of distance." There is always a good deal of disagreement about details of justice, but that may only indicate just how far we agree about what is wanted in a theory of justice more generally. Disagreement indicates not incommensurability (in which no talk at all would be possible, let alone vigorous disagreement) but a merely apparent relativism that is really substantive disagreement capable of being overcome. Justice is precisely the value that can be shared and talked about in the way MacIntyre denies—across traditions. This view marks an advance on the bare-bones modus vivendi approach by picking out an aspect of all individual and group commitments that is shared, and therefore worthy of respect and admiration. An example of such a view is given by Walzer, who argues that a notion of "reiterative universalism" is available as a basis for transcultural

---

39. And, to that extent, this reply may suggest a view similar to Rawls's idea of "overlapping consensus."

notions of respect and justice.[40] Unlike "covering-law universalism," which sets out the limits of right and finds all people on the wrong side of these limits at fault, reiterative universalism allows a complex series of manifestations of right that are each equally worthy of respect. Though substantially different, these manifestations share enough characteristics for it to make sense to speak of a transcultural or transtraditional value of justice, despite the variations in manifestation and deep differences on other moral issues. Commitments within traditions and groups are maintained here, but justice is rediscovered as a value that, precisely because its purview is intergroup relations and respect, extends beyond the limits of this or that view, set of virtues, or tradition.

I suggested that these replies to MacIntyre's critical project appear to reform the liberal approach to justice by assimilating the notion of tradition to the common contemporary starting-point of competing conceptions of the good. Once accomplished, this assimilation allows either (1) construction of a theory of just interaction that takes coexistence as a supreme value and simply leaves intact substantive (and incommensurable) commitments to deeper notions of justice and ethics generally, or (2) picks out what is common in tradition-based notions of justice in such a way as to show how the value of justice is indeed transcontextual. MacIntyre professes to find both strategies antithetical to his theoretical project of demonstrating the inescapability of traditional commitments. To see why, and to see whether a more convincing reply is possible, it is necessary to look more closely at his notion of the conversation among traditions.

III. TALKING TO EACH OTHER: TRADITIONS IN CONVERSATION

1. Crisis and Translation

Traditions are not to be understood as monolithic. Indeed, MacIntyre's explicit aim is to show just how a tradition is a story of ongoing conflict, synthesis, and

---

40. See Michael Walzer, "Two Kinds of Universalism" (unpublished paper, October 1989). In contrast to Rawls's view, this reiterative universalist position on justice extends beyond the boundaries of a single society. Instead of the perception of certain circumstantially common moral commitments, Walzer suggests each culture manifests its own version of (a value called) justice.

argumentation. On his view, traditions seep into and through one another not only in the larger pattern of historical development, but also to the extent that the remains of a particular tradition survive its general synthesis or disintegration. This is why, for instance, Thomists and Humeans may coexist, however uneasily, in the universities of contemporary North America long after their respective forebears were the dominant tradition of a society. Traditions therefore represent *both* the moments in time in which they held general sway *and* the cultural inheritances within which individuals and groups still work and live today. It is precisely because the second point is true that we have an interaction problem of the kind interpretive justice theory is concerned to deal with. There are many traditional holdovers in our culture, and it is just these notions that will serve to infect and destroy any facile unity of inquiry advanced by the inheritors of the Enlightenment project.

How, then, are we to make sense of these conflicts, conceived now not as hitches in the general (that is, universal) progress of reason but as the incompatibility of notions deeply embedded in traditions of inquiry? MacIntyre's answer is that by critically examining how traditions arise, come into conflict, mature, and are overcome, we will acquire a sense of what happens when one tradition encounters a challenge to its legitimacy. This large historical picture will help us understand the actual conflicts of our own era. And what we shall find is that the general *conversational* structure discernible in the conflict between traditions works to exhibit the *rational superiority* of one tradition over another, including in that superiority its notions of justice and practical rationality. "Rationally superior" will be taken to mean, on this view, that a given theory is *the best theory produced so far,* by a general conversation, and tested against the demands of epistemological adequacy and explanatory ability.

The notion of adequacy indicates immediately MacIntyre's central presumption, that traditions can fail in their own terms to answer questions arising in moral and epistemological inquiry. Things go wrong in traditions of inquiry, and so *crisis* within a tradition, which initiates the kind of self-reflection that can demonstrate rational superiority, is a necessary if sometimes tragic feature of our lives as moral and rational agents. Crisis results from a felt inadequacy of the categories employed by a tradition—an inadequacy most often, but not always, made evident by conflict with another tradition of inquiry. It is, moreover, essential for MacIntyre's view that moral crisis (crisis in the terms and practices of moral discourse) be related in complex ways to epistemological crisis (crisis in the terms and practices of rational inquiry generally). In the modern era, a moral crisis is thought to be evident in the unreconstructed emotivism of moral debate and the poverty of the view of the self. If we accept such a diagnosis of contemporary moral discourse, it would in turn indicate a wider crisis in the practices of practical rationality. Not being able to agree on what is right or wrong also means, here, not being able to agree on what sort of argument would be adequate in deciding such a question.[41]

Is there a way out of such a moral-epistemological crisis? MacIntyre notes two stages of reaction when traditions of inquiry contact, and conflict with, one another. In the first stage, each tradition "characterizes the contentions of its rivals in its own terms"[42]—perhaps deciding in the process that the rival has some interesting things to say about certain marginal issues. But because there is no direct or deep challenge to the first tradition's legitimacy, this phase is no more than a rephrasing of contentions in a straightforward process of assimilation. We take on board anything that we can use from your tradition of inquiry, but the core—and so the basic stability of our tradition—remains untouched. In the second stage of conflict, however, this attitude can no longer be maintained. Here, MacIntyre says,

> the protagonists of each tradition, having considered in what ways their own tradition has by its own standards of achievement in enquiry found it difficult to develop its enquiries beyond a certain point, or has produced in some area insoluble antinomies, ask whether the alternative and rival tradition may not be able to provide resources to characterize and to explain the failings and defects of their tradition *more adequately* than they, using the resources of that tradition, have been able to do.[43]

Now the picture is clearly more complicated. In this second stage there is a recognition of difficulties, a willingness to accept outside aid in resolving them, and a presumed ability truly to *translate*—and not merely assimilate—notions from one tradition into another.[44]

The move to stage two depends greatly on a kind of humility on the part of

---

41. MacIntyre explores these notions in an early paper called "Epistemological Crises, Dramatic Narrative, and the Philosophy of Science," *The Monist* 60 (1977): 453–72.

42. *Whose Justice?* p. 166.

43. Ibid. (emphasis added).

44. As we shall see in a moment, MacIntyre's notion of translation is significantly conversational, which is to say that true translation is not the simple reduction of one set of terms into the language of another. It involves, in a manner similar to Gadamer's interpetive model in *Truth and Method*, an expansion on the part of both talkers—the creation, in effect, of a third language.

one tradition's members. At the least, there must be a recognition, however unwilling, that their own tradition is inadequate in its own terms. Often, of course, if there is any advance beyond stage one in the contact between discrete traditions, it will not be to the richer possibilities of stage two, but rather to open conflict between the traditions or to the disintegration of one or both of the rivals into smaller, even less viable fragments.[45] MacIntyre notes:

> In controversy between rival traditions, the difficulty in passing from the first stage to the second is that it requires *a rare gift of empathy* as well as of intellectual insight for the protagonists of such a tradition to be able to understand the theses, arguments, and concepts of their rival in such a way that they are able to view themselves from such an alien standpoint and to recharacterize their own beliefs in an appropriate manner from the alien perspective of the rival tradition.[46]

Individuals possessing this gift of empathy are bound to be infrequent actors on the historical stage, and unusually influential ones. This is why, for example, MacIntyre thinks Thomas Aquinas, with the benefits of his unique education, understood both the Aristotelian and the Augustinian traditions of rational inquiry, and moreover understood them in a way that allowed him to synthesize their claims. Aquinas spoke the languages of both traditions and therefore was able to translate them one to another, not content merely to rephrase the contentions of a rival tradition in the existing locutions of his own.

Now, it is crucial to MacIntyre's argument that there is no *neutral* standpoint from which Aquinas—or any other gifted individual—can adjudicate between the rival claims of the Aristotelian and Augustinian world-views. Aquinas did not move to a higher vantage point when he effected his world-historical synthesis. Instead, he synthesized while always staying within *both* traditions. Only thus were the theses and arguments of both intelligible to him, and only thus was he able to make sense of arguments that only count as good arguments to someone who is, in some sense anyway, an Aristotelian or an Augustinian. For MacIntyre, the attempt to move to a higher vantage point is always an illicit one, for it always opens up an infinite regress; a further vantage point, above both the first and its object of inquiry, is always theoretically possible. And above that new vantage is yet another. There is, in other

---

45. See *Whose Justice?* pp. 12 ff.
46. Ibid., p. 167 (emphasis added).

words, no adequate "stopping-rule" for the ascent to neutral viewpoints.[47] Perhaps more important, such viewpoints remain a theoretical fiction, impossible to find in practice, for we can never actually transcend the boundaries of our own viewpoint.[48] We can only hope, and this but rarely perhaps, to expand those boundaries. Yet, if for MacIntyre there is no neutral standpoint available to traditions in conflict, how is rational superiority ever assessed? From which vantage point do questions concerning adequacy become intelligible? Where are we standing when we decide one tradition is more adequate than—which is to say rationally superior to—another?

The answer is tied to the notion of epistemological crisis—that moment when inconsistencies and inadequacies embedded in the tradition show themselves in antinomies or blocks to further rational progress. These problems are systematically intractable, not just small obstacles in the general progress of rational inquiry. A tradition in the throes of genuine epistemological crisis simply cannot solve the problems it identifies, and realizes that it cannot. So an *adequate* response to a genuine epistemological crisis must meet three basic requirements: (1) it must provide a *solution* to the problems that have proved systematically intractable; (2) it must provide an *explanation* of what rendered those problems intractable, and thus made the tradition incoherent, in the first place; and (3) it must perform these two goals in a way that preserves fundamental *continuity* between the new theory and the tradition's precrisis state. In solving an epistemological crisis from within a tradition, then, "*imaginative conceptual innovation* will have had to occur. The justification of the new theses will lie precisely in their ability to achieve what could not have been achieved prior to that innovation."[49]

Once again, because conceptual innovation is likely to be very rare, much more likely than internal reform is a scenario in which the theses necessary for

47. This point will be familiar from recent attacks on the so-called detachment model of objectivity, found in both moral and (especially) epistemological inquiry. This model is, according to some critics, a misleading inheritance of the seventeenth-century scientific outlook. See, for some examples, Thompson Clarke, "The Legacy of Skepticism," *Journal of Philosophy* 69 (1972): 754–69; Bernard Williams, *Descartes: The Project of Pure Inquiry* (New York: Penguin, 1978); Nagel, *View from Nowhere*; Jonathan Lear, *Love and Its Place in Nature* (New York: Farrar, Strauss, Giroux, 1990), esp. ch. 7. I have been helped on these issues by discussions with Christopher Dustin. For more on the peculiar limitations of the detachment model, see my "The Plain Truth About Common Sense: Metaphysics, Skepticism, and Irony," *Journal of Speculative Philosophy*, forthcoming.

48. It is worth noting here that MacIntyre's thought on issues of viewpoint, placement within a tradition, and the conversation among traditions all bear resemblance to Gadamer's seminal work in *Truth and Method*.

49. *Whose Justice?* p. 362 (emphasis added).

solving the crisis come from a *rival* tradition of inquiry. In this way, contact with rival traditions of inquiry may hasten crisis, and ongoing contact between traditions is a fundamental precondition for any general progress toward the best available theory. Consider a highly schematic example. Tradition A is in crisis, unable to solve certain problems that arise naturally in its project of inquiry. As a result of this inability, its rational progress is stalled, its movement blocked. But then adherents of A encounter some members of rival Tradition B, at present free of this sort of crisis and offering different answers to some of the same questions the A-people are asking. During the comparing of notes that ensues, Tradition B adherents point out—very generously or very arrogantly, depending on your point of view—that their system of rational inquiry both solves the problems Tradition A cannot *and* explains why Tradition A came to be in its state of crisis in the first place.

Yet the third condition of adequacy cannot be met here, for there is no obvious fundamental continuity between Tradition A and its rival, Tradition B. Precisely here lies the possibility of demonstrating rational superiority. "In this kind of situation," MacIntyre says, "the rationality of traditions requires an acknowledgement by those who have hitherto inhabited and given their allegiance to the tradition in crisis that the alien tradition is *superior in rationality* and in respect of its claims to truth to their own."[50] In other words, to the extent that adherents of a tradition are participants in an extended argument, a process of inquiry, they *cannot avoid* the conclusion that a tradition able to solve problems they could not themselves solve, *and* able to explain why this is so, is rationally superior to their own[51]—even though it is a rival tradition, one whose arguments were not necessarily intelligible, and certainly not straightforwardly acceptable, before the crisis encounter.[52] MacIntyre concludes: "It is in respect of their adequacy or inadequacy in their responses to

50. Ibid., p. 365.

51. The force of this "cannot avoid" may be similar to Habermas's notion of the "performative contradiction" in rational debate. In both cases, a commitment to rational assessment is presumed in one's participation in a certain kind of talk. I can only deny that commitment at the cost of coherence, by saying I am not doing what I am in fact doing. I assess the force of this commitment at greater length in the next chapter. See also the illuminating discussion by Michael Kelly, "MacIntyre, Habermas, and Philosophical Ethics," *Philosophical Forum* 21 (1989–90): 70–93.

52. MacIntyre considers the challenge that can be brought against this sort of view by so-called irrationalists—persons for whom rational superiority is not a desideratum and who will not, therefore, see any point in the conversation among traditions. His examples—Nietzsche, Sartre, Deleuze, Derrida—indicate that this irrationalist objection is perhaps more serious than he allows, such thinkers being central figures of modern (and postmodern) thought. See MacIntyre, *Some Rival Versions of Moral Enquiry*, where this question is explored again at greater length.

epistemological crises that traditions are vindicated or fail to be vindicated" as rationally superior.[53] Without crisis we will not find ourselves in the position of wondering whether the tradition to which we belong is superior to any other. And if the question does not arise, we can be confident in our tradition's adequacy only in a blinkered fashion, with no rational sanction.

It is perhaps already obvious from the parameters of this model and its reliance on translation that encounters between traditions are always mediated by language, but what is less obvious is exactly how, and with what limitations, adherents of rival traditions are able to talk to one another at all. In general, MacIntyre's analysis of the intertradition conversation deepens the conventionally recognized problems of translation (distortion, loss of idiomatic charge) by insisting that we view language as always embedded in a set of "beliefs, institutions, and practices" that are constitutive of a social community. Like Ackerman, MacIntyre believes the inescapable mediation of political and moral claims in language is at least prima facie reason to investigate our deepest practices in the way we talk to one another. But here the matter is complicated by certain real-world problems absent in Ackerman's "transmitter-shield" model of painless and perfect translation. The language of a tradition cannot be learned, on MacIntyre's view, apart from some measure of painful commitment to the practices of which that language is an expression. Translation among traditions, if it is possible at all, will *not* be mediated by interpreters who can easily recast the utterances of one tradition into those of another. That is straightforward assimilation, and it never succeeds in seeing beyond the limitations of a given version of what MacIntyre calls "language-in-culture."

MacIntyre therefore offers the view that genuine translation must involve learning what he calls a *second* first language. In this comparatively rare process, particularly gifted individuals can acquire not only a new set of linguistic signifiers but also a welter of connections to beliefs, practices, and institutions of which the second language is an expression. When these connections are in place, when one has truly learned a second first language, what was previously called translation is shown to be, in its only real form, a matter of *thinking in two languages*. And so, paradoxically, it is only traditions that have already recognized the great extent of untranslatability that will succeed in translating well, because only they will explore other avenues than the conventional distortion of matching word for word in an apparently *unproblematic* act of translation.[54] Pessimism about straightforward translation is just

53. *Whose Justice?* p. 366.
54. Ibid., p. 388.

what opens the way to a more effective approach, namely the cultivation of the empathy and conceptual innovation demanded by learning a second first language. By contrast, those cultures or persons confident in their ability to translate all claims into their own language will succeed only in a systematic distortion of those claims. A recognition of translation's limits is therefore, in the conversation between traditions, just what sets us free to succeed in translating well. What chastens us is also, here, what brings success.

2. An Example

How does the translation conversation play out in practice? And in this model, what has become of our main concern, justice? MacIntyre's view is that justice is one of those beliefs/institutions/practices of which a particular language-in-culture is an expression. Because it a value that orders a great many others, it is also a central or basic feature of a tradition. So what happens when adherents of different traditions meet to talk about justice?

First of all, we can expect their conversation to be blocked, probably quite quickly.[55] Even if they appear to speak the same natural language, their languages-in-culture are quite different. For example, Person A may mean the following by "justice": giving each person what he or she is entitled to by certain formal rules of material acquisition and transfer. By contrast, Person B means by "justice" something that is quite different: giving each person what he or she needs for minimum well-being, established in a rule that guarantees that only the inequalities that maximize the well-being of the least-well-off group will be just. The conflict here is both subtle and tricky, for while the signifier employed is in both cases the same one—"justice"—the problem is actually one of translatability. Translation is, as we have seen, not always or simply a matter of interchanging different signifiers. Real translation between languages-in-culture is always a question of *conceptual* shifts, of attempting to imagine oneself in another scheme of belief where, as it may be, all the words sound the same but have different meanings. This act of imagination need not imply any strong commitment to the different meanings, but it does demand an openness to the possibility that they may be valid—perhaps even more valid than mine. Perhaps more important, it demands that an interlocutor recognize that his or her dialogic partner *is* committed to these different

---

55. MacIntyre illustrates such a block in the first part of *After Virtue*, using (as I have) notions borrowed from Rawls and Nozick.

meanings, and that such commitment is not necessarily maintained for irrational or nostalgic or otherwise indefensible reasons.[56]

When A and B meet and converse, then, they do not simply reach a point at which A says, "Oh, *that's* what you mean by my word 'justice.' You see, here we mean something else"—and the two part laughing at the funny world of conceptual differences. Implied in their different meanings of "justice" is a genuine disagreement about what justice really is, or should be. They are also, presumptively, dealing with the fact that they cannot simply part laughing, for they must find some way of ordering a society they both happen to share. (There are of course other reasons to begin talking to an adherent of a rival tradition—simple curiosity, perhaps—but this pragmatic question of coexistence is the most pressing one.) So, if they are to go on talking together, and possibly decide which of them is right, something must happen. Several options are available. A and B can each decide the other is simply wrong, misusing the word "justice," which in fact retains a single correct meaning. Conversation blocked: they may keep talking, but the first principles they are committed to (needs versus entitlements, let us call them) are rival and incompatible and will prevent them from circumventing their initial disagreement. But perhaps A sees, in a moment of MacIntyrean insight, that their disagreement is not about the single meaning that "justice" purportedly has; he sees instead that he and B actually have radically different commitments, cultural histories, and notions of what counts as a good argument. Though they *seem* to be members of a single "tradition-free" society, they in fact belong to rival traditions within that society. A new set of options is now presented. B might simply turn his back on A. Or the two might choose to escalate their disagreement into a fight.

Suppose, however, that they both desire to live together, or find that neither sets much hope on ordering society through violent suppression of disagreement. They disagree about a lot, but on this much they agree: they need to get along with each other.[57] In a heroic "act of empathic conceptual imagination,"[58] A puts himself in the place of B. He tries to see things as B

---

56. I am diverging from MacIntyre here, since his version of learning a second first language has a strong component of taking on my rival's commitments. I believe this view is too strong, and I suggest a more convincing model, based on openness and interpretive sensitivity, in Chapter 6.

57. I am overdetermining the issue somewhat by putting it this way, for MacIntyre never identifies this kind of pragmatic imperative in his account of conversation. But to the extent that our problem is that rival traditions occupy common social space, it is an accurate depiction. I have more to say about this presently.

58. *Whose Justice?* p. 395.

does, to learn how his use of "justice" is embedded in a complex of commitments and reasoned beliefs about morality and rationality; B's use of "justice" is, he finds, part of a whole series of practices of which he took a different view. At the same time, perhaps, B is following A's lead, and making the same conceptual shift necessary for translation. Armed with the new insights gained by their leaps of imaginative reason, A and B can now continue their conversation in a way that will eventually demonstrate the rational superiority of one or the other view. The block that threatened to stall them at a level of disagreement over first principles is effectively circumnavigated by their willingness, first, to see traditional commitments as real and to the point—a willingness that then allowed them, second, to look beyond the limitations of their own traditions and thus both understand and question rival claims initially thought unassailable.

MacIntyre cannot say in advance what the translation conversation will look like in detail, of course. He can only say that it is the single possible route of advance when rival and incompatible traditions, with their respective languages, practices and beliefs, notions of justice, and practical rationality, come into conflict. In such a conversation, it is supposed that the rationality of the various traditions will eventually play itself out, though perhaps over long stretches of time, and issue in the best possible theories of rational and moral inquiry. Many inadequacies that were invisible to adherents of one tradition will be noticed. Epistemological crises will be hastened by conflict, as I noted earlier. More adequate answers to tough questions will compel acceptance. All of it will be done by—and only by—our talking together. In MacIntyre's words, each member of a tradition "has to become involved in the conversation between traditions, learning to use the idiom of each in order to describe and evaluate the other or others by means of it."[59] Only in this way can we deal with the disagreement about moral issues (now including issues of justice) that was the starting point of our discussion. No particular outcome can be guaranteed in advance. It can only be hoped that the "more rational" tradition, and its understanding of justice, will win out in the end.

This is an attractive picture, and I have dwelt on it in order to make that attraction evident in its clearest expression. However, it is not clear what the actual results of MacIntyre's rationality-of-traditions conversation will be. Nor is it clear, as I shall now suggest, that such results can ever be vouchsafed in anything more than general terms.

59. Ibid., p. 398.

IV. THE LIMITS OF CONVERSATION

1. Force and Deception

MacIntyre's picture of the clash between two traditions is a detailed one, but it nevertheless fails to account for several serious problems. The most damaging of these is the possibility that the intertradition dialogue may be ruled by strategic deception and not by any presumptively shared criteria of adequacy. That is, stronger or more wily agents will simply dominate "more rational" (but less strategically able) agents. This is not to say that the two traditions in question will launch immediately into war—which is the option MacIntyre considered when dialogue fails because there is not enough agreement to disagree. Rather, the situation I am imagining is one in which adherents of a tradition engage in intertradition dialogue deceptively, or self-deceptively. In a simple scenario of this kind, A approaches B and indicates a willingness to talk about the things on which they disagree, including what "justice" means. A has taken care to learn B's language, sees the extent of B's traditional commitments, and professes to see no other option than to talk about it together until some kind of route around their previously blocked conversation is found. They begin talking.

But A is not *rationally committed* to the conversation, in the important sense that he is not open to real assessment and correction of his beliefs. He is not in fact willing to shift his views if or when evidence indicating the limitations of them is produced. Indeed, although the fact remains unknown to B, one of A's central commitments is never to surrender his views under any circumstances and always to dominate over other views. The truth, then, is that A is participating in conversation only because he realizes it is the best way to open up B to domination. In other words, he is participating in an *apparently* rational conversation, but in a way that is systematically distorted with respect to the ends imagined by other participants in the conversation. (We want to say that he is not *really* participating in the conversation, that he is being deceptive, but from what viewpoint can this judgment be delivered?) B's problem here is that he may be unable to make any critical judgment of A's sincerity with respect to the common goals of the conversation until it is too late. He has been systematically deceived; or he has been deceived just long enough for a possible use of force by A, when and if it happens, to go largely unchallenged. A's view wins out—by deception if possible, by force if necessary—through strategic means that seem to have no place in rational conversation but that nevertheless were played out precisely there.

Some observers (call them political realists) will see no difficulty in this scenario. The rationality-of-traditions conversation was supposed by MacIntyre to demonstrate, over time, the "more adequate" tradition. Here, A's tradition is simply the more adequate: it has shown its superiority by virtue of dominating the less wily and less bold adherents of B's view. The conversation between traditions is on this view really a process of natural selection and, like natural selection, is no more than tautologous when stated as a principle: the fittest to survive turn out to be those who in fact survive. Nothing more can be said about results generated in such a process, for the "more adequate" tradition simply is the tradition that more adequately meets the demands of survival, by whatever means necessary. There is no neutral standpoint, MacIntyre has insisted, from which the rationality of traditions can be adjudicated, and the move to this imaginary place of judgment was just what was thought wrong with modern liberalism.[60] Therefore, *whatever* results issue from the rationality-of-traditions conversation are the best results available. We cannot judge them by any other standard than that they proved themselves more adequate, in some factual sense, to the demands of conversation and epistemological crisis.

But somehow the example given is not adequately explained by this rather cynical position. The scenario is predicated on the fact that B's view is still, to observers like us, in some sense rationally superior to A's view. If nothing else, we want to say, B is genuinely engaged in a rational conversation in which A is engaged only distortedly. So here it is possible for us to imagine a "rationally superior" tradition that does not win out in the conversation *precisely because it is superior*—the eschewal of strategic deception being a mark, we might say, of good faith in joining the conversation in the first place. The force of the example, then, is that because MacIntyre's view fails to take account of agents who will systematically deceive, participating in a conversation only for instrumental reasons, we cannot say, without a more detailed picture of the conversation, that such deception could be ruled out by rational conversation itself. That is, it is not clear on his view that, or how, A's deception could be (for instance) exposed once the talk got going; we cannot be sure that genuineness in talking will be readily discernible. To the extent that this is true, MacIntyre's view of the rationality-of-traditions conversation is incomplete and pos-

60. Stated this way, the judgment may remind us of Raymond Geuss's effective arguments against Frankfurt School *Ideologiekritik*, namely that its judgments of "false consciousness" were never made from an epistemological platform stable enough to vindicate the critical outlook. See Geuss, *The Idea of a Critical Theory: Habermas and the Frankfurt School* (Cambridge: Cambridge University Press, 1981).

sibly incoherent. It could conceivably commit him to saying that a less rational tradition was actually *more* rational because it emerged victorious from the conversation.

Consider a reply to this charge. It is not bare survival that marks the rational superiority of a tradition, but instead how adequately it justifies its beliefs to adherents in the crucible of conversation. So, for quite independent reasons, a more rational tradition might cease to dominate—but that does not mark its *rational* inferiority. The conversation between traditions is not a contest to decide which one survives but a process by which each assesses its own claims and arguments to see how adequate they are, given the challenge that exposure to another tradition always brings. Seen this way, deception and self-deception cease to be difficulties for the view because we can expect them to be routinely uncovered in the self-reflective conversation brought on by contact with another tradition. Rational superiority is not a feature of traditions seen from outside (for there *is* no outside) but a feature seen from within, by adherents convinced of the need for reform when epistemological crisis is upon them. The tactics of deception are assessed, and presumably found wanting, precisely as features of a tradition's ability to answer to internal concerns about its rationality, concerns that, *as* rational members of such a tradition, we must share.

While such a reply renders the current problem less serious, it exposes an even more telling one. MacIntyre has turned much of his theory's critical force on the view that there is no universal rationality, and no supratraditional viewpoint, from which traditions (and their virtues) can be judged. And yet he now appears to have a strong sense of what it means to have rational commitments across the board—that is, as a member of *any* rational tradition committed, as it must be, to assessing its own degree of rationality. The rationality-of-traditions conversation is predicated on a certain highly successful kind of interaction, in which rational agents with diverse commitments meet to take account of their disagreements and on that basis decide internally which tradition of inquiry is the more adequate. Embedded in this view is the controversial notion that common rational commitments will allow adherents to decide which tradition is more adequate and therefore more rational—the final goal being a kind of self-transparency reminiscent of elements in the Hegelian tradition. Only thus will blocked conversations, including those about moral issues, be unblocked. Yet this notion of a "common commitment to rationality" was just what MacIntyre refused to countenance in his indictment of the modern project of liberal justice theory. Is MacIntyre involved in a self-contradiction?

2. Rational Commitments

MacIntyre said epistemological crisis could be solved only with the benefit of "imaginative conceptual innovation," and further suggested that in a crisis brought on by a tradition-to-tradition clash a "rare gift of empathy" would be necessary to make translation possible. His idea of a successful intertradition conversation therefore depends, in one reading, on the highly contingent fact of there being a certain number of people around with the special talent of being able to see beyond themselves. Dialogue assesses justice only with the added benefit of traits that are necessarily uncommon. (This picture of dialogue may be contrasted once more with Ackerman's model, in which interaction, because it was effectively governed by strictly enforced rules of dialogic interchange, requires no empathy at all.) If, on the other hand, MacIntyre wants to say that "imaginative conceptual innovation" and "empathy" are more common than that, he commits himself to a view of transtraditional rationality at odds with his general critical stance. Now the cultivation of empathy and imagination, qualities that take us beyond our present categories and interests, begins to look like other models of interaction that depend on a base level of transgroup or transtradition understanding.[61] To the extent that MacIntyre wants a *normative* conversation between traditions, the rational force of "the more adequate tradition" indicates a commitment to transcontextual reason.

MacIntyre's critical analysis in *Whose Justice? Which Rationality?* was predicated on the belief, arguably substantiated by historical research, that "different and incompatible conceptions of justice are characteristically closely linked to different and incompatible conceptions of practical rationality."[62] Both notions are deeply embedded in particular traditions. So, at the same time a moral notion arises as to how a community ought to structure itself with respect to desert and distribution, there also arises a rich idea of how to decide practical questions, of what constitutes a good argument for action, and of which actions or principles are justified. Practical rationality varies with traditions, running from the Aristotelian practical syllogism and *phronesis* to Augustinian voluntarism to Humean community standards. These versions of practical reason, like the versions of justice to which they are wedded, are at

61. Owen Fiss suggested in a unpublished talk (New Haven, 1991) that this commitment was not dissimilar to Rawls's idea of a rationality operating apart from particular interests in the original choice situation. This comparison is overdrawn, but Fiss was right to suggest that MacIntyre courts self-contradiction in this area.

62. *Whose Justice?* p. ix.

odds. MacIntyre's insistence on the integrity of traditions means that what counts as a good reason for an Aristotelian to act will not count as a good reason for a Humean so to act.

What this deep disagreement with regard to practical rationality hides is a different sense of rationality, one driven by adequacy in the intertradition conversation. Which tradition's theses, beliefs, and institutions are more equal to the demands of the world, whatever they may be?[63] The more adequate theory-set is the one understood as *rationally* (and not merely evolutionarily) superior. Presented with a theory that answers a question mine cannot, and why, I must recognize the new theory as rationally superior. (The corollary point, though it is one MacIntyre does not separate off from this moment of recognition, is that I will transfer my allegiance to the new theory-set. But this is harder to justify—I may recognize the rational superiority of a new theory but cling to mine anyway, out of nostalgia, insecurity, or sheer bloody-mindedness.) MacIntyre has assumed a good deal with this notion of common rational commitments in members of traditions, certainly as much as some of the modernist theorists he is concerned to criticize. Indeed, these minimal common commitments to rationality seem not very different from some of the criteria of rationality employed by such characteristically modern thinkers as Rawls and Habermas. The ability to reform beliefs in the face of new evidence is precisely what many conceptions of rationality desire, and the pivot on which many modern moral/political projects are turned.

My concern here is not to criticize MacIntyre for the use of this pivot, but rather to indicate that his project cannot rationally avoid a version of the commitment he wished to challenge and discard as the unwarranted transcendentalism of modern liberalism. What else is this common commitment to rationality than an extracontextual fact that extends past traditional boundaries? If it did not extend beyond traditional boundaries—if Aristotelians no less than Thomists did not recognize the need to reform belief in the face of superior evidence—there would exist no ground for the conversation among traditions. And that conversation is necessary to the extent (which MacIntyre

---

63. MacIntyre's view of rational progress is significantly influenced by the work of Thomas Kuhn, whose *The Structure of Scientific Revolutions* (Chicago: University of Chicago Press, 1962) sets out a detailed model of scientific progress not unlike this one. Theories are challenged as a whole, not piecemeal, and "revolutions" in the sciences—as here in moral epistemology—are the result of imaginative responses to crisis in the status quo ante. Richard Rorty (*Philosophy and the Mirror of Nature*) argues persuasively (if somewhat tendentiously) that the notion of the "best theory so far" provided under such a view is essentially pragmatic, a way of going on, and that no extravagant claims—such as claims of realism—should be made about it.

has emphasized) that traditions persist through time, creating the issue of social coexistence that is ever in the background of our discussion. Without the ability to talk to one another about our rival and incompatible claims, without the ability to put each other's claims and theories into question, all conversation is blocked. And blocked conversation was just the problem MacIntyre's theory of tradition was put forward to solve. Though, as mentioned, he cannot say in advance what the outcome of such a conversation will be, except in terms of his own beliefs and traditional commitments, it is nevertheless crucial that he be able to demonstrate the possibility of conversation. Without that possibility, MacIntyre's laborious historical analysis is no more than a very detailed statement of incommensurability in the modern world.

The possibility of this conversation is one we desire no less than him. It is the ground of our ability to go on living together in a manner that takes account of rival commitments and incompatible conceptions of the good life. Now the question is posed in this fashion: can this possibility be maintained only by positing a common commitment to rationality? Are we only able to talk to one another to the extent that we are all rational beings? In pursuing this issue further, I want to decide whether such a commitment is ultimately any different from the universalist rationality used by some modern theorists of justice.

V. THE LIMITS—CONTINUED

1. The Better Argument Alone?

MacIntyre argued that the moral residue of the Enlightenment was in fragments, shards of a past coherence that could today no longer carry the ethical weight implied by their surface uses. Disagreement, not consensus, was the central fact of modern moral debate, a disagreement born of deep incoherence and lack of vision in the debate's practitioners. Claiming to be the heirs of no tradition at all, these practitioners obscured the fact that their beliefs, institutions, and languages of morality stem precisely from traditional sources. A liberal retreat from this state of moral incoherence to a position of alleged abstraction from disagreement merely deflected the hidden commitments from one realm to another, no less infected, one. The neutral standpoint in politics is as much a fiction as the impartial standpoint and the impersonal or punctual self in ethics.

This view of contemporary moral and political discourse is of course a caricature, and MacIntyre has justly endured the opprobrium of critics who point this out. For example, the aspirations of modern morality (and, by extension, of liberal justice theory) are not everywhere so high as MacIntyre likes to suggest. The goal for many is not a set of unquestioned rules of universal morality, but rather a discussion that makes clear central theses and principles all reasonable persons can accept. It is possible to speak of (some kinds of) rational commitment within a framework that grants traditions, and even tradition-based notions of "justice," their due. Indeed, most theorists who want to rehabilitate the priority of right are engaged in some version of just this project: silent on the question of intratradition goods, they seek instead general principles of interaction that will govern the necessary transactions between individuals and groups of diverse conviction. They may never attempt, like Kant or the early Rawls, to derive those principles from the general character of all rational agents. They nevertheless believe that it is rational to engage in political dialogue to the extent that we share a general project of social coexistence.

A good deal hangs, then, on just how these theorists delineate our rational commitments, and how they generate the principles of social interaction. There is going to be disagreement—it was to such disagreement, among theorists *and* practical advocates, that MacIntyre first pointed. But, *pace* MacIntyre, the fact of disagreement is not sufficient prima facie evidence to establish the futility of the project. Nor, once we realize how exaggerated MacIntyre's picture of the Enlightenment heirs is, are we likely to be convinced by the general historical arguments. In rehabilitating tradition-based virtues, MacIntyre did manage to point out the pallid nature of justice as it is commonly understood today. When contemporary theorists speak of justice, they most often mean distributive justice, and its rules of dividing up goods, with that procedural fiction "the individual" at the center of some decision procedure, either demanding rights or receiving commodity-like social goods. Of course this image of a demon distributor doling out commodities to eager materialist citizens is a straw man, a cartoon. What MacIntyre's critical analysis ultimately shows is that the issues of justice are better viewed as matters of general interaction: an ebb and flow among spheres or traditions of conviction, rule-governed but open to reform, that covers not only material distribution but also contracts, hierarchies, nonmaterial goods, and daily interface among citizens.

But, having opened up this expansive critique, MacIntyre has to deal with this set of problems as much as any liberal justice theorist. The general conversation among traditions, I suggested, appears to reintegrate into MacIntyre's system just the sort of universalist rationality he was at pains to show up as illusory when employed by the liberal justice theorist. It appears that MacIntyre, though insistent that justice must be reclaimed as a tradition-based virtue, cannot avoid addressing the issues of political interaction in a way that is at least similar to the strategies employed by the modern theorists he reviles. And so, to the extent that these problems of interaction *are* the problems of modern justice, his theory works ultimately against its own stated goals. If traditions do indeed inhabit common social spaces today, interaction in a conversation guided by at least minimum rational commitments cannot be avoided. Justice is precisely the conversational interface among traditions that is governed by (1) the need to talk in general, as a way of avoiding open conflict, (2) general rationality and the larger project of rational inquiry, and (3) a commitment on the part of citizens to adopt the superior theory when confronted with evidence supporting it. [64]

But perhaps these issues of interaction among traditions or conceptions of the good are not, finally, the concerns of justice. Perhaps the conversation among traditions is rather a matter of scientific adequacy, and nothing to do with the issues traditionally governed by the virtue of justice. If this is so, traditions would not, in the end, compete for social goods in the way Ackerman's space colonizers do—there is tradition-to-tradition conflict, but it concerns the adequacy of theories only, and not the parceling out of resources. This would seem to be an escape hatch for MacIntyre. Adherents of a tradition do not see themselves as involved in a general conversation about *justice* with adherents of other traditions. Instead they remain as much as possible within the framework of that tradition, venturing conceptually out of it only when epistemological crisis comes knocking. Even then, the conversation is a way of testing the adequacy of their beliefs and arguments *to themselves,* not defending them in some larger court of appeal (for there is none). Traditions are, for

---

64. Such a definition of justice may strike many observers as all too thin, and therefore not only of limited interest but also of limited effectiveness in the task of assessing particular norms and/or actions undertaken on the basis of norms. If this is justice, in other words, many persons may be inclined to reply, "Thanks for nothing." This issue will also arise in the discussion of Habermas's theory, which, though in many respects superior in detail to MacIntyre's (at least as understood here), has difficulty overcoming the danger of emptiness in formalism—at least on a practical-political level. In the final part of the present work, I meet this problem with an account of justice that is minimal enough to work prior to any particular conception of the good but is also based on certain demonstrably actual aspects of moral interaction in a society like ours. (Surrendering the strong universalist aspirations traditionally enshrined by modern theorists of justice will be a necessity.)

the most part, free-floating spheres whose edges rarely, if ever, touch. When they do touch, conflict is generated and the rationality conversation is set in motion; but justice, to the extent that it means anything, means whatever the internal goods of Tradition A or Tradition B demand. On this view, traditions are opaque and impermeable, coexisting uneasily in the limited and tenuous background of minimal rationality, a background against which no common principles of justice, however minimal, can be erected.

This reading of MacIntyre bears an interesting similarity to the view attributed by Habermas to Wittgenstein. In Wittgenstein's ahistoricist picture, according to Habermas, a plurality of language-games is seen to exist at time t with certain unavoidable connections, but in general language-games are separate and distinct. "In [Wittgenstein's] hands," Habermas remarks, "the language game congeals to an opaque unity." Yet this congealing treatment is misleading, for

> [a]ctually, language spheres are not monadically sealed off but inwardly as well as outwardly porous. . . . Both translation (outwardly) and tradition (inwardly) must be possible in principle. Along with their possible application, grammatical rules simultaneously imply the necessity of interpretation. Wittgenstein failed to see this; as a consequence he conceived the practice of language games unhistorically.[65]

Wittgenstein's congealed view of language spheres likewise retains a too positivistic picture of language, and a sense that interpretation rules are fixed rather than flexible in context. On all three counts, Habermas considers Gadamer's view, and especially his own communicative-action reading of it, superior.[66] Yet an impermeability thesis of the Wittgensteinian type would nicely avoid the difficulty I have been illustrating for MacIntyre's theory. Impermeable spheres would never face the problem of shared commitments to rationality, or anything else. Of course, without such shared commitments, they would never converse with one another either, and so it is hard to hold on to this thesis as a reading of MacIntyre's theory. Most obvious, its implied

---

65. Habermas, "A Review of Gadamer's *Truth and Method*," in his *Zur Logik der Sozialwissenschaften*, p. 252.

66. We should note that this defense of Gadamer, and Habermas's characterization of himself as significantly Gadamerian, is of early vintage and preceded the so-called Gadamer-Habermas debate. Yet there is a commonality here that persists past all the points of difference. For a good survey of this terrain, see Bernstein, "What Is the Difference That Makes a Difference?" (as noted earlier), in Wachterhauser, *Hermeneutics and Modern Philosophy*.

ahistoricism is anathema to MacIntyre, for whom what Habermas calls the "inward porousness" of traditions (the conveying of arguments and language through generations) is essential.

Even more to our point, the so-called outward porousness is likewise central to MacIntyre's view. Consider the fact of *traditions within a single society*. One of MacIntyre's most telling initial points was that the remnants of various traditions are alive within single polities, especially the culturally diverse ones found in Europe and North America. Here conflicts among citizens are not disagreements about how to apply, say, virtues they all agree on; they are more likely to be the fundamental divergence found in the abortion example from the previous chapter. In MacIntyre's reading of moral commitments, what looks like a disagreement about where to apply a single concept—"person," let us say—is really a deep conflict about what that concept means and how it fits into larger moral schemes and narrative links. At least part of the problem is that the agents cannot recognize that they are employing the same word to pick out fundamentally different notions. Their traditional commitments are obscure to each other, and, more problematically, to themselves.

Within one political association, then, the impermeability thesis cannot be maintained. Epistemological crisis, though once perhaps a rare occurrence for a strong and coherent tradition like the Thomistic synthesis of Aristotle and Augustine, is today an everyday fact of life. Every time a moral or political debate is blocked, such a crisis, however minor in scope, is indicated. Georgia Warnke sees the issue in terms of "strands" of traditional commitment, but the point is the same because Warnke's single tradition is understood as the tradition of a political association like the United States. "Just as the rationality of a tradition requires that it test itself against other traditions and be willing to learn from them," she says, "the rationality of one strand of a tradition seems to involve its testing itself against and learning from other strands of the same tradition. Moreover, just as one tradition must assume that another might be rationally superior to it, one interpretive perspective within a tradition must assume that another can offer it insights into interpreting shared social meanings."[67] The translation conversation is supremely important because problems of interaction are not distant possibilities, but daily imperatives. Intratradition justice—that is, justice as a virtue—though it might tell me all I need to know about treating other members of my group, tells me

---

67. Warnke, *Justice and Interpretation*, p. 124. This claim is one basis of Warnke's argument for a "hermeneutical conversation" in public debate.

nothing about the pressing concerns of the society as a whole. Internal justice may indeed specify treatment of out-groupers, but it does not say anything about how we are all to get along together in a single, well-ordered social space. True, telling me to eliminate all out-groupers violently specifies conditions for ordering a society, but most of us do not, and would not, adhere to a tradition with *that* kind of version of internal justice. With a sense of the imperatives implied by shared social space, the intertradition conversation need not become a free-for-all of competing claims and morally sanctioned war. What might now be thought of as the ongoing epistemological crisis of modern society therefore forces the emphasis onto the interaction among adherents of traditions. We cannot adopt a hands-off isolationism here, for traditions are not separate countries.[68]

Consequently, we are right to emphasize MacIntyre's rationalist characterization of the conversation among traditions and to point out its defects in advancing notions of "imagination" or "insight" that may be obscure or controversial. In the end MacIntyre commits the crime so ruthessly prosecuted by his own work: he employs hidden rational commitments. To be sure, these commitments are not identical to those on which some inheritors of the Enlightenment project chose to lean; they make no extravagant claims about all rational agents or any processes of self-reflection that will call out structures of morality from the character of rationality itself. In that sense, MacIntyre's theory marks a genuine advance over the deracinated versions of the moral self generated in some modern theories of morality. Moreover, the thesis that standards of practical rationality (if not of rationality more generally) will be tied always to moral commitments in traditional context is worthy of serious attention. The restoration of the virtue of practical wisdom to moral decision-making, with its inexplicitness and sensitivity, seems to reflect accurately our actual experience of matching convictions to principles, and principles to situations in moral life. But even here, general rational commitments—once combined with an orientation to social coexistence shared by a given group of social actors—make impossible any policy of intratradition isolationism.

The conversation model offered by MacIntyre gives no advance answers to the problems we recognize as the problems of modern (that is, structural) justice. Indeed, there is no rational way to generate those answers except by

---

68. In a world such as ours is now, with complex economic and political interrelations between nations, we cannot even be hands-off in many conflicts that arise country-to-country. We needn't talk to Iranian fundamentalists, for instance—until they begin attacking our sources of oil or begin killing our nationals. Then conflict is unavoidable and must be mediated somehow (we hope peacefully).

actually engaging in the translation conversation, however difficult that will turn out to be. That the conversation is rational, that it will generate results over time, are tenets of faith for MacIntyre. But that faith is based on the close historical study of which his recent work is mainly composed. The progress of conversation simply is the progress of rationality—including in that, necessarily, the rational treatment of problems of social interaction. Whether, like Hegel, MacIntyre envisions a time when that progress will reach its end, an ultimate human *telos* convincing to all rational talkers, is unclear.[69] What is clear is that the conversation is everything, a conversation that will continue only if liberalism takes up its status as a tradition among others. In concluding this chapter, I want to examine briefly why this is so.

2. Talking Traditions

MacIntyre ultimately suggests that if we want to go on talking we must locate our traditional commitments, pledge allegiance, and join in the larger conversation. Our choice of traditions is not necessarily limited to those sketched by MacIntyre, but what we cannot do is continue to talk in a supratraditional fashion, hoping thereby to avoid disagreement.[70] "It follows," says MacIntyre, "that only by either the *circumvention* or the *subversion* of liberal modes of debate can the rationality specific to traditions of enquiry reestablish itself sufficiently to challenge the cultural and political hegemony of liberalism effectively."[71]

In one respect, this comment is based on the standard historicist criticism of liberalism, that it ignores narrative continuity and depends on such philosophical fictions as general rationality and human nature per se. It also brings full circle the sweeping critique of liberalism with which not only *Whose Justice? Which Rationality?* but also *After Virtue* began. But we can now see that the picture is more complicated than that. To the extent that liberalism commands the commitments of many fully rational persons, and sustains too a coherent notion of practical rationality, MacIntyre now feels compelled to admit it as a

69. There is at the end of *Whose Justice?* some provocative but finally ambiguous talk about how the conversation will play itself out. MacIntyre is being cagey there, defending his own traditional commitments while at the same time still talking in a philosophical fashion that is, however minimally, directed at all rational agents (or at least at that portion of them who read and consider texts in philosophy).

70. The bulk of *Whose Justice?* is taken up in detailed historical examination of Aristotelian, Humean, Augustinian, and Thomistic traditions of inquiry—a choice that says more about MacIntyre's intellectual obsessions than about the state of contemporary moral and political debate.

71. *Whose Justice?* p. 402 (emphasis added).

tradition of inquiry in his own sense. It can no longer be considered the grand enemy in a general historicist push to take traditions seriously.[72] Liberals can be part of the conversation just to the extent that they will admit their tradition as one among many. In other words, as long as liberals can lower their theoretical aspirations and see themselves as just one more tradition of inquiry, they must be part of the general rationality-of-traditions conversation.

This is an odd move for the champion of traditions to make. The reason liberalism was the enemy of tradition-based understanding was precisely that it denied the particularity of context and tried to transcend difference with illusory rationalist constructions. Now, by trying to cut liberalism down to size in traditional terms, MacIntyre draws the sting of his original critique. More seriously, at the same time he is insisting the liberal gaze must lower in this way, his own gaze seems to be rising—to a hidden, largely undefended notion of common rationality that guides the conversation among traditions. What was once thought a creation of hubristic liberal theorists—human rationality—is now a kind of background against which floating, sometimes permeable, bubbles of traditional belief and inquiry move around and interact. What MacIntyre achieves here is not the elimination of liberalism—neither the circumvention nor the subversion of liberal modes of debate—but instead the reform of liberalism, and a contextual deepening of its modes of debate. This reformed liberalism is not conceptually limited by being one tradition of inquiry among many. It is still what it hoped to be, the mediating commitments of the interaction among traditions—but no longer in the hyper-thin, hyper-rationalist terms of MacIntyre's caricature. It is a political theory, not a moral one, concerning how the conversation among persons and groups of diverse commitment can and must carry on. MacIntyre, no less than any other citizen of a pluralistic society, is committed to this conversation.

We can see this more clearly by asking what *status* MacIntyre's contributions to contemporary theoretical debate must have. Neither *After Virtue* nor *Whose Justice? Which Rationality?* can itself be considered a document in the rationality-of-traditions conversation. Instead they precede it, general works of ground-clearing that find their place somewhere *before* the pledging of traditional allegiance. Choices are not posed until the end of each book, and

---

72. See ibid., ch. 17. Yet it remains unclear how liberalism can be a tradition on the MacIntyrean view and still remain what it wants to be: a political defense of plurality and not a theory of ultimate human ends. MacIntyre's rehabilitation of liberalism as a tradition is similar to Galston's suggestion, cited earlier, that neutral liberalism can find no rational defense, and so we should just give up that attempt and defend liberalism as a substantive conception of the good—one among many, and (in MacIntyre's terms anyway) a failed one at that.

though MacIntyre is never *not* a member of the tradition of Thomistic inquiry to which he is committed, he must at least for the purposes of communicating come out of his traditional mode in order to write books such as these. In other words, to all appearances these documents find themselves in a general field of rational inquiry that is not yet tradition-based; they appeal to diverse readers on the basis of a notion of rationality, of what constitutes a good argument. What constitutes a good argument for MacIntyre is, in general, just what constitutes a good argument for Bernard Williams, or Donald Davidson, or any other practitioner of contemporary philosophy.[73]

The arguments, then, have been read and understood by precisely the people MacIntyre is criticizing. Indeed, it appears crucial that they are more addressed to these people than to those who already find traditional commitments salutary. The arguments advanced here are intended to convince, and so they are part of a general conversation known as contemporary philosophy that is governed by standards of rationality in argument that at least *appear* to extend beyond moral contexts. Here we see most clearly the paradoxical status of MacIntyre's project. If MacIntyre is right about traditions, rationality, and justice, he cannot advance any theses except *from within* a tradition; but he must advance theses *in the absence of* a tradition, namely in the apparently ahistorical mode of contemporary philosophy, in order to show that he is right about traditions, rationality, and justice.[74] Such a conclusion may be modified somewhat by the fact that (as noted) MacIntyre's method is mainly historical. He also consciously restricts himself to discussing traditions of which his own culture (and ours) is an expression. But I do not believe that these considerations wholly blunt the paradox, and the contradiction it threatens. If MacIntyre's argument is addressed to all of us, in a way he thinks must be at least intelligible, if not automatically convincing, there

73. This may suggest the view that philosophy, or analytic philosophy, is itself a tradition of inquiry. What remains unclear in so suggesting, however, is what cultural or historical context and narrative such a tradition lives in, and what its (presumed) rational limitations would therefore be.

74. This is the sense in which MacIntyre himself may be ensnared in what Habermas will call a performative contradiction. By his very arguments against liberal rationality, he appears to commit himself to a version of rationality that is impersonal, strong, and potentially universal. To the extent that this is true, it cuts against the substance of the points advanced for consideration in those very arguments. In addition to this potential contradiction, of course, I have been suggesting that MacIntyre's substantial points themselves entail commitment to a general theory of rationality. See Habermas's discussion of MacIntyre in "Remarks on Discourse Ethics," in *Justification and Application: Remarks on Discourse Ethics*, trans. Ciarin P. Cronin (Cambridge, Mass.: MIT Press, 1993), esp. Remark No. 12.

is strong prima facie evidence he is assuming a notion of general rationality that is not tradition-bound.

I have mentioned that such a result is damaging to MacIntyre's attempts to distance himself from liberalism and the general rationalism of the modern justice project. But for the purposes of our general inquiry, it helps to illuminate more fully how interaction among individuals and groups *must* be mediated in some kind of rational political conversation. In general, MacIntyre may be seen as (unwillingly) agreeing with Ackerman that certain pragmatic-political considerations ultimately govern the project of talking together from within rival and incompatible conceptions of the good life. Cohabitation makes conversation inevitable. Where MacIntyre advances this understanding is in seeing that this conversation must proceed out of deep moral commitments, and not simply rule them off the agenda by external means. Conversation among traditions is not to be constrained in a manner justified somewhere "above" traditions themselves, but only from within the shared political values we all have as citizens. Ackerman also began with the political difficulties prompted by moral difference, but elements of his theory, as we saw, obscured the substantive depth of moral commitments and the difficulties we will encounter in abstracting from difference in the interests of social coexistence. In particular, the constrained dialogue model did not seem to provide the kind of moral commitment that might in itself prompt a move to the realm of neutral talk and, moreover, excite loyalty and allegiance for that realm. MacIntyre's analysis, though it does not achieve what it sets out to do, works for our purposes to add moral depth to just talking.

We may want to assume, with MacIntyre, that the justice conversation will ultimately issue in the best theory so far, and in a tradition of inquiry that edges us closer and closer to the moral ends of humankind. That hope could well be unfounded. It is in any case unnecessary for political success in the conversation. MacIntyre's apparent cognitivism about ethics leads him, I might say, to underestimate the practical-political difficulties of mediating social interaction in the time between now and any realization of human moral ends. This is a criticism I shall likewise want to bring against Habermas's more detailed and careful analysis of common rational commitments in talk. A signal benefit of Habermas's idealizing reconstruction of communicative competence is, we shall see, that it shows effective ways of dealing with force and deception in talk. MacIntyre erred by *assuming* the rationality of the intertradition conversation, and therefore failed to see how damaging deception, coercion, and open violence could be to a dialogue of legitimation. Indeed, it was the uncovering of these limitations in MacIntyre's model of conversation that showed how much, in the form of rational commitments, he was assuming. The defective treatment of force and deception can be traced to the hidden nature of MacIntyre's commitments to rational dialogue and the unexamined but crucial status of his notion of general rationality.

In the next chapter, therefore, I examine a view that begins by uncovering precisely what is covered over in MacIntyre, namely the assumption of success (in the form of rationality) within conversation. Habermas's theory of communicative action may, to this degree, offer the possibility of remedying defects noted in MacIntyre's otherwise compelling view. It may likewise advance our understanding of the conversation about justice by demonstrating just what is rationally anticipated in any discourse oriented to the assessment of norms. And where it fails to be fully convincing, I shall suggest, it has the important effect of leading us back to a fuller sense of civility's value in the social conversation about justice.

5

Justice and
Communicative Action

This chapter examines Jürgen Habermas's theory of communicative action and an explicit version of the rational-commitments theory that was hidden in MacIntyre's view. Some of the controversy surrounding the model of norm justification known as discourse ethics, with particular reference to the issues of justice, is presented along with some of its benefits. Habermas, because he wants to radicalize and reform just the rationalist project MacIntyre found incoherent, is able to advance a more effective model of dealing with deception and force in dialogue. He also demonstrates convincingly the unavoidability of idealizing presuppositions in discourse.

But these presuppositions do not seem to offer much in the way of political payoff, given the issues of disagreement and diversity we face in a pluralistic society. I therefore discuss some objections to the theory, in particular that the idealizing force of Habermas's model does not appear usefully applicable in real situations of political decision-making. I suggest, ultimately, that the theory must be modified by reintroducing political-pragmatic imperatives of the kind Ackerman considered central, and a version of practical judgment that depends on more than transcontextual rational commitments. These features then become the basis of justice as civility.

I. INTRODUCTION

In the previous chapter, I suggested that MacIntyre's attempt to bring justice and practical rationality back inside the rich context of traditions was limited by general rational commitments that he, no less than other theorists of justice, could not avoid. In the conversation among traditions, standards of rational appraisal and adequacy may be seen to extend past tradition boundaries, *even when rational assessment is carried on only internally*. Moreover, the notions of "conceptual imagination" and "empathy" upon which MacIntyre leans in the description of a successful intertradition conversation also indicate a commitment, however weak, to transtraditional rationality. While MacIntyre's reform of the wider hopes of Enlightenment-style liberalism (in the form of guaranteed rational agreement) is indeed timely, and his revitalization of the moral self as a locus of narrative and judgmental continuity is richer than any deracinated maximizer of preferences, MacIntyre fails in his general attempt to demonstrate the incoherence of neutral liberalism and right-over-good theories of justice. Social coherence, for him, is the smooth interaction of diverse traditions engaged in a successful conversation.

Because that conversation in MacIntyre's model is not externally or explicitly constrained, in the manner of Ackerman's, it may answer to certain concerns about ideality and commitment brought up in the earlier discussion of Chapter 3. It may, that is, accomplish its avowed goal of giving us a more accurate picture of our moral and political interaction. Yet MacIntyre's presumed refusal to see the theory in the terms I have suggested makes it unlikely that his model of talking can go much further in accomplishing this discussion's main goal, namely the provision of a dialogic theory of justice that is both theoretically adequate and real to our experience. We saw that the presumption of rationality in MacIntyre's conversation failed to make explicit some pressing limitations on talk—limitations of force and, especially, deception. It is precisely because he *assumes* that the intertradition conversation will be rational that these distorting factors do not show up as difficulties for him.

I turn to Habermas, therefore, not only because his theory of communicative action is a richer demonstration of how a structure of assessing norms of justice may be derived from rationality and its presumptions, but also because it is an explicit one. I will ultimately suggest that the idealizing force of this theory cannot be adequately imported into the practical-political sphere without the addition of some more substantive moral and political-pragmatic elements, and that more-modest goals should therefore be set for justice theory. For now it is crucial to examine in detail what I regard as the most systematic attempt to ground justice in talk, and thereby to fulfill in a radicalized fashion the aspiration of what MacIntyre called the Enlightenment project.

In the following, I can consider only one aspect of the recent work Habermas has undertaken in the larger field of critical social theory, namely what I take to be his *theory of justice* and how that theory depends on a model of *dialogic interaction*.[1] This will naturally lead to the wider implications of the aspects of his recent thought that Habermas has labeled the "formal-pragmatic analysis of speech-acts," the "theory of communicative action," and "discourse ethics." As we shall see, Habermas's general theory of communicative action includes two features crucial for understanding how dialogue plays a role in determining principles of justice. These are, first, a "move to discourse"—the resort, when disagreement develops about substantive matters of truth and rightness, to a kind of talk in which reasons are given and arguments weighed; and, second, the threefold nature of speech acts: that they implicitly advance claims to truth, to normative rightness, and (since communicative claims are inseparable from one's actions in making them) to sincerity.

The force of these (typically only implicit) claims is modeled in what Habermas has called the "ideal speech situation," that conceptual space toward

1. Habermas has no single place in which he articulates a theory of justice comparable to that of, say, Rawls or Nozick. But to the extent that normative validity claims, justice central among them, are part of what is available to be criticized in discourse—rational argument oriented toward agreement—his theory of communicative action is likewise a theory of justice. The dialogic aspect of the theory is not merely a matter of discourse being something that happens in talk. Habermas's claim is that norms and truth-claims are criticizable only in dialogue, not in the sort of philosophical monologue imagined, for instance, by the Kantian project. See Jürgen Habermas, *The Theory of Communicative Action*, 2 vols., trans. Thomas McCarthy (Boston: Beacon Press, 1984 and 1987) (hereafter: *TCA1* and *TCA2*). Recent formulations and replies are collected in Jürgen Habermas, *Moral Consciousness and Communicative Action*, trans. Christian Lenhardt and Shierry Weber Nicholsen (Cambridge, Mass.: MIT Press, 1990), and his *Justification and Application: Remarks on Discourse Ethics*. A generally good series of comments on Habermas's normative work is available in Seyla Benhabib and Fred Dallmyer, eds., *The Communicative Ethics Controversy* (Cambridge, Mass.: MIT Press, 1990), and in David Rasmussen, ed., *Reading Habermas* (Cambridge: Basil Blackwell, 1990). See also Seyla Benhabib, "In the Shadow of Aristotle and Hegel: Communicative Ethics and Current Controversies in Practical Philosophy," *Philosophical Forum* 21 (1989–90): 1–31, and Stephen K. White, *The Recent Work of Jürgen Habermas: Reason, Justice, and Modernity* (Cambridge: Cambridge University Press, 1988).

which discourse aims, if never reaches, by considering only the force of the better argument.[2] In other words, the speech-acts routinely marshaled in dialogue, if and when disputed in the normal course of communication, can be *rationally* accepted or rejected by the affected interlocutors on any or all of these three grounds:

1. Their propositional truth
2. Their rightness with respect to existing norms, or the rightness of the norms themselves.
3. Their sincerity with respect to the real goals of the speaker[3]

"Communicatively achieved agreement," then, which is the rational end of communicative action, is "measured against exactly three criticizable validity claims," and "someone who rejects a comprehensible speech-act is taking issue with at least one of these validity claims."[4]

In this complex realm, *justice* will reside in the rationally testable validity of norms and actions that concern distribution of social goods, access to freedom, recourse in the event of force, and so on—actions and norms that are always justified in the crucible of discursive speech.[5] "Justice" is the general name we give to a certain complex of principles, the validity of which is put into question, usually implicitly but sometimes explicitly, when someone acts on their basis. When I say, for example, "Taxation is theft," I raise by my speech-act a criticizable validity claim concerning the justice of taxation. The normative claim, articulated clearly in the context of the dialogue in which the speech-act occurred, might be expected to garner routine support—we are a community of libertarian true believers, say, and the claim merely expresses something we all uncontroversially take to be true. But suppose a voice is raised in favor of taxation. It is true that this voice can be quickly stifled with force, but when I

2. The notion of an ideal speech situation appears early in Habermas's work on communicative action, and in its potentially universal extension is indebted to C. S. Peirce and Karl-Otto Apel. Briefly, the ideal speech situation is meant to capture the implicit claim or orientation, operative continuously in actual conversation, that only the better argument *should* be decisive. The move to discourse when disagreement arises is meant to approach, if never actually reach, such an ideal.

3. See *TCA1*, p. 307.

4. Ibid., p. 308.

5. It should be noted that Habermas considers together, as elements of a single class of claims, two claims other theories strive to keep apart, namely those about actions based on norms and those about norms themselves. In other words, we might want to distinguish first-order normative claims (Did the action in question conform to a rule we accept?) from second-order normative claims (Does the rule conform to our wider notions of rightness?).

claimed that "taxation is theft," I did not mean that I (and my fellows) could *force* everybody else to assent to, or abide by, that claim. What I meant, really, was that there were good reasons for thinking it was so—better reasons, in fact, than any pro-taxation view could ever marshal in its own defense. If we begin talking about those reasons—assessing the force of the better argument—we are engaged in discourse. Every claim that is made in this way therefore anticipates, Habermas believes, a discursive move in which it can be tested for its validity.

Since this move to discourse is implicit in any claim of a normative type, such testing always also anticipates, according to Habermas, a *rational consensus* about norms. This consensus is ideally available to us through unconstrained discourse. Each of the affected participants in the conversation can give a yes/no answer to the claim I have raised, and we will ideally reach understanding and agreement about the norm under consideration—in this case the norm that a graduated income tax is a violation of my right to keep what is mine. Because it reflects the rational commitments of all concerned, the rational agreement that issues from our unconstrained conversation about justice is what serves to justify the norm in question or, contrarily, to overturn it convincingly.

Of course, the justification of norms through consensus is only one of the goals anticipated in the resort to discourse, only one of the commitments implicit in the kinds of speech-act that characterize what Habermas calls communicative action.[6] Rational claims to truth are also assessed in the same way, while truthfulness or sincerity is assessed in terms of behavior, that is, how actions relate to claims. One of the benefits of bringing sincerity claims inside the purview of rational assessment in this fashion is that it will allow the effective uncovering of ideological manipulation or deception. As we shall see, Habermas resorts to a therapeutic model similar to Freud's and a model of *Ideologiekritik* derived from earlier analyses in critical theory to deal with instances of deception and self-deception that "systematically distort" communication.

This first glance at Habermas's rich theory may suggest he holds out hopes of rational agreement in discourse and the resulting justification of norms of

---

6. Habermas contrasts communicative action, which is oriented toward understanding and agreement, with instrumental action, which is oriented toward success. Someone who converses to, say, score points or build self-image is acting strategically, not communicatively. Understanding the other interlocutor(s) is not his or her central motivation. These points are made in *TCA1* with reference to some classics of argumentation theory; see esp. Stephen Toulmin's *The Uses of Argument* (Cambridge: Cambridge University Press, 1958), which Habermas probes and expands on in fascinating ways.

justice that are excessively optimistic. Indeed, the ideality of his theoretical strategy should be already apparent. Is the gossamer thread of our pragmatic[7] orientation to communicative action really strong enough to suspend the norms of justice? What we shall find, I think, is this: properly understood, the idealities Habermas wishes to discuss cannot be avoided in the rational commitments of argument. Each of us exhibits these commitments, and the rational anticipations that come with them, on a daily and even hourly basis. The discernment of these idealities, furthermore, is not of merely theoretical interest, for they will indicate what is at stake in our actual processes and practices of norm justification. These processes—the discursive testing of claims governing who, how, and why we judge—are deeply wedded to the moral and political projects that shape our lives as persons and citizens.

In general, any initial impression of excessive or bizarre abstraction must be tempered by an awareness of Habermas's methodological commitments. Habermas depends in his analysis of communicative action on the force of "reconstructive sciences." These are investigations undertaken on the basis of empirical evidence but with a strong degree of evaluative force. Through the rational reconstruction of social phenomena—a kind of principled and normative interpretation—their findings extend beyond the "merely" empirical and in effect bridge philosophy's traditional fact-value distinction. The examples of such reconstructions to which Habermas habitually refers are the developmental psychology of Jean Piaget and the moral psychology pioneered by Lawrence Kohlberg.[8] I shall examine in the next section of this chapter the status of communicative-action theory and discourse ethics as such a reconstruction, and discuss the ways in which it may have telling rational force for us. In particular I suggest that Habermas's provocative reconstruction of communicative competence may indeed allow us to clarify what is at stake in the project of

---

7. What Habermas means by pragmatic is not what Ackerman meant by it: not the political imperative to find ways of cohabiting in limited social space, but instead the implied commitment to the better argument contained in speech-acts. The latter is considered universal; I consider the most compelling version of the former to be of more limited scope. (More on this later in the chapter.)

8. The bridge between Habermas's critical social theory and the moral psychology of Lawrence Kohlberg remains unclear. Kohlberg's project of distinguishing among the stages of moral development has been criticized for mistaking Western, middle-class developmental traits for something universal. It is nevertheless the most powerful analytic tool yet developed in the field of moral psychology. See Lawrence Kohlberg, *Essays on Moral Development*, 3 vols. (New York: Harper & Row, 1981–84). For a dissenting view from a feminist perspective, see Carol Gilligan, *In a Different Voice* (Cambridge, Mass.: Harvard University Press, 1982). Interesting new work on psychology and justice is surveyed in Barbara Mellers and Jonathan Baron, eds., *Psychological Perspectives on Justice: Theory and Applications* (New York: Cambridge University Press, 1993).

rational justification of norms. It may also show how infidelities and infections in that project can be in principle eliminated, on the basis of our rational commitment to it.

I have already mentioned (Chapter 1) certain figures, particularly Richard Rorty and Jean-François Lyotard, who find Habermas's project of rational agreement both incoherent and potentially dangerous. These and other objections to Habermas's theory are discussed in the penultimate section of the present chapter. Though I believe Habermas's theory can withstand the main force of these criticisms, they will prompt a shift of focus in the chapter's final section: from the ideal conditions initially investigated by Habermas to the practical-political problem of justifying norms of justice in a real democratic decision process. I believe we shall find that the ideal conditions of norm assessment are, as it were, too thin to have the concrete application we desire in a political solution to the problems of justice. At that stage I suggest how our general investigation of just talking can proceed from that point of limitation.

II. JUST SPEECH ACTS

What has come to be called the theory of communicative action has had a long genesis in Habermas's work and has received numerous more-or-less complex treatments over two decades or more. I choose to begin my investigation of the theory with an early statement of its scope and main insights. I do this partly because it will allow fruitful comparison with later versions and, perhaps more important at this stage, partly because here the more nuanced and detailed treatments in, for example, *The Theory of Communicative Action* and the essays of *Moral Consciousness and Communicative Action* are effectively foreshadowed in relatively simple outline.

1. Competence and Distortion

In an early article, "Towards a Theory of Communicative Competence," Habermas argues against the then-dominant Chomskian model of "linguistic competence" and in favor of his own model of "communicative competence." He claims to find the former too "monological" in its tendency to view "the general competence of a native speaker" as a matter of "the mastery of an abstract system of linguistic rules."[9] Communication, Habermas suggests, is also crucially a matter of *interpersonal dialogue.* Here participants possess, in addition to mastery of linguistic skills, the ability to create and shape speech situations, take up and explore roles, and determine meanings together in discourse. "[A] situation in which speech, i.e. the application of linguistic competence, becomes in principle possible, depends on a structure of intersubjectivity which is in turn linguistic." An awareness of this structure is thus part of what it means to be communicatively competent; and such awareness has more than merely linguistic force, since the intersubjectivity presumed in competent communication makes evident our anticipation of the "ideal speech situation," that discursive space in which rational commitments demand that only the better argument hold sway.[10] "[C]ommunicative competence means," says Habermas, "the *mastery of* an ideal speech situation."[11]

Habermas discovers this ideal not through any deduction, and still less as the result of imposing a self-created limit. Instead he depends on the speech-act analysis of performative verbs pioneered by J. L. Austin and revised and expanded by John Searle, among others.[12] That analysis indicates, in Haber-

9. Jürgen Habermas, "Towards a Theory of Communicative Competence," *Inquiry* 13 (1970): 366 (hereafter TTCC). The Chomskian view is also criticized for its "a priorism" (seeing language as a set of elements that exist before acquisition) and its "elementarism" (seeing language as a finite set of rules and atomic parts). See ibid., p. 363. The charge that such a theory is "monological" will also be familiar from my earlier discussion. This reform of the Chomskian model shows, perhaps even more clearly than Habermas's critiqiue of Cartesian reflection, why the picture of the single isolated consciousness fails to capture the essence of language acquisition, language use, and indeed epistemological reflection. For a skeptical answer to these claims concerning communicative competence, see Joseph Beatty, " 'Communicative Competence' and the Skeptic," *Philosophy and Social Criticism* 6 (1979): 267–88. See also Thomas McCarthy, "A Theory of Communicative Competence," *Philosophy of the Social Sciences* 3 (1973): 135–56.

10. As noted, the ideal speech situation, and the possibility of its universal extension to all rational agents, are notions Habermas takes on from Karl-Otto Apel and his discursive treatment of insights from G. H. Mead about "ideal role-taking" in justification. See Apel's *Dialog als Methode* (Göttingen: Vandenhoeck & Ruprecht, 1972) and, for a treatment of the "transcendental-pragmatic" argument in favor of this universalism, his *Kommunikation und Reflexion: Zur Diskussion der Transzendentalpragmatik* (Frankfurt: Suhrkamp, 1982) and *Understanding and Explanation: A Transcendental-Pragmatic Perspective,* trans. Georgia Warnke (Cambridge, Mass.: MIT Press, 1984).

11. TTCC, p. 367 (emphasis added).

12. We shall see, in Chapter 6, that the sociolinguists of politeness, whose own reconstructions provide key foundation stones in my interpretation of civil communicative competence, also refer back to the ground-breaking analyses offered by Austin and Searle. See J. L. Austin, *How to Do Things with Words* (Oxford: Oxford University Press, 1962) and *Philosophical Papers* (Oxford: Clarendon Press, 1979), esp. "A Plea for Excuses" and "Three Ways of Spilling Ink." See also John Searle, *Speech Acts: An Essay in the Philosophy of Language* (Cambridge: Cambridge University Press, 1969) and *Expression and Meaning: Studies in the Theory of Speech Acts* (Cambridge:

mas's dialogical rereading, that pragmatics as well as linguistics can be sub-jected to formal analysis. In other words, we can determine the formal struc-tures governing not only how words work in language but also how we do things with words. Austin tells us that such verbs as *promise, announce, warn, report, desire,* and *determine* can be used actually to perform the acts they define, provided certain contextual features are given. When, for exam-ple, the guard says to students in the reading room at five o'clock, "The library is closed," he has *by his very utterance* closed the library.[13] This ability of some words to *do* something (and not merely *say* something) is what Austin calls their "illocutionary force."[14]

By thus extending himself beyond the "monological" theory of language competence, Habermas is seeking to build on this pioneering analysis of illocutionary force:

> When [speakers] use performative expressions, the speech acts are linguistic representations of that illocutionary force, i.e. the universal pragmatic power of utterances. Expressions of this kind retain no given pragmatic feature of contingent speech situations; *they explain the meaning of certain idealized features of speech situations in gen-eral,* which the speaker must master if his competence is to be ade-quate for participating at all in situations of potential speech. A theory of communicative competence can thus be developed in terms of universal pragmatics.[15]

So while performatives in particular depend on context to function, in general they point to "universal" pragmatic features of language as a whole. (Habermas's brand of the pragmatic implications of dialogue is not the same, clearly, as Ackerman's political imperative.) What Habermas here labels "dialogue-constitutive universals" establishes the general features of dialogue, including the ability to do things with words. The ideal speech situation is therefore nothing more than the implied ability of competent communicators

---

Cambridge University Press, 1979); and John Searle and Daniel Vanderveken, *Foundations of Illocutionary Logic* (Cambridge: Cambridge University Press, 1985).

13. I owe this example to David Eustis, who once pointed out the illocutionary force used by the guard in David Hume Tower, Edinburgh University, to kick us out of the philosophy library.

14. See his "Three Ways of Spilling Ink," among others, for a characterization of what, and how, words do.

15. TTCC, p. 367 (emphasis added).

to establish the terms of mutual understanding in a dialogue—an ability that is anticipated by their very acts of communication.

That communication is in practice often distorted, that it may be influenced by motivations operating outside the view of public communication, does not alter the fact that speech-acts exhibit in their very structure a formal orientation toward mutual understanding. That orientation includes an anticipated reciprocity between speakers. Yet frequently that reciprocity will have to be bracketed, if, for example, the distortion likely to affect the cooperative achievement of goals is *systematic*. In the companion article to "Towards a Theory of Communicative Competence," entitled "On Systematically Distorted Communication," Habermas investigates Freudian therapeutic analysis and its ability to bring systematic deception, of the kind likely to distort the goals of understanding and cooperative goal-direction and truth-seeking, to the full awareness of affected speakers.[16] Here, in contrast to communicative action operating without distortion, the interlocutors may have to assume superordinate and subordinate positions in order to expose, and eliminate, distorting elements of the talk. This is so because the distortions of communication can be such that a speaker cannot come to a realization of them simply by submitting locutions to reciprocal testing of validity. My self-deception may be, for example, on the order of a psychological delusion. The force of this kind of self-deception is that no standards for evaluating the distortion of language are available "from the inside"—it is *systematically* distorted in that its self-justifications, designed to keep the self-deception going, go as it were "all the way down."

Indeed, as the Freudian literature amply indicates, speakers working within this sort of delusional distortion may have an infinite and infinitely inventive capacity for recasting locutions in such a way as to support, and never challenge, the dominant delusion. The therapeutic point, then, must be to bring the delusional speaker to a self-awareness about the fact of his own communicative distortion *from within* that distortion, and this can be done only by prompting an internal account of its genesis and manifestation in delusional symptoms. Such prompting can only be undertaken by assuming, with refer-

16. "On Systematically Distorted Communication," *Inquiry* 13 (1970): 205–18. Here Habermas draws effectively from the Freudian model. The investigation of therapeutic modes of communication is also taken up again, and in greater detail, in Habermas, *Theory of Communicative Action* and in "The Hermeneutic Claim to Universality," in Josef Fleicher, ed., *Contemporary Hermeneutics* (London: Routledge & Kegan Paul, 1980), pp. 181–212. The latter piece is a conflated and condensed version of the two *Inquiry* papers; it can also be found in Müller-Vollmer, *Hermeneutics Reader*, pp. 293–319.

ence to the deluded speaker, a therapeutic position. This leaves reciprocity aside for the time being, true, but only because the goals of communicative action cannot be pursued until the disruption, in the form of distorted communication, is healed. Any other course, including the simple continuance of discursive give-and-take, would do no more than perpetuate the delusion.

Habermas argues that the case is similar in instances of ideological deception and self-deception. Here, once more, we are dealing with systematic distortions of language that can be expected to have an infinite capacity for casting reciprocally critical evaluations in their own self-justifying terms.[17] In a simple case, any instance of criticism of an ideological world-view constitutes, for inhabitants of that world-view, not genuine criticisms to be assessed for their rational force but instead further evidence that those tenets of the world-view predicting hostile reaction to its adherents were correct. ("The prophet said we would be attacked, and here it is happening.") Or, in a related form of ideological deception, all judgments of understanding are in effect reduced to expressions of agreement. ("You must have misunderstood if you still refuse to accept what I say.") Given such situations, reciprocity may have to be surrendered once again, until such time as the adherents of the ideological world-view can be shown, to their own satisfaction, that, say, the world-view does not really answer to needs that they have and instead makes someone else's needs appear to be theirs. This critique of ideology could involve, for example, attempts to show that the high priests of the world-view are practicing a communicative deception by distortedly recasting their own self-interest in terms of the general interest. Such a demonstration would appeal, Habermas says, to standards of sincerity. One large chink in ideology's armor will be discernment of actions undertaken by a speaker that do not correspond to the speech-acts he or she conjointly employs with those actions.

The rational assessment of sincerity shows that more routine elimination of deception and force in communication need not involve bracketing the reciprocal nature of communication: we can always appeal to our shared, and symmetric, standards of sincerity when actions and communication do not seem to reinforce each other. These assessments, part of the routine processes of keeping discourse on the rails, are not usually therapeutic in the structural sense. We do not actually change our roles to heal such minor distortions. So when you say, for example, "I believe x," it will be a relatively straightforward matter for me to

---

17. I have pursued this parallelism, and its implications for the place of "madpeople" in dialogues of legitimation, in my "Madpeople and Ideologues: An Issue for Dialogic Justice Theory," *International Philosophical Quarterly* 34 (1994): 59–73.

assess your actions in regard to x to see whether you have indeed comported yourself in such a way that indicates belief about x. I may find that your statement of belief in x conceals an agenda of control, for you want me to think you believe x even while you in fact believe y. (Such instances of deception need not always be malign, of course. Insincerity has its social uses, but also its social limits. I have more to say about this issue in Chapters 6 and 7.) If, on the other hand, you say, "I am doing x" even while it is clearly observable that you are doing y, the situation may be one in which standards of sincerity have little purchase. You may sincerely believe you *are* doing x, but I (and others) judge that you are deluded in so believing because, by common consent, what you are doing is not actually x. Here my reciprocal appeal to any shared standards of truth, normative rightness, and sincerity will do little in furthering communication. And so the therapeutic or critical standpoint may have to be adopted—a standpoint that is by definition not reciprocal.

It is worth noting how much of an advance over MacIntyre's model of dialogue is shown by both the routine and the therapeutic modes of dealing with deception and force. Though therapy bears some conceptual relation to adequacy in traditional conflict—therapy shows me, like a more adequate theory does, just why my own view is no longer good enough—MacIntyre's failure to admit the possibility of severe irrationalities in communication makes the inadequacy of his model apparent. Habermas is frequently criticized for the degree of ideality he employs in speaking about our rational commitments. Yet here it is just that way of speaking that makes possible salutary and rational elimination of distortions in communication—distortions that threaten the project of justifying norms or principles of justice in dialogue. MacIntyre's apparent presumption of rationality in the conversation among traditions begins to seem, by contrast, superficial and excessively optimistic.[18]

2. Discourse Ethics

To be sure, Habermas does not investigate the full implications of communicative reciprocity, its normative function, or the therapeutic elimination of distortion in these short articles. But these early efforts are significant for introducing the notion of *criticizable validity claims*, raised implicitly in speech and

---

18. This may not be surprising: if, as I believe is the case, MacIntyre is recapitulating many of the tenets of Gadamer's translation and horizon-fusion models, the critical points marshaled by Habermas are, by implication, here the same as those that are operative in the celebrated Gadamer-Habermas debate. In both cases, the failure to account for force and deception—the failure to incorporate *Ideologiekritik*—leads to an uncritical support of the status quo ante.

action. This is where we may now locate "discourse ethics" and what I want to call Habermas's dialogic theory of justice. Discourse ethics speaks to a kind of dialogue that, in contrast to the talk defended in Ackerman's theory and in the general strategy of liberal theorists, is *externally unconstrained*. Its goal is univeral consensus, a consensus vouchsafed by the anticipation of the ideal speech situation—a situation "necessarily implied in the structure of potential speech, since all speech, even intentional deception, is oriented towards the idea of truth."[19]

Discourse ethics can be seen to develop directly from this idea of a presupposed rational consensus. The early sketch contains in outline three crucial elements that will be of interest to us in that deeper analysis:

1. An initial empirical and reconstructive investigation of speech acts
2. The notion of criticizable validity claims, raised implicitly (but sometimes challenged and defended explicitly) in dialogue
3. The ideal of a universal consensus, achieved through an unrestrained discussion in which interlocutors may raise (and also challenge) any opinion or normative claim.

These three features, highly schematic though they appear, constitute the basis of Habermas's "rational reconstruction" of communicative action. Building on an empirically testable orientation in speech, Habermas has constructed a notion of universal consensus with rational force. To assess this force more closely, I now turn to more complex analyses of communicative action, and the place of the norms of justice within them.

In *The Theory of Communicative Action*, Habermas's sense of the centrality of communicative action is based in large part on his view of what constitutes rationality. But he likewise believes that any strategy of examining rational commitments and orientations in an artificial state of inward-looking self-reflection (like Descartes's, or Kant's—or Rawls's) will fail to take sufficient account of the social character of rational belief and action, the fact that we are always *oriented to the world and to others* in our rationality. A good part of what it means to be rational is to be both able and willing to give reasons, to interlocutors, for performing our actions and holding our beliefs. Rationality is not a state entered into as the result of, so to speak, a bargain between me and myself; rationality is an orientation that presumes at least one other person with whom I am exchanging information and coordinating actions.

19. TTCC, p. 372.

Habermas begins this account by considering what it is that makes assertions (i.e., truth claims) and actions *rational:*

> An assertion can be called rational only if the speaker satisfies the
> conditions necessary to achieve the illocutionary goals of reaching an
> understanding about something in the world with at least one other
> participant in communication. A goal-directed action can be rational
> only if the actor satisfied the conditions necessary for realizing his
> intention to intervene successfully in the world.[20]

These sets of conditions vary with context and are established not a priori but
rather by the pragmatic expectations of the communication community. Both
assertion and action may fail to fulfill the given conditions, whatever they are,
but such failure can then in turn be explained *in terms of* the conditions—a
failed action shows forth what a successful one would have been. Rationality
therefore consists, on this view, in being able to orient one's assertions/actions
to understanding/success. The advance of communicative rationality as a
theory is that it takes account, in a way that a monological self-reflection
could not, both of "cognitive-instrumental reason" (the orientation toward
success in autonomous action) and of the common, dialogically achieved goal
of maintaining and reproducing a shared lifeworld. Because this goal is conceived as a collective one—one about which no member of a community could
reasonably be indifferent—it implies that *responsible* actors are those who
orient themselves to adding to the stock of shared understanding and coordi-
nated action.

Such an account of rationality is still only partial, unless it includes in the
field of criticizable validity claims, in addition to claims about truth, claims
about "normatively regulated behavior" (following rules, justifying actions on
the basis of legitimate expectations) and "expressive self-presentation" (making desires or intentions known, expressing a feeling or mood, sharing, confessing). Since our main concern is justice, and the normative claims grouped
under its auspices, I put aside any further discussion of the aesthetic and
therapeutic significance of the latter type of claim.[21] I also forgo detailed
discussion of the type of communication Habermas calls "explicative dis-

---

20. *TCA1*, p. 11.
21. But see ibid., pp. 20–22. I also suggest later that some critics of Habermas believe he
undervalues these elements of communicative action in terms of their normative importance,
especially with regard to characterizing public discourse.

course," which deals with the well-formedness and correctness of expressions. But together these various *forms of argumentation* mark the field in which validity claims are raised and criticized.

The important notion for our purposes is that claims to truth and to normative rightness can be assessed rationally in the processes of argumentation. Indeed, the claim is more than a "can": these claims cannot, it is argued, be assessed anywhere else, for rational assessment means the process of having those affected by a claim argue without constraint about its validity. Recognition of this rational compulsion makes for the "move to discourse" noted at the outset of this chapter—that is, the shift from routine communication to argumentation that occurs when success is blocked in the common run of talk. "Thus," says Habermas, "the rationality proper to the communicative practice of everyday life points to the practice of argumentation as a court of appeal that makes it possible to continue communicative action with other means when disagreements can no longer be repaired with everyday routines and yet are not to be settled by direct or strategic use of force."[22] Argumentation depends on the force of reason-giving, on a recognition that the validity of the better argument is the proper, and sole, criterion by which to judge a claim. Rationality, understood in this communicative fashion, is therefore a principled responsiveness to arguments, a willingness to have one's own claims criticized, to grant rational assent to the better argument, and to correct mistakes. But this orientation is not voluntary; it is simply what is implied, unavoidable, in our competences as communicative actors. We avoid communicative rationality only at the cost of silence and isolation.

Habermas now sets out clearly the features of the ideal speech situation first sketched in his "Towards a Theory of Communicative Competence." In the ideal speech situation there is no force but that of the better argument, no motive but that of a cooperative search for truth. The situation is anticipated, if never actually achieved, in all argumentation. The commitment of the ideal speech situation is, at bottom, no more than the primary philosophical project of transforming *doxa* into *episteme*. It follows—if we are all rational participants in discourse, seeking to transform opinion into knowledge—that no extra force, no external constraint however powerful, will be needed *or justified* in giving the better argument force. Since we are rational participants if and only if we are communicating participants, there is no magic to the reality of the ideal speech situation. It simply isolates a claim implied in our acts of talking themselves, namely that the *force* of the better argument comes with

22. *TCA1*, pp. 17–18.

its being better, given—and this is to say a great deal—our shared context of discursive communication.

That force can be summarized in what Habermas calls a "fundamental principle of universalization" (*Universalisierungsgrundsatz*, otherwise known as "U"). "U" is understood here to be a *discursive* reformulation of the Kantian categorical imperative and, though very different in derivation, intended to achieve the same ends as Kant's principle. It is, in other words, "a bridging principle that makes agreement in moral argumentation possible."[23] Habermas's "U" therefore reads, in one version: "Every valid norm must satisfy the condition that the consequences and the side-effects which foreseeably follow from its general compliance can, for the satisfaction of the interests of every individual, be accepted without force by all those affected." What this principle seeks to capture is the essence of discourse about norms: when we can all agree without external force or constraint that the norm in question is acceptable to us, the norm may be considered argumentatively justified. Habermas is able to derive from the principle of universalization (which is meant to apply to argumentation in general) a stronger *practical* principle of discourse ethics, "D," which reads: "Only those norms can claim to be valid that meet (or could meet) with the approval of all affected in their capacity as participants in a practical discourse."[24]

What I do when I propose a norm in such a discourse, Habermas suggests, is implicitly demand that *everyone* affected by it should be able, under reasonable ideal conditions, to give his or her assent to it. The "reasonable" ideal conditions are just those implied by the structure of communication itself: that the better argument is the single compelling factor in the generation of rational agreement, given our inescapable rational presuppositions (implied by communicative competence) and our general orientation to a cooperative search for truth (given by our communicative, as opposed to strategic, action). "Participants in argumentation," says Habermas, "cannot avoid the presupposition that, owing to certain characteristics that require formal description, the

23. Jürgen Habermas, "Discourse Ethics: Notes on a Program of Philosophical Justification," in his *Moral Consciousness and Communicative Action*, p. 57. Habermas notes at that juncture that "U" is formulated in such a way that any *monological* application is impossible; it is on this basis that he criticizes Rawls's attempt at neo-Kantian derivation of principles through individual self-reflection. See also Habermas's "Morality and Ethical Life: Does Hegel's Critique of Kant Apply to Discourse Ethics?" in ibid., pp. 195–215.

24. The best discussion of this derivation of "D" (a practical principle) from "U" (a principle of argumentation) is in Habermas's "Discourse Ethics," pp. 64–68. There Habermas also discusses his debts to Stephen Toulmin in the theory of argumentation (debts apparent in the parallel treatment in *TCA*) and to, e.g., Kurt Baier, Bernard Gert, and Marcus Singer in the treatment of moral rules.

structure of their communication rules out all external or internal coercion other than the force of the better argument and thereby also neutralizes all motives other than that of the cooperative search for truth."[25] On the basis of these "inescapable presuppositions," Robert Alexy has formalized the rules of discourse at this level in the following terms: (1) Every subject with the competence to speak and act is allowed to take part in a discourse. (2)(a) Everyone is allowed to question any assertion whatever; (b) everyone is allowed to introduce any assertion whatever into the discourse; (c) everyone is allowed to express his attitudes, desires, and needs. (3) No speakers may be prevented, by internal or external coercion, from exercising their rights as laid down in (1) and (2).[26]

Discourse ethics thus represents the communicative process of rationally assessing a succession of (naturally arising) normative claims, each serving to orient ethical action. Understanding is reached in discourse in the form of agreement about the validity of claims raised by our normative speech-acts.[27] Our yes/no responses to these claims serve ultimately to justify norms, and actions done on the basis of norms, as we proceed toward agreement—that is, toward the shared and rational moral truth. Says Habermas:

> Processes of reaching understanding aim at an agreement that meets the conditions of rationally motivated assent to the content of an utterance. A communicatively achieved agreement has a rational basis; it cannot be improved by either party, whether instrumentally through

25. Ibid., pp. 88–89.

26. Robert Alexy, "Eine Theorie des Praktischen Diskurses," in *Normenbegründung, Normendurchsetzung*, ed. W. Oelmüller (Paderborn: Schöningh, 1978); adapted from Habermas's "Discourse Ethics," pp. 87–89. Alexy also specifies rules that apply at more basic levels of communicative competence—e.g., rules of noncontradiction, consistency, and that reasons must be given for exclusions. See also Alexy's "Probleme der Diskurstheorie," *Zeitschrift für Philosophische Forschung* 43 (1989): 81–93. It might be thought that such rules are cognate with Ackerman's rules of dialogic neutrality, but Habermas wants to argue "that these rules of discourse are not mere *conventions*," but rather, "inescapable presuppositions" of rational communication itself ("Discourse Ethics," p. 89). Ackerman never makes his claim so strong, nor does he base it on communicative competence.

27. This fusion of understanding and agreement, which overturns part of the dispute between Habermas and Gadamer, has suggested to some critics that Habermas's communicative rationality is itself ideological. If, in other words, I have not understood until I come to agree, are we not dealing here with a form of rationalist domination? But here the freedom from external constraints is crucial. If the only force in play is the force of the better argument, and "better" means freely accepted as superior by all affected participants, there is no question of hidden or ideological coercion, and no reason to continue holding open a distance between understanding and agreement. I shall have more to say on this issue below.

intervention in the situation directly or strategically through influencing the decisions of opponents.[28]

So such an agreement is for Habermas rationally binding and can never be the
result of force or strategic deception. It is also, he wants to say, potentially
universal in that the discourse giving rise to it can always in principle extend to
include all those affected by the norm or its side-effects, presuming of course
their rational willingness and ability to engage in the discussion.

Of course, discursive argumentation is not necessarily common in the spheres
of actual social interaction. And, as we saw, discourse may arise only when
controversial claims stall the routine processes of reaching agreement. The
move to discourse therefore happens only when there are blocks in general
agreement. Even here, there must be a supposition "that a rationally motivated
agreement could in principle be achieved, whereby the phrase 'in principle'
expresses the idealizing proviso: if only the argumentation could be conducted
openly enough and continued long enough."[29] By so basing validity on a process
of discursive assessment of claims by a group of interlocutors, Habermas has
shifted validity from semantics and semantic units (sentences) and into the
realm of pragmatics and pragmatic units (actions).[30] But these units, no less than
semantic ones, can be usefully subjected to a formal analysis.

In the sphere of practical argumentation, where the norms and actions of
justice are under consideration by interlocutors, discourse ethics professes to
find rational commitments that have been denied by ethical noncognitivists,
including both MacIntyre and, as we will see presently, Lyotard.[31] These thinkers argue that moral discourse of the kind Habermas is concerned to defend is
either impossible, or if possible then dangerous. In other words, the anticipation
of agreement in moral debate is either mistaken (MacIntyre) or politically
charged (Lyotard). But Habermas, though he is willing to admit that rational

28. *TCA1*, p. 287.
29. Ibid., p. 42.
30. See ibid., p. 276.
31. This is one reason that such apparently very different theorists as these should both be
labeled conservative. Premodernism and postmodernism agree with respect to the incoherence of
modernism and its commitment to universalist rationality. An outline of this charge as it applies
to Lyotard can be found in Section III.3 below; as applied to MacIntyre, it is compactly expressed
by Roger Paden in "Post-Structuralism and Neo-Romanticism, or Is MacIntyre a Young Conservative?" *Philosophy and Social Criticism* 13 (1987):125–44.
MacIntyre does not view himself as a noncognitivist in ethics, if that term is taken to describe
one who denies that we can ever know the moral truth. What he denies is that we can ever know it
on the basis of a rationality shared by all rational actors.

agreement is difficult and even unusual, does not agree that it can be considered impossible. Paradoxically, the expansiveness of his aspiration here—an aspiration MacIntyre fought shy of—leads him to a more detailed, and more accurate, reconstruction of the rational commitments underlying moral and political talk. "In everyday life," he maintains, "no one would enter into moral argumentation if he did not start from the strong presupposition that a grounded consensus could *in principle* be achieved among those involved."[32]

Because on this view each of us, by participating, shows himself or herself always already committed to the project of reaching agreement about normative validity claims, valid norms will be accepted just in case we are sincerely participating. "Reaching understanding," Habermas says, "is the inherent telos of human speech."[33] However distorted *actual* attempts at moral discourse may be, ruled by passion and hidden commitments and even systematic self-deception, the in-principle claim still holds. What it means to speak rationally about the justifiability of norms is (1) to orient oneself to understanding, (2) to consider only the force of the better argument, i.e., the stronger justifiable true claim, and (3) to presume the ideal possibility of universal consensus. Like claims about the truth of propositions and about the well-formedness of symbolic expressions and logical theorems, claims about the rightness of moral norms are, Habermas argues, *by their very meaning* universal in extension.[34]

Habermas further argues that, once pointed out, the rational commitments we all exhibit in discourse can help to sharpen our argumentation, bringing us closer to an ideal situation in which every opinion is assessed and either accepted or rejected on the basis only of its validity. For the special problems of justice, this would naturally mean an ongoing process of rational assessment of rules and norms that affect distribution of goods and offices, treatment of individuals and groups, and relations among individuals and groups.[35] Haber-

32. *TCA1*, p. 19 (emphasis added).
33. Ibid., p. 287.
34. Ibid., p. 42.
35. Agnes Heller has, with a definiteness that is not always desirable, asserted that the three spheres to which the norms of justice traditionally and uniquely apply are: distribution (of material goods, services, honors); retribution (punishment and reparation); and the declaration and waging of war. See Agnes Heller, *Beyond Justice* (New York: Basil Blackwell, 1987), ch. 4. Heller reads these concerns back into the issues of group-to-group interaction, especially in the notion of in-group/out-group behavior, and the norms that govern it, but she does not explicitly make the relations *among* groups a matter of justice. That is, her procedural version of justice governs only how group members treat out-groupers, not how they conceive of intergroup relations generally.

mas's reconstruction of speech-acts about justice (and other normative matters) is therefore meant to show that rational yes/no decisions about particular rules and practices can be made in dialogue, provided there are no artificial constraints and all the interlocutors are aware of their rational commitments to the force of the better argument—that is, not ideologically dominated or self-deceived. Ideally modeled, each participant in discourse has free and equal access to the forums of discourse where the force of the better argument can be demonstrated. Reciprocity, which is presumed in any discussion about justice,[36] is here built into the conditions of speech itself. As Alexy's formalization of the "D" rule implies, we must all have equal access to the podium of communicative action.

Habermas readily admits that his use of speech-act theory here is idiosyncratic. Whereas Austin broke the field of speech-acts into types of verb (vindictive, exercitive, commissive, behabitive, expositive, etc.), and Searle divided it by illocutionary aim (assertive, declarative, expressive, directive, commissive, etc.), Habermas wants instead to classify speech-acts on the basis of contexts or social situations.[37] However unusual, such a classification has the advantage of providing more insight into the processes of forging understanding and agreement in social communication, and allows the initially empirical investigation about particular locutions to gain normative significance. Habermas believes he can reconstruct on this basis a tenable universality claim without relying on metaphysical grounding or a belief in rational progress. This is the sense in which communicative competence, our very ability to undertake actions in language, indicates the universal-pragmatic presuppositions of discourse, especially the anticipation of agreement. Rational reconstruction has force in this realm because it begins with the rational commitments evident in our actual speech-acts, and, by submitting them to a formal analysis, brings to the fore the precise nature of those commitments and their determination of norm assessment. We get, in short, the results of the Enlightenment project without having to accept the metaphysical schemes that raised the hackles of contextualizing critics like Gray and Walzer, Taylor and MacIntyre.

---

36. The argument goes back at least to Thucydides: justice is the principle marshaled to govern interactions among equals. This is why justice does not apply to either friends, family, and lovers (who receive more) or to inferiors like slaves (who receive less). I have followed Bernard Williams's use of this point in presuming reciprocity throughout this discussion—that is, we care about what justice is only *after* it is established that we all care about justice.

37. See *TCA1*, pp. 319–21.

III. REPLIES AND REACTIONS

1. Universal, Transcendental, Rational?

Habermas is well aware that some features of discourse ethics are going to appear alien, and perhaps indefensible, to our view of communication. Consider first the *universalism* embedded in the theory of discourse ethics. One of the supposed advantages of Habermas's theory is its freedom from the sort of external dialogic constraints found in Ackerman's model. According to Habermas, all we need is a keen analysis of what is implied by the structure of communication itself: the "conversational implicature," to borrow H. P. Grice's term, on which rational agreement can be founded.[38] The argument is that those actually engaged in argumentation, by virtue of their very participation, commit themselves to a cooperative search for truth in which only the unforced force of the better argument is convincing. The extension of the group of talkers is, according to the "U" principle, potentially universal—however difficult it may be actually to achieve such discourse, even in small groups. With its Kantian heritage, the demand for universality in Habermas's "U" will not be surprising. But is it supportable?[39]

Habermas follows Karl-Otto Apel's "transcendental-pragmatic" line of argument in defending "U." That is, we emphasize the inescapability of rational commitments by pointing out a "performative contradiction" in those who deny them.[40] This line of defense is commonly used by prorationalist philosophers against so-called irrationalist thinkers, such as Nietzsche or Derrida or

38. I argue in Chapter 6, on the basis of Grice's analysis, that conversational implicature also generates a shared anticipation of civility, something lacking in Habermas's too-rational reconstruction.

39. In these particulars, I am following the argument of Kelly, "MacIntyre, Habermas, and Philosophical Ethics," pp. 70–93. Kelly argues that there is a "methodological convergence" between MacIntyre and Habermas concerning their desire to defend "philosophical ethics," which, "like hermeneutic ethics, is tradition-bound but which is, at the same time, rational and critical, like Kantian ethics" (p. 72). There has been a good deal of recent debate on universalism in ethics. For an illuminating collection of positions, reprinted from the journal *Philosophy and Social Criticism*, see David Rasmussen, ed., *Universalism vs. Communitarianism: Contemporary Debate in Ethics* (Cambridge, Mass.: MIT Press, 1990).

40. For a strong statement of this argument, see Habermas, "Discourse Ethics," sec. 3, esp. pp. 82–86 and 90–98. In the same paper, Habermas makes a convincing reply to the muteness of a Nietzschean skeptic about communicative action and its presuppositions: the stance cannot be maintained consistently without courting suicide or sociopathology. See ibid., 98–102. This reply is stronger than, e.g., MacIntyre's simple refusal to engage in rational discussion with the genealogist. Being a strong cognitivist in ethics means, among other things, that Habermas can assert that the rational commitments of ethical life cannot be sanely avoided.

Rorty in some of his moods, who seek to undermine rational discourse while still employing the forms of rational discourse. In Habermas's version the defense is compellingly directed toward the "universal pragmatics" of discourse itself, turning on the presuppositions I cannot avoid when engaged in the discursive practices of argumentation. Habermas wants to ask of any interlocutor, If you are not asking for universal assent when you propose a norm, then what *are* you doing? To deny the demand for universal assent when arguing in favor of a norm is to have misunderstood what it means to "propose a norm for assessment." Universal assent may be neither actually expected nor actually achieved by the particular speakers involved, but it is always *anticipated* in the rational assessment of norms carried on in discourse. In other words, anyone seriously engaged in argumentation is by the same token accepting certain universal-pragmatic presuppositions about the nature of argumentation itself.

Habermas is thus able to point out that any denial of these pragmatic conditions in fact presupposes them, because arguments that make a denial rationally compelling share the anticipation of all arguments, namely that they will convince those genuinely engaged in a free and equal assessment of the better argument's force. The performative contradiction resides in using the rationally compelling force of argument to deny that argument has rationally compelling force. The status of my argument, as argument, shows the performative force of my argument to be self-contradictory. And this is a commitment I cannot avoid. It is, moreover, a commitment that has universal extension in the field of rational agents—all those who use arguments give reasons for the propositions they hold. This is why Habermas can speak (once more following Apel but also G. H. Mead) of an "ideal speech community"—the group of all those rationally committed to the unforced force of the better argument and the free and cooperative search for truth. This universalism may strike us as overstretched, especially when it comes to normative questions, but Habermas's argument is that, on the ideal level anyway, we cannot rationally avoid it.

There is also a controversial whiff of universalism in Habermas's reconstruction of communicative competence. As we have seen, that reconstruction is intended to have universal application in human life: wherever and whenever people talk together about norms and actions, *these* are the features anticipated by their discourse (with the important rider that the idealized conditions of such discourse may not be realized). But can this presumption of universality be maintained when we consider the narrowness of Habermas's empirical sample and possible differences in human language acquisition, patterns of discourse, and notions of practical rationality?[41] The same objection will be familiar to readers of Kohlberg's moral psychology, one of Habermas's models in reconstructing the features of communicative action. The evidence for such reconstructions, the charge goes, is in fact drawn from a limited field of Western, industrialized social and political life. Their universalist aspirations are just a newer, more apparently empirical, version of the exclusive modernist universalism associated with the Enlightenment. A single narrative of human development, moral or communicative, is here erected as the basic or fundamental story of what it means to be human, to be moral, to be a communicative actor.

Habermas attempts to disarm this objection by accepting that his universal conclusions, just because they are based on empirical and therefore fallible evidence, must always be provisional. And such provisionality should be seen as a result of rational reconstruction, not in opposition to it. "[R]ational reconstruction," one supporter of the view suggests,

> being subject to fallibilism, cannot support a strong universalism (e.g., that communicative competence is universal and discourse is necessary). Habermas may still draw universal conclusions, but only so long as it is clear that they are provisional (inductive, empirical—or simply, hypotheses, as Habermas sometimes calls them) rather than strong (universal and necessary).[42]

In other words, if rational reconstruction is to be empirical, it must face the consequences of empirical investigations: that they are open to error. Habermas's "U" is precisely *not* a strong universalist notion if that is taken to mean one based on a priori or transcendental arguments. It is true that, when it comes to the actualities of real norm assessment, Habermas may be casting his net too wide in wanting to speak of the set of all rational actors; but that is not yet reason to suppose that the idealizing universalism derived from his rational reconstruction is illicit. If the reconstruction of communicative compe-

41. This criticism is offered, in different forms, by Anthony Giddens and Thomas McCarthy. See McCarthy's "Rationality and Relativism: Habermas's 'Overcoming' of Hermeneutics," in *Habermas: Critical Debates*, ed. John B. Thompson and David Held (London: Macmillan, 1982), p. 69; and Anthony Giddens's "Reason Without Revolution? Habermas's *Theorie des kommunikativen Handelns*," in *Habermas and Modernity*, ed. Richard Bernstein (Cambridge, Mass.: MIT Press, 1985), pp. 112ff.
42. Kelly, "MacIntyre, Habermas, and Philosophical Ethics," p. 77.

tence proves to be in error, it will be modified. Fine-tuning is already evident in the many revisions and clarifications of the theory.

This reply has not convinced some critics, notably Richard Bernstein, who believes that the strong universalist baggage in Habermas's theory is evidence of ambivalence about the empirical nature of the central reconstruction.[43] Consequently, Bernstein suspects Habermas of stipulative definition when it comes to practical discourse, and suggests that claims for the "scientific" status of the theory of communicative action are dangerously overplayed: it is not, in the Popperian sense, falsifiable, for there is no way to specify relevant evidence to refute claims that, contrary to fact, we all aim at rational agreement in discourse. If this is so, Habermas's insights should seek another, more defensible, status—as rich interpretations of practices, not universalist scientific theses—and therefore be seen as claims made in what Bernstein calls "his pragmatic voice" and not "his transcendental voice."

This objection, though not always as ably expressed, is common. Many people worry that Habermas is importing an indefensible *transcendentalism* into his theory of communicative action. The insistence on retaining certain features of the Enlightenment project, namely its ability to criticize and justify norms across cultural boundaries, seems to ignore hermeneutical arguments that all judgments, norms, and discussions about them are historically and culturally conditioned. At the same time he or she recovers the structure of understanding, the sensitive interpreter must surrender ultimate or universal truth—to the extent that such notions of truth are conceived as extending beyond traditional boundaries or appealing to a standpoint detached from his or her own. Habermas, who wants to speak of agreement, not merely understanding, is therefore depending on notions of truth and rightness that extend beyond our individual or group experience. The legacy of Kantian reasoning in Habermas's theory is expressed in a transcendental standpoint that is impossible to reach and therefore dangerously misleading. It follows that the "U" principle is just the sort of principle whose substantive emptiness, while advanced as the proper route to justification, is better understood as committed to strong metaphysical claims about universal truth. In the words of Richard Rorty, Habermas, by attempting to appeal to rational standards embedded in

---

43. See Richard J. Bernstein, "What Is the Difference That Makes a Difference?" in Wachterhauser, *Hermeneutics and Modern Philosophy*, esp. pp. 354–56. Bernstein's survey of the debate, its consequences in mutual revision, and Rorty's departure from a modernist project shared by both Gadamer and Habermas is an effective blend of summary and critique.

the structure of communication, just "goes transcendental and offers principles" of dubious justification.[44]

This argument is often overstated, and sometimes misses the point of rational reconstruction and the ideal features that are formally derived from it. Habermas is careful to avoid, in the formal-pragmatic analysis of speech-acts, any features that might be considered to extend beyond the boundaries of actual human competences and the anticipations and presuppositions of rational speech.[45] Isolating the goal of rational agreement in discourse need not, in other words, court this illicit transcendentalism, since our participation in argument actively anticipates that goal. Understanding the discursive claims of an interlocutor is, properly viewed, a matter of anticipating a *rational* agreement either on those claims or on rival claims supported by better arguments. Since the ideal speech situation merely models these commitments explicitly, and in addition models the important proviso that dialogue should (under ideal conditions) continue long enough to generate agreement, there need be nothing *transcendental* in the theory. It begins by indicating what is presupposed and pragmatically unavoidable when you and I argue—namely an orientation to truth and the unforced force of the better argument. It ends by building those features into an explicit version of what we presume inexplicitly and often badly—namely an ideal speech situation and a universal community of affected speakers.[46]

To be fair, Habermas's manner of speaking about these claims made the objection inevitable, and Bernstein is right to emphasize the pragmatic (or, as I would put it, interpretive) aspects of the theory. The real advantage of Habermas's rational reconstruction is that it isolates the presuppositions of *our arguments*, and models them in a way that formalizes what we, as rational actors, anticipate in our discursive claims. Here our practices of rational assessment are, by way of sensitive interpretation and close discus-

44. Richard Rorty, "Pragmatism, Relativism, Irrationalism," in his *Consequences of Pragmatism*, p. 173. Habermas's attempt to derive rational standards from our talking is, according to Rorty, an example of philosophy's "scratching where it does not itch."

45. See, e.g., "What Is Universal Pragmatics?" in *Communication and the Evolution of Society*, trans. Thomas McCarthy (Boston: Beacon Press, 1979), where Habermas discusses the nontranscendental status of his reconstruction of communicative competence.

46. This version of Habermas's reply, where he discusses the shortcomings of Apel's "transcendental-pragmatic" arguments, can be found in his "Discourse Ethics," pp. 83–86. Habermas believes Apel asks for too much in his pragmatics and that as a result Apel's argument appears less compelling. The "universal pragmatics" uncovered in Habermas's reconstruction of communicative competence are meant, *contra* Apel, to generate universal principles without any recourse to transcendental argumentation.

sion, lifted to an unusual degree of theoretical clarity. As a theory of justice, this procedure follows MacIntyre's sort of route rather than Ackerman's: instead of specifying the principles of justice that can be expected to issue from dialogue, it specifies only the rational commitments we all anticipate in any discursive assessment of norms (including norms of justice) that can be thought rational.

By refusing in this way to overdetermine the justification of norms with excessive control by the theorist—a control that would indeed prove illicit, since it would prejudge the rational possibilities of choice—Habermas believes he can exempt discourse ethics from the force of Hegelian-spirited objections to transcendentalism and empty universalism. Indeed, he explicitly defends his theory against other neo-Kantian versions of procedural ethics, prominently that of Rawls, that allow theoretical control to outstrip what can be rationally reconstructed from our common commitments.[47] The disadvantages of Rawlsian procedural ethics, the "fiction" of the original position and the constraints it places on actors in the theory, are—it is argued—avoided in the unconstrained conversation at the heart of discourse ethics. Here the "moment of insight" about how justification of norms is carried out is not denied the actors performing the justificatory task. Participants in discourse ethics are fully constituted, embedded in real forms of life, and fully aware of the task they are undertaking in dialogue. As a result, they face no debilitating problems concerning the strains of commitment, and do not depend on a crippling and limited conception of moral selfhood.

Habermas thus cannot say in advance which norms and actions will come up for justification in the conversation, for these must proceed from the lifeworld and the deep concerns of those engaged in discourse. Though discourse points beyond itself in the sense of presupposing commitment to rational force of argumentation and agreement, the matters under discussion arise from the real-world concerns of those affected. And though ideal in orientation, discourse ethics is meant to retain critical purchase by addressing only those matters of real concern to the interlocutors. By revolving around the analysis of actual speech-acts, discourse ethics is nowhere as much a matter of constructed conversation as is Rawls's original position, or indeed Ackerman's unreconstructed version of the Assembly Hall—both of which, as justificatory

---

47. These arguments are contained in two recent articles by Habermas: "Justice and Solidarity: On the Discussion Concerning Stage 6," *Philosophical Forum* 21 (1989–90): 35–52, and "Morality and Ethical Life: Does Hegel's Critique of Kant Apply to Discourse Ethics?" in *Moral Consciousness and Communicative Action*, pp. 195–216.

thought-experiments, blind their participants to any insight about their situation and its constraints.

2. Self and Solidarity

These advantages in the status of Habermas's theory point to two features of the norm-assessment project that have not, in the discussion so far, received their due. The first concerns Habermas's view of the self. His discussions of this issue resonate with worries about loss of context that motivated MacIntyre in the previous chapter. Free of the Anglo-American liberal tradition that leads theorists to conceive of human actors as "radically deracinated" maximizers of their own interests, Habermas paints a richer picture of a community of actors who determine their interests together in an ongoing conversation about themselves. Beginning with the assumption that we are always already embedded in a real community of real interests, he views the task of justification as a matter of clarifying and assessing our norms in discourse. The project is understood as both collective and critical. On this view, conversation is not just the forum in which interests and conflicts about them are mediated; it is also the locus of determination for those interests, and for the identity of those holding and (perhaps) sharing them. We do not have a set of interests in advance of any social interaction, an agenda of needs that is met well or poorly once we enter into society. (We are not Hobbesian, or Lockean, selves.) On the contrary, the communicative-competence view shows us coming to full participation in social interaction as a learning process parallel to, and determined by, our growing ability to talk with others, to discern pragmatic universals, and to tell one context from another. "The theory of communicative rationality," one commentator puts it, "does not posit a self-sufficient subject, confronting an object-world, but instead begins from the notion of a symbolically structured life-world, in which human reflexivity is constituted."[48] We must learn to be social actors, which means in part learning how to assume the roles proper to the variety of situations each of us inhabits in the course of a day, and a life.[49]

This role-taking ability, including the ideal role-taking ability associated with discourse, is based on our being able to distinguish one kind of speech-act from another. It might therefore be supposed that the view Habermas has of

48. Giddens, "Reason Without Revolution?" p. 109.

49. This is one feature of Habermas's theory I will be concerned to retain in the analysis of civility that follows, since my reading of politeness emphasizes its socializing and educative role in bringing us to full social awareness of varying contexts and the demands of communicative situations.

the human actor is similar to Ackerman's role-taking picture in "Why Dialogue?" But whereas Ackerman seemed to view role-taking as a check, however essential, on the otherwise rampant self-interest of his social actors, Habermas chooses to see role-taking as an organic ability that arises with the formation of the individual as a member of his or her lifeworld. Since it is not cutting against natural inclination, as in Ackerman's picture, there is less difficulty in solving motivational problems associated with the liberal view (i.e., why should I restrain my urge to get all that I can?). This is in effect the difference between external constraints, including those of "society" perceived as the Other, and internal constraints associated with social maturity. We may find that it is misleading to speak of Habermas's brand of dialogue as unconstrained; nevertheless, it has the advantage of being constrained on the basis of real commitments shared by participants in discourse. I argue later that constraints on conversation are a necessity in talk about justice that is to issue in more than endless disagreement. But I will also argue that constraints that arise together with social and communicative competence are more plausible than any descending, via theoretical fiat, from outside.

The second advantage of Habermas's discourse ethics is that its rational reconstruction strategy never faces the liberal dilemma of being too substantive to compel agreement. Instead of articulating principles of justice, discourse ethics, as we saw, articulates principles of argumentation. These principles are based on pragmatic assumptions—i.e., "that in principle all those affected participate as free and equal members in a co-operative search for truth in which only the force of the better argument may hold sway."[50] Thus, while Habermas believes "it must be possible to decide on firm grounds which moral theory is best able to reconstruct the universal core of our moral intuitions,"[51] he does not believe that it is possible to say in advance which particular norms will arise for assessment and justification in discourse. Moreover, the intuitions Habermas believes are modeled in discourse ethics do not seem as problematic as those of impartiality that Rawls, for example, wanted to begin with. Instead he begins with morality as a structure holding sway "in situations where it is in our power to counteract the *extreme vulnerability* of others by being thoughtful and considerate."[52] Here the *facts of socialization* show forth the dual concerns of any moral theory: the individual, and the intersubjective lifeworld of which he or she is a part.

50. Habermas, "Justice and Solidarity," p. 40.
51. Ibid., p. 33.
52. Habermas, "Morality and Ethical Life," p. 199.

Various responses to these dual concerns have been advanced, among them Carol Gilligan's addition of an "ethics of care" to an "ethics of justice," and Kohlberg's attempt to conjoin "benevolence" with "justice." Habermas seeks to advance this discussion with the allied notions of justice and solidarity. His view is that the linguistic community or form of life involved in a moral argument advances simultaneously as individuals and as a whole. "Every autonomous morality," he emphasizes,

> has to serve two purposes at once: it brings to bear the inviolability of socialized individuals by requiring equal treatment and thereby equal respect for the dignity of each one; and it protects inter-subjective relationships of mutual recognition in requiring solidarity of individuals as members of a community in which they have been socialized.[53]

A dialogic conception of norm-justification clarifies these two related projects, then, because it exhibits individuals in search of justice relating to each other as members of a speaking community. My very search for equal rights in the larger discourse of ethics is a recognition of all those with whom I argue—the community.

3. Conversing, Modern and Postmodern

But what is the range of that community? As might be expected, postmodern reactions to the modernism radicalized and rehabilitated in Habermas's theory of communicative action have claimed to find the prospect of full disclosure tyrannizing, not liberating. How, they want to ask, is conversational power governed, and by whom? Can we not expect that we (or somebody else) will feel that the conversation is proceeding in all kinds of ways we do not like? Will any amount of irony or role-taking ability concerning my public and private selves solve this problem? Should we be extending the compass of conversation in this fashion, claiming ever more for its ability to get to the "way things are" about truth, justice, and sincerity? In following the latter course, as we have seen, Habermas has dispensed with external constraints of the type that drove Ackerman's theory to conclusions ultimately hard to countenance. Only "unconstrained" dialogue can produce the sort of legitimat-ing discourse that grounds our criticizable validity claims in rational consen-

53. Habermas, "Justice and Solidarity," p. 50.

sus. It is worth noting that, with this move, Habermas provides only a *negative* answer to the charges brought against him by thinkers like Lyotard and Rorty. How so?

Postmodernism charges Habermas with a nostalgia for the misplaced aspirations of the Enlightenment, an unseemly regard for the project of universal morality. The details of the indictments differ—Lyotard claims to find legitimation *tout court* oppressive, essentialist; Rorty only balks at universal rationality and old-style epistemology—but this shared objection is stark enough to constitute the heart of the postmodern position.[54] It is contempt for nostalgia that characterizes postmodernism, but nostalgia of a very particular kind, namely for such generalized and context-independent notions as Truth, Rationality, and The Moral.[55] The progressivism associated with modernism, the desire to change social relations by grounding and justifying them more fully, against, for example, the forces of tradition or superstition, is on this view the product of misplaced arrogance. It does not take difference seriously enough, and therefore does not see that, for us today, the project of enlightenment initiated by *les philosophes* must be considered over, no longer seriously an option. Or, more subtly, it mistakes a common concern from a variety of quite different human practices—the concern to get things right, to say what is the case within the practice—for a general question concerning human reasoning and a metaphysical category called Truth.

Habermas's explicit response to this accusation, in contrast to the implicit reply given by his theory itself, is an *ad hominem* charge against the political nullity of postmodernism. "The disillusionment with the very failures of those [modernist] programs that called for the negation of art and philosophy has come to serve as a pretense for conservative positions," he argues in a celebrated article. These positions can be distinguished as "the antimodernism of the young conservatives, . . . the premodernism of the old conservatives

---

54. See Lyotard's *The Postmodern Condition* and (with Thébaud) *Just Gaming*. Richard Rorty's postmodern theorizing arguably begins with the defense of "hermeneutics" in his *Philosophy and the Mirror of Nature* and runs throughout his subsequent work. A concise treatment of the relevant figures is given in Rorty, "Habermas and Lyotard on Postmodernity," pp. 32–44 (also in Thompson and Held, *Habermas: Critical Debates*, pp. 161–75). See also Albrecht Wellmer's useful essay "On the Dialectic of Modernism and Postmodernism," *Praxis International* 4 (1985): 337–62.

55. Postmodernism may also be accused of nostalgia, of course, in its sometimes slavish regard for the styles (in art, literature, design, clothing) of earlier eras. It is attitude or stance, if anything, that saves postmodernism from the force of this charge: playful, ironic, noncommittal, postmodernism employs everything while taking nothing seriously. In certain manifestations, it is trendiness elevated to a dogma.

and . . . the postmodernism of the neoconservatives."[56] What is conservative about postmodernism? Habermas provides few clues in that brief analysis, but an answer can be sketched out on other evidence, especially that provided in his later, more systematic engagements with postmodernism.[57] Postmodernism is conservative because it surrenders the quest for justification and legitimation, finds naive the desire to challenge the status quo with regard to how well it can justify itself in its own terms.

The feature of the postmodern outlook most frequently cited, its playful mixing-and-matching of cultural references and surface phenomena, is a case in point. The cultural grab-bag attitude gives up all pretensions to the critical stance, finding anything and everything available elements of a not-yet-constructed cultural pastiche. "Eclecticism is the degree zero of contemporary general culture," Lyotard avers in an oft-quoted reply to Habermas and other critics. "One listens to reggae, watches a western, eats McDonald's food for lunch and local cuisine for dinner, wears Paris perfume in Tokyo and 'retro' clothes in Hong Kong; knowledge is a matter of TV games."[58] This eclecticism, this "realism of 'anything goes' is in fact that of money," Lyotard admits candidly. Here art, and culture more generally, have given up all aspiration to social comment, community sense, collective experience, or unity. The only value is exchange value—as Lyotard says, the realism of money.

A main aspect of Habermas's concern with the modern/postmodern issue is therefore just this recognition that contemporary culture no longer speaks to the concerns of the community, that community itself is fractured. Social unity has been lost in the separateness of cultural spheres (art, politics, morality) that are ruled by experts and governed by "systemic" imperatives: efficiency, profitability, rationalization. (This fracturing and domination of spheres by imperatives of system is what he means by "the colonization of the lifeworld.") So the cultural unity posted in modernism *is* given the lie in the state of contemporary social life; Habermas does not deny it. The ques-

---

56. Jürgen Habermas, "Modernity Versus Postmodernity," *New German Critique* 22 (1981): 3–14.

57. See esp. *The Philosophical Discourse of Modernity: Twelve Lectures*, trans. Frederick G. Lawrence (Cambridge, Mass.: MIT Press, 1990). In these lectures, Habermas traces postmodern thinking as following two paths that open up from Nietzsche's critique of rationality (itself a result of Hegel's conception of modernity): the path of Heidegger and Derrida, which traces philosophy to its pre-Socratic origins, and the path of Bataille, Lacan, and Foucault, which, more deeply skeptical of philosophy, employs genealogical techniques to investigate reason. In criticizing these positions, Habermas is concerned among other things to point out the performative contradiction in their condemning reason with the tools of reason.

58. Lyotard, *Postmodern Condition*, p. 76.

tion then becomes one of the appropriate response. Put simply: pastiche or reform? Accept ironically, or seek (perhaps quixotically) to improve?

If we opt, like Habermas, for the goal of recovering cultural unity via some kind of justificatory dialogue, what are the implications? Lyotard expresses his view of the stakes quite clearly:

> Jürgen Habermas . . . thinks that if modernity has failed, it is in allowing the totality of life to be splintered into independent specialities which are left to the narrow competence of experts, while the concrete individual experiences "desublimated meaning" and "destructured form," not as a liberation but in the mode of that immense *ennui* which Baudelaire described over a century ago. . . .
>
> My question is to determine what sort of unity Habermas has in mind [in reforming the modern project]. Is the aim of the project of modernity the constitution of sociocultural unity within which all the elements of daily life and of thought would take their places as in an organic whole? Or does the passage that has to be charted between heterogeneous language games—those of cognition, of ethics, of politics—belong to a different order from that? And if so, would it be capable of effecting a real synthesis between them?[59]

In the view of Lyotard, still smarting here from the charge of neoconservatism, both possible paths close down under the force of a postmodern critique. But I believe, with Rorty in his more qualifying moments, that Lyotard is too quick to surrender the value, and possibility, of social critique and the real community it may produce. It may be that such community is best understood as ironic and tolerant, rather than deeply corporate and ethically "thick." But this is more, and moreover *worth* more, than the hands-off eclecticism championed by any uncritical brand of postmodernism. It is, furthermore, just this possibility that I will take more seriously in continuing my critical assessment of Habermas's theory.

IV. PRACTICAL POLITICS AND NORM ASSESSMENT

I have suggested that not all the criticisms alluded to in the previous section actually hit the mark, or hit it as squarely as their purveyors sometimes

59. Ibid., pp. 72–73.

suppose. All the same, we are now entitled to wonder, on the basis of challenges to Habermas's theory of rational consensus concerning norms, whether
the ideal speech situation is equal to the tasks of practical politics. That is, even
if we accept, on pain of performative contradiction, the unavoidability of the
ideal speech situation as a presupposition of rational discourse, is it enough to
shape real democratic decision-making about justice? So wondering, and given
the facts of disagreement that have been our concern throughout this discussion, we may begin to doubt the usefulness of Habermas's reconstruction of
certain ideal intuitions about what practical discourse ought rationally to be.
Such doubts, which coalesce in a sense that rationality may be the wrong place
to look for political guidance, can take a number of forms, as we have seen.

For example: we may suppose, with a pessimistic Ackerman, that without
the addition of explicit dialogic constraints to screen out certain types of
justification, the social conflict that stalled dialogue in the first place will never
be resolved with rational discourse, however lengthy. Modeling the fragile
insights of communicative rationality in the ideal speech situation cannot, in
other words, by itself address the difficult real-world problems of reaching
actual agreement on controversial questions. The bare commitments of rationality are never enough, or never explicit enough, to ensure that certain types
of justification will not be used in discourse. So, for example, my claim that
goods should be distributed on the basis of the intrinsic superiority of my
group's goals cannot be considered rationally convincing—yet I certainly consider it a good argument, one better, indeed, than any you have. So it is not
clear that my own commitments to rationality, whatever they are, will be
enough to show me in practice that this is a bad argument, even given world
enough and time. In my view it answers to your interests in just the right
way—by making it clear that they are best realized in serving mine. This
objection is based on an empirical claim, certainly, and not an ideal one, and it
does not allow what Habermas said the ideal speech situation demanded,
namely that all affected participants had to be accounted for in justification.
But seeing this is small comfort, if it is true that our actual talk could well go
on forever without producing concrete results unless and until we prohibit
some kinds of justification. This, after all, threatens the project of finding and
justifying a just society.

From a slightly different vantage, we might suppose with MacIntyre that
disagreement will go on forever, the result of conversational blocks, unless and
until our real traditional commitments are made clear, and any aspirations to
rational discourse as such and its possible universal extension are surrendered.
Here, once more, the transcontextual and unconstrained commitments associ-

ated with the ideal speech situation are viewed with misgiving, even suspicion. They begin to look like just the sort of philosophical solution we could have expected a Kantian-influenced thinker to offer to pressing problems of political conflict and difference. As Gray said, this sort of attempt to free us from our real commitments and actual selves, in favor of universally shared rational commitments that seem, at least on first glance, to have no real force, is another example of the way Kantian political philosophy has "condemned itself to political nullity and intellectual senility."

Both of these objections take the form of what I will call *realist curbs* on the idealism to be found in Habermas's theory of rationality. Realist curbs on Habermas's idealizing provisos claim to find the rational reconstruction of the ideal speech situation either (1) empirically suspect, based on faulty evidence or inferences, or (2) too fragile to do the work for which we desire decision-procedures, namely the rational assessment of normative claims about justice. Though they do not separate cleanly, I would suggest that MacIntyre's (presumed) objection to Habermas's strategy tends toward (1): he thinks Habermas has mistaken conflicts between adherents of different notions of rationality, for those between adherents of an (in-principle) universal notion of Rationality. Ackerman's tends toward (2): he thinks Habermas's prohibition on constraints will consign us to perpetual disagreement about norms, not free assessment of them. Let us examine the force of such objections more closely.

1. Discourse Ethics in Practice

It is from these critical perspectives, of the realist type, that Habermas's project of anticipating rational consensus in norm assessment seems too ideal to be practically illuminating. The criticisms turn, first of all, on an empirical claim, namely that rational persons do not necessarily demand universal *assent*, even by implication, when advancing or employing a norm of justice in practices of decision-making. And this is so even if it is also the case that the *form* of their claims cannot avoid anticipating rational assent. Interlocutors may, in other words, fully expect other rational persons to disagree with them, and be under no threat to their performative consistency by so expecting. An interlocutor may know that the disagreeing person holds a conception of justice that varies from his as a result of commitments held at another level. Indeed, perhaps the two share no standards of moral assessment.[60] Their commitment to a neces-

---

60. This may be a result, as MacIntyre suggests, of our notions of practical rationality varying from tradition to tradition. But even here we may expect that in the confrontation between

sary dialogue, such as one about the norms governing their common social space, will not be ruled by any of the strong universal conditions presupposed in Habermas's characterization of the ideal speech situation. They argue intending to compel with rational force, certainly, for they could not do otherwise; but they also argue with a full, and equally unavoidable, awareness that notions of normative rightness will vary as the result of commitments (say traditional ones) not open to question in this dialogue. This awareness of difference may impair their discussion in all kinds of ways, though that is far from clear (it may do the opposite). What is clear is that such an awareness does not make their claims to rightness performatively contradictory.

Now, this sort of empirical claim about practical discourse may not actually damage Habermas's theory at the level it was assessed in the first part of this chapter. He has also, in recent expansions and revisions of this theory, especially the remarks in the collection *Justification and Application*, defended a distinction between the pragmatic, ethical, and moral uses of practical reason which goes some distance to avoiding the force of this kind of objection.[61] That is, he has suggested that in pragmatic rounds of reaching actual agreement on norms, the pure rational commitment to the better argument alone—the commitment to seeking and finding rational moral truth—is not the sole issue of our discourse. This introduction of nuance makes his views more compelling, but it also confuses the issue somewhat. We now have to face questions of practical application concerning the ideal speech situation.

Habermas argued that an awareness of the universal presuppositions of argument is indeed enough to make discourse compelling as the court of rational appeal when assessing norms of justice. That was all that discourse ethics was in the business of proving, and it did so in a way that stopped well short of denying the numerous ways in which actual discourse can be impaired. All discourse ethics could provide was an awareness of ideal possibilities, and the fact that those possibilities were built into communicative action itself. But when we understand what justice is, and what kind of norms discourse ethics can generate, that is quite a lot. It follows that if we could ever

adherents of different traditions some sort of rational superiority will show itself. More problematic still would be claims—say, those of feminists—that rationality is itself an ideological construct whose parameters, so far from being universally compelling, are limited in their force to a certain segment of the population.

61. See Jürgen Habermas, "On the Pragmatic, the Ethical, and the Moral Employments of Practical Reason," in his *Justification and Application*, pp. 1–17. One consequence of this clarification on Habermas's part is that the phrase "discourse ethics" is really a misnomer and should be understood to mean "a discourse theory of morality."

achieve an agreement under conditions approximating those modeled in the ideal speech situation, that agreement would then count as rational. Nonagreement would never be rational, of course, but neither would agreement achieved under other conditions (say those of ideological deception or coercion or, say, sentimental convergence on a value like patriotism). So while it is true that other kinds of commitment may obscure the possibility of agreement here, and indeed make the universal range of rational commitments appear politically irrelevant, that does not impair for Habermas the necessary and in-principle ability of discourse (properly understood) to extend to all rational agents *insofar as they are rational*. The agreement forged in this kind of practical discourse will not concern the practical goals (pragmatic) of persons, nor their sense of themselves (ethical), but only the abstract (moral) principles of justice: which is to say, principles that hold for everyone, regardless of whatever other commitments and differences they have.[62]

This clarification may still be small comfort when we are faced with a highly contextualized political problem, such as our ever-present abortion debaters. Here it is not clear that advocates of the divergent positions could ever, even if they wanted to, phrase a norm in such a way that it would command the rational assent of all those affected. Indeed, it is not clear that any such norm exists here. Consider the hard questions: Who are "all those affected"? Does it include the unborn? Can a woman claim sole control of her body's reproductive functions, or do others have a say? Is there a state interest in the fetus? Always? Never? How—in what sort of public discussion—could we ever decide?

With the prospects of rational consensus so slim—though certainly never absent, so long as we are rational—other factors may have to be introduced to forge actual decisions. Like other critics of Habermas, I would like to suggest here that another type of pragmatic consideration must come into play, revolving around the question of sharing and supporting common social space. This kind of *political-pragmatic commitment* will not be founded on rationality nor, unless we are positing the prospect of world government, will it be universal in extension. (Even then it might be better expressed as applying to

---

62. In offering this distinction, Habermas is continuing in ever more explicit terms his general project of reforming Kantian universal morality in a discursive form. If we separate off practical and ethical considerations, and so restrict ourselves to universal principles of morality—that is, principles of justice or right—we do not confront the objections generated by communitarian and neo-Aristotelian critics of universalism. See Habermas's "On the Pragmatic, the Ethical, and the Moral Employments of Practical Reason" and "Remarks on Discourse Ethics," in *Justification and Application*, where he offers detailed reports on engagements with these critics.

all citizens, not to all rational agents.) These political-pragmatic conditions, although they do not defeat universal pragmatics in terms of its anticipation of rational agreement, actually cut along a different dimension, such that in practical terms any strong or global understanding of universal rational extension in dialogic norm-assessment will have to be modified or surrendered. Habermas himself seems to move in this sort of direction when he offers his detailed distinction between *justification* of norms, which is in-principle universal, and *application* of them, which depends on institutions and citizens structured in particular ways.[63] Yet even here there remains a difficulty.

For the most part, Habermas's recent defenses of his moral theory have involved a revision of expectation. Like most expectation-lowering tactics, this one is intended to sidestep certain objections. Do not think that moral theory can by itself generate substantive principles, Habermas implies, or provide motivation and guarantee the adherence of citizens—for these goals we need other conditions to be met. Those conditions concern institutions of law and policy, citizens of determinate ability and orientation, forums for actual justificatory talk, and so on—in other words, the conditions associated with what I called a moment ago the political-pragmatic. This seems to indicate that, in offering the justification/application distinction, Habermas is taking the problems of practical politics seriously and usefully wedding his abstract theory to a keener sense of them. But the appearance is misleading. The point of this distinction is to separate two levels, or rounds, of discursive assessment: that concerning the justifiabilty of a norm, and that concerning whether the norm should be applied in *this* concrete situation. However, *pace* Habermas, these two issues rarely separate so cleanly, if they separate at all. And it is his sense of an easy separation that contributes to the unease some critics, myself included, retain in the face of these late revisions of the theory. If we cannot say whether a norm is justified except by reference to situational constraints— and with norms of social interaction, we cannot—the role of purely moral assessment is severely curbed, if not rendered irrelevant.

Another strand of this line of criticism, concerning the excessive abstraction of Habermas's justificatory conversation, makes the point still clearer. Although the objection appears in various forms,[64] Walzer's brisk "Critique of

---

63. See Habermas, "Remarks on Discourse Ethics," esp. Remark No. 4.

64. See, e.g., David Ingram, "The Possibility of a Communication Ethic Reconsidered," *Man and World* 15 (1982): 149–61, where Ingram criticizes Habermas for a conception of language that leaves out rhetoric, authority, preverbal play and other "real" elements. As a result, Ingram considers that the theory fails as a justificatory procedure or ethical theory, succeeding only as a limiting force on ideological manipulation.

Philosophical Conversation" applies most clearly.[65] Habermas has argued that under ideal conditions discourse issues in rational agreement, and so justifies the norms considered in conversation. Walzer is quick to point out the constraining features operating in Habermas's "unconstrained conversation," features that in his view make it a *designed* conversation. "Habermas," he says,

> argues for "unconstrained communication," but he means only (!) to exclude the constraints of force and fraud, of deference, fear, flattery, and ignorance. His speakers have equal rights to initiate the conversation and to resume it; to assert, recommend, and explain their own positions; and to challenge the positions of other speakers. . . . [T]he universalization requirement is a powerful constraint.[66]

What such hidden constraints do, according to Walzer, is artificially narrow the field of possible locutions in practical discourse to those that produce the results desired in advance—a version of Bernstein's stipulative definition argument, alluded to earlier. Habermas's ideal speech is not recognizable as what we know as actual human conversation oriented to practical questions. Not enough account is taken of differences in rhetorical or argumentative ability; the complexity of human talk is narrowed into a limited discursive space in which only a certain kind of talk can carry on.[67]

Walzer suggests that no truly convincing results will be generated for justice theory unless and until theorists either (1) design conversations that are more like our actual ones, full of ambiguity, uncertainty, power plays, senseless repetition, rhetorical flourishes and wit, or (2) give up the aspiration to design and instead investigate real talk about justice as a kind of descriptive/ interpretive undertaking. Habermas believes that his rational reconstruction of communicative competence satisfies (2), but the success of this undertaking has not been fully demonstrated. The conditions modeled in the ideal speech

65. Walzer, "A Critique of Philosophical Conversation," pp. 185–87.
66. Ibid., p. 186.
67. A pointed version of this point is made by John B. Thompson in "Universal Pragmatics," in Thompson and Held, *Habermas: Critical Debates*, pp. 120ff. Thompson's charge is that Habermas has concentrated too exclusively on "standard form" speech-acts in his reconstruction of communicative competence, rendering the presupposition of the ideal speech situation questionable. This objection is also minimally related to Derrida's critique of speech-act theory, and its reliance on the "normal" over the "deviant," in *Limited Inc*. For Habermas's reply to this critique, in which he defends the centrality of the normal or standard, see "Excursus on Leveling the Genre Distinction Between Philosophy and Literature," in his *The Philosophical Discourse of Modernity*, pp. 185–210.

situation appear both too strong and not erected in the right place to allow actual normative results in practical discussion. A designed conversation of this kind, even though explicitly derived from the reconstruction of features evident in communicative competence, may prove to be ineffective in our real justifications—not because the presuppositions modeled there do not exist, but because they will not act as a real procedural grid through which we must pass our actually contested norms of justice.

To sum up: the general objection is that rational reconstruction of communicative competence is not effectively normative, because too ideal; it will not, in practical terms, generate the sort of justifications we require from a theory of justice. So stated, this objection captures the frequent criticism of Habermas that the ideal speech situation is too formal to provide norms, or even procedures, for real situations of social conflict. It also reprises the Hegelian criticisms of Kantian, and neo-Kantian, attempts to ground morality in procedural rules: objections that Habermas claimed his theory could avoid.[68] The universalization principle and the symmetric reciprocity among interlocutors are, like the categorical imperative, notions not "thick" enough to have critical bite in framing and applying principles of justice. They may prove so stringent that *no* norm or action can be justified on their basis—or, if justified, they would not make obvious how the norm ought to be applied.[69] Or, from a different critical perspective—and here we see the Kantian legacy in Habermas coming home to roost once more—they may prove so formal and ideal that *any* norm can be justified.[70]

Without a more concrete picture of discourse, then, one that pertains meaningfully to our actual political practices (and is not merely something to which our actual commitments ideally point), it is unclear what role Habermas's theory can have for us. It may be that, as Larmore and Bernstein suggested in

---

68. Habermas believes, as we saw, that the strategy of rational reconstruction gives him good reason for thinking that such Hegelian criticisms—as, e.g., against universalism and formalism—do not hit the mark with discourse ethics. See his "Morality and Ethical Life," in *Moral Consciousness and Communicative Action*, and "On the Pragmatic, the Ethical, and the Moral Employments of Practical Reason," in *Justification and Application*.

69. Georgia Warnke makes this point effectively by emphasizing that the "U" principle depends centrally on consequences and interests. "Once we focus on consequences, circumstances and interests, however," she says, "it is not clear that we can ever agree on which interests are generalizable in this way unless we already share interests and circumstances" (*Justice and Interpretation*, pp. 96–97).

70. For various versions of this objection, see Giddens, "Reason Without Revolution?" pp. 112; Ingram, "Possibility of a Communication Ethic," p. 159; and the contribution by Richard Bernstein in *Habermas and Modernity*, p. 317.

reforming Kantian ethics, we need to rehabilitate a notion of *phronesis* or practical judgment as a supplement to these formal conditions of justification.[71] Without his concrete notion of judgment, we have no interpretive measure of success in our actual discursive encounters, and no standard by which we can judge the value of continuing the search for agreement on one level or, perhaps, moving to other spheres of discussion. Lacking such a standard, the commitments we share simply on the basis of our genuine willingness to argue will not be enough to generate rational agreement—and will make any circumstantial agreement nonnormative. Indeed, in addressing the criticisms of one prominent neo-Aristotelian thinker, Bernard Williams, Habermas appears to grant just this point.[72] Yet this granting of the point leads, as we saw, to a problematic picture of practical discourse split into discrete and airtight levels, rather than to a revision of a coherent single notion of practical discourse.

I suggested earlier that we ought to supplement any awareness of (universal) pragmatic commitments of discourse with an equally important awareness of the (political) pragmatic commitments of coexistence. Here I suggest we likewise supplement an awareness of a commitment to the better argument's force with an awareness of the value of practical judgment in discerning and feeling that force. This notion of practical judgment cannot, however, be recovered from the abstract structure of communicative rationality as Habermas understands it. Nor can it, therefore, be considered to have universal extension without further delay. Indeed, I do not believe that a notion so concrete will be universal in the strong sense. It is nevertheless necessary for the effective achievement of normative agreement by discursive means. Appeals to general principles of argumentation may be, by themselves, an unsuitable place to look for an effective theory of justice.[73] If we suspect that Habermas's ideal speech situation is incapable of *ever* generating practical content, we have good reason for wondering if more is necessary even in the

71. As noted in Chapter 2, Steven B. Smith also makes this point in a short critical passage on Habermas found in his *Hegel's Critique of Liberalism*, pp. 244–46.

72. See Habermas, "Remarks on Discourse Ethics," no. 1. The work by Williams in question is *Ethics and the Limits of Philosophy*, where he criticizes "the peculiar institution," morality. Habermas also engages with other prominent critics of Kantian-driven moral theory, including J. L. Mackie. See Mackie's *Ethics: Inventing Right and Wrong* (Harmondsworth: Penguin Books, 1977). In replying to them, Habermas denies that they can help themselves to an unproblematic notion of *phronesis*.

73. This judgment also applies to a more recent attempt to build procedural justice on a foundation of "cross-frontier and therefore rational standards of fair argumentation." See Hampshire, *Innocence and Experience*, p. 74.

dialogic clearing.[74] The objection is intended, as Hegel's was against Kant, to emphasize the importance of context, even in procedural ethics. Such ethics require concrete criteria of judgment in order to be sufficiently incisive, that is, to justify *some* norms but not others. We want justificatory talk to be, crucially, both binding and real.

2. Approximation and Compromise

Of course, Habermas is aware of these difficulties. He knows full well that the practical payload of idealities offered in discourse ethics may be small, or even nonexistent. The remarks provided in his latest work clarify his own sense that the ideal speech situation is not *meant* to generate results, but merely to clarify the ideal toward which all rational assessment of existing norms (and practices based on these norms) is directed. And Habermas is aware that instituting and applying the ideal speech situation will inevitably involve compromise. "[I]nstitutional measures are needed to sufficiently neutralize empirical limitations and avoid internal and external interference," he has written recently, "so that idealized conditions always already presupposed by participants in argumentation can at least be adequately approximated."[75] He has, moreover, emphasized the inescapability of ethical life as a matter of real communities, and not the set of all rational agents, concentrating especially on the forms of socialization that make for citizens willing and able to assess norms dialogically, and on the institutional necessities—law and public policy, primarily—that will put norms into practice. Indeed, the orientation of most of his recent work is to provide just this sort of "shading-in" reply to contextualist and other antiuniversalist critics.[76]

But what constitutes an "adequate approximation" of discourse's ideal commitments, and on what basis is it to be decided? Habermas notes that presumed in this move to an approximation is the fact that "fair compromise calls for morally justified procedures of compromising." Yet this assurance might seem

74. So, e.g., replies that moral theory is saved from this charge because it is not in the business of generating such content are not satisfying. The objection is not about the role of theory *tout court*, but about the possibility that discourse ethics may be counterproductive because it models our rational commitments too abstractly. Ciaran P. Cronin's "Translator's Introduction" to *Justification and Application* is quite helpful on these points, esp. pp. xxiii–xxvii.

75. Habermas, "Discourse Ethics," p. 92.

76. The lengthy "Remarks on Discourse Ethics," cited earlier, constitutes the most sustained engagement with these critics, who, in addition to those mentioned already, include Klaus Günther, Ernst Tugendhat, Stephen Lukes, Charles Fried, and Günther Patzig. See "Remarks," p. 19 and passim.

to invite a circularity, since if we have irreconcilable differences on the disputed matter we may well have them on the standards of moral justification in
erecting compromises.[77] By the same token, the "institutional measures"
Habermas speaks of so confidently are open to their own tricky questions of
legitimacy, effectiveness, and fairness. "We seem to move in a circle," Georgia
Warnke has accurately noted;

> If, in our attempt to determine fair procedures of compromise, we begin
> with different notions of what counts as a sufficient approximation to
> an ideal speech situation, we shall need to come to an initial agreement
> about the elements of such a sufficient approximation. But if this initial
> agreement is itself to be legitimate it must itself be acceptable to all
> under conditions that already sufficiently approximate an ideal speech
> situation.[78]

The question here is no less than by what standards of practical rationality we
will in practice assess our normative claims. It is just these institutional measures, in other words, that have been a main object of study in this investigation. And as we have seen, justifying them effectively—in both theoretical
and practical-political terms—is no small feat. Separating the processes of
justification from those of application will not do the trick.

I do not believe Habermas underestimates these difficulties, but neither
does he address them convincingly. His conviction throughout has been that
no theoretical answer to actual justice issues could ever do more than risk
controversy: moral theory must here give way to our actual attempts at
justification. We forge our ways of going on only by talking together, and no
theory can do that for us. Yet the force of the objections I have been rehears-
ing in this chapter is that the orientation of Habermas's theory is not directed
in the right quarters—not so much because his theory is ideal as because the
idealities embraced there do not leave adequate room for, or incorporate
convincingly, the pragmatic and phronetic concerns that are so crucial in
understanding our real political problems. His recent attempts at what one
could cynically view as spin control do not significantly alter the basic prob-

---

77. Larmore, like Hampshire, doesn't think so; for them, standards of fairness in debate are
universal in the strong sense. See Larmore's *Patterns of Moral Complexity* and Hampshire's
Innocence and Experience.

78. Warnke, *Justice and Interpretation,* p. 100.

lem, which is that universalism in the Kantian tradition appears to generate a transcendental standpoint that may be at odds with particularistic commitments of actual citizens.

It may be that reforms of the kind discussed above will instead entail an approach to "weak" universalism. That is, instead of implying global acceptance, defense of a norm could take more seriously the limitation, not emphasized sufficiently by Habermas, that is built in to "U." The phrase "all concerned" could act in a reformed practical model of discourse as a curb on the more excessive universalist tendencies in discourse ethics.[79] Actual norms are, after all, advanced and assessed not by an ideal speech community but by members of actual communities, societies, who face pressing problems of coexistence and the erection of justified practices of distribution, judicial assessment, crime and punishment, and reparation. Such a curb would then echo Rorty's celebrated claim that we should offer justifications only to those with ears to hear them, and there are moments where Habermas, too, seems to think this prospect the one avenue left open to him. To that extent, his renewed emphasis on procedural justice within an interlocking set of pragmatic and ethical, as well as moral, uses of practical reason, together with the emphasis on law, public policy, and a particular socialized citizenry, constitutes his own attempt to meet the problem of moral pluralism by contextualizing the priority of right over good—the project with which this study began.

This kind of curb will not solve all difficulties with the ideality emphasized in Habermas's view, of course, since rational persons within a community may still disagree literally endlessly about certain norms and practices. But it will make for a reading of "U" that shows it applicable and valuable in the actual, day-to-day difficulties of living together with other people. What we need is a conjunction of universal pragmatics with political pragmatics, the result of which would be (I am suggesting) a modified version of universalism that takes full account of the practical political problems justice most centrally addresses. These problems would not always be restricted to members of a single society, since global coexistence and global justice are themselves goals of just talking; but in the first instance the task of justice would be, as ever, to frame a well-ordered society, meaning here one in which citizens are discuss-

---

79. Donald Moon has helped me to see this point more clearly. "Universalization requires only that *all affected* be able to accept the norm in question," he wrote, "and some norms will affect only people who are members of particular cultural or social formations" (private correspondence, August 1993).

ing in binding and real ways the pressing political questions of their lives together.

As interlocutors participating in a practically normative conversation of this kind, any simple or pure orientation to rational consensus will prove insufficient and possibly misleading. Gadamer chides Habermas for seeking universal agreement when understanding was all that could be, or ought to be, sought in dialogue. More than this, he suggests that Habermas's penchant for ideal speech actively undermines our trust in one another as real interlocutors. In Habermas's view, we orient ourselves to universality, for just this is our rational heritage—what we mean by saying, for example, that human beings are free and equal is that *all* human beings are. And yet this very orientation, which seeks somehow to take us beyond ourselves, may serve to make "real talk" appear pallid and ineffective in its actual political sphere. Under this compulsion to orient ourselves to the universal, nothing real is good enough any more. Actual talk cannot have justificatory force. We must employ what amount to idealizing *constraints* on our actual conversations, and such constraints, apart from being difficult to justify, only make our real dialogues look less important than they might be.[80]

This cannot be the royal road to justification. When we disagree—as we must—the real task is to examine the prospect of our common desire to understand one another's diverse commitments, and to assess the political solutions that are possible on their basis. For this we need a kind of sensitivity and openness to diverse claims that extends beyond the strict orientation only to the unforced force of the better argument. My interlocutor and I are members of a real community, with pressing needs of social cooperation. Our disagreement must be mediated, not overcome in a rational consensus predicated on the anticipations of agreement we (perhaps undeniably) exhibit in our arguments. Since our real differences are irreconcilable ones, we also exhibit the difference between real community and any ideal speech community anticipated by our rational commitments.

Ultimately, then, as a matter of practical politics, the insights modeled in the ideal speech situations do not, of themselves, give us a powerful enough decision-procedure for assessing norms of justice. Discourse ethics lacks the complexity we associate with particular forms of practical rationality, and does not factor in the powerful (and in practice inescapable) cohabitation imperative. It must fail to convince as a fully workable model of dialogic justice.

80. I am here following the argument made by Walzer in "Critique."

Different versions of this claim, and different responses, are available in the critical literature. Warnke suggests that we recall Habermas's other versions of communicative action: not practical discourse, with its transcendental rational demands, but aesthetic criticism and therapeutic critique, with their emphasis on history, sensibility, and culture. Importing these kinds of talk into the moral domain may seem to threaten universalizability, or to indicate "merely" a problem of application, but Warnke thinks the conclusion is unavoidable. Our interests and interpretations are part of political debate, a debate that is not always discursive in the sense of testing validity claims for their ability to generate ideal agreement. Our interpretations and evaluations are part of us in a way that no appeal to universal testing can alter; at the same time, they play a strong role in political debate.

It is possible, indeed, that these interpretations and interests are even more important in that debate than our rational commitments. "[A]lthough reasons may play a role in revising them," Warnke says,

> they play only an indirect role. Neither the process of coming to inter-
> pret ourselves and our relations to others differently, nor the process of
> changing the evaluative terms with which we understand our world
> depends on the force of the better argument alone; rather both also
> involve transformations [of] orientation that depend on experience and
> an education of our sensibilities.[81]

This emphasis on the aesthetic model, where debate is a matter of appealing not to rational presuppositions but to the possibility of widening the scope of understanding and increasing sensitivity, recalls Galston's claim, quoted in Chapter 3, to the effect that political debate more resembles a conversation among critics than it does a set of purely rational appeals. In turn this reminds us, effectively, that political debate is a real social practice with fuzzy edges, lots of messiness, and appeals that are rarely, strictly speaking, rational.

81. Warnke, *Justice and Interpretation*, p. 107. By opening up this line of reply to Habermas, Warnke underwrites her own commitment to just talking in the notion of a "hermeneutic conversation" guided by Gadamer's "anticipation of completeness" and informed more by Habermas's critique of ideology (as modeled in psychoanalysis) than by his neo-Kantian rationalism. By using MacIntyre and Gadamer as realist curbs on Habermas in the sense I indicate above, she arrives at a point similar to mine by a reverse route. Her proposed solution, however—a conversation governed by "the standards of fairness, equality and democracy"—suffers, in my view, from a lack of concreteness. It is just this lack, noted at the outset of the present study, that I attempt to remedy in the final section.

3. The Way Forward

In conclusion I want to suggest, in MacIntyrean fashion, that our task is to cultivate an even keener sense of the limitations erected by particular contexts. In what follows, I shall continue to speak of conversational constraints—and it is worth taking a moment, here, to clarify what I mean. We saw, in Chapter 3, that Ackerman's external constraints on dialogue were open to objection on several grounds. While I defended the merits of Ackerman's voluntaristic version of the constraints, they nevertheless possessed a formality and rigidity that made many critics uneasy—so uneasy, in some cases, that an alternative of "unconstrained" dialogue was sometimes offered. But here a confusion creeps into the debate. When Habermas speaks of "constraints" on conversation he means specifically those of manipulation and deception—the forces of ideological distortion. These constraints must of course be eliminated, or at least we must possess means by which their elimination can be pursued.

But it does not follow that our justificatory conversation will therefore be, as Benhabib (and sometimes Warnke) has it, free of *all* constraint. Nor is Benhabib's "moral-transformative" conversation of full disclosure, which tends toward a kind of Hegelian "self-transparency," necessarily a goal we all desire in political theory.[82] No less than Ackerman's external rigidity, this forcibly unconstrained conversation seems to force certain voices off the roster—those voices, in particular, that want to maintain a private realm of purely personal conviction. "[M]oral-transformative discourse involves a commitment to self-disclosure that is incompatible with important values such as privacy and personal integrity," J. Donald Moon has argued. "[B]ecause it rests on a demand for self-disclosure, [it] can take institutional forms that involve domination or imposition."[83] With these extremes in mind, then, I shall be searching in what remains of this discussion for what can be called *justified dialogic constraints*. My goal, as always, is to articulate and defend a real political conversation of legitimation: one that has the power to transform speakers through their interactions, yes, but that nevertheless maintains a defensible (if always challengeable) public/private distinction.

Contextual limitation on the scope of justice will entail a reformation of the goal of universalism. Without going as far in the opposite direction as either Lyotard (whose "pagan" pragmatism means a kind of anarchic atomism) or

---

82. Cronin believes it is not a goal Habermas desires either, since Habermas is concerned only with transparency in the strict sense of principles of (just) social interaction; see "Translator's Introduction" to *Justification and Application*, pp. xxv–xxvi.

83. Moon, "Constrained Discourse and Public Life," pp. 220–21.

Rorty (whose pragmatism is merely a matter of "what we do"), we may nevertheless find that globalism can be replaced by a weaker notion of universalism based on the shared commitments of forming and maintaining a society. In what follows, I therefore assume that justice is best reformed on a model of "limited" or "weak" universalism and the sort of pragmatic commitments we saw operative in liberal theories like Ackerman's. I argue that taking account of the details of context means grounding dialogic justice in a fairly particular set of ethical commitments, commitments whose range is limited. That is: I shall locate talk about justice in certain *sittlich* details of life and talk, those of politeness and civility, which constrain talk without the ideality that hinders Habermas's theory or the externality and rigidity that afflict Ackerman's.

I am aware that civility may appear to be an odd place to locate our hopes for justified principles of social interaction. The advantage of this approach, however, is that it joins abstract rational features that have wide extension with a concrete social notion, the concern for the needs of others, that we can locate in the particularities of our form of life. What I am calling civility will, it turns out, be familiar to us in numerous other guises. We shall also see that only its combination of general and particular will answer *both* to the aspirations of rational justice, to reach defensible positions on the assessment of norms and principles, *and* to the concerns of particularistic criticisms, that such decisions are always limited by the divergent commitments of ethical and political context.[84]

---

84. Compare Warnke (*Justice and Interpretation*, p. 133) on the stakes for political debate: "Thus, the discussion of different interpretations of our goods and practices need not take the form either of practical discourse or of hermeneutic justification as understood by such theorists as Rorty and Williams. We need be neither Kantians nor communitarians in moral and political theory. . . . We need neither try to purify our discourse of interpretive elements nor talk only to those who already share our interpretations. Instead we can try to learn from the understanding of meaning others possess and try to develop our own understanding through conversation with them."

PART THREE

6

Justice as Civility

I. INTRODUCTION

I began this study with an awareness of certain factual premises concerning the politics of pluralism: that there are rival and incompatible conceptions of what constitutes a good human life; that adherents of these conceptions nevertheless might easily have to inhabit a single polity, certainly the same world; that conflict might ensue as a result of this, might even be a central fact of social life. I have therefore argued that justice is best understood as the mediation of such conflicts, operating as it were at the troubled interface of rival conceptions of the good. Affinities among many contemporary theories of justice, only some of which have been explored at length, show this so-called structural understanding of justice to have widespread support, despite divergences in content and conclusion. Through sometimes stiff challenges to its legitimacy, especially those of MacIntyre and other communitarians, I have further argued that we have good reason to retain the priority of right over good that marks these structural theories—but in a form that meets the charge, from the other side, that justice theory has grown arid and thin.

The second prong of the initial argument concerned dialogue and its place in models of procedural justice. I hoped to find an interpretive version of the priority-of-right claim, one that would not sacrifice context for the sake of theory. Following Habermas's understanding of the dialogic turn as a paradigm shift, I likewise hoped to avoid certain deficiencies and one-sidedness in "monological" justice theory by examining models of justice with dialogic interaction at their center. To this end, I examined three theories in detail in Part Two and assessed their advantages and disadvantages. The general conclusions to be drawn from this examination can be expressed in the following way. A successful theory of justice must provide a procedure for the assessment of particular social norms and practices. That procedure must be centrally a matter of matching the norm or action against the interests of all capable participants in the society, with those interests expressed in dialogue. To be normative, this dialogue must be free of all unjustified constraints; at the same time, to be practically effective, some constraints will prove necessary if talk is not to go on forever without producing results. The essential task of dialogic justice theory, then, is the articulation of *justified constraints* on talk about norms and principles.

What it means for a constraint to be justified needs still to be determined, but two limits should be clear. The first is what we may call *interpretive responsiveness:* only those constraints are justified that can be drawn from, and accurately reflect, the in-play commitments of actual participants in dialogue. In other words, we must try, so far as it is possible in theory, to take talkers as they really are. Attempts to isolate their communicative commitments with a reconstruction of talk must steer around excessive ideality. It follows too that wholly external constraints, however powerful, will remain only problematically or ideally justified. In general, though we cannot say in advance (that is, theoretically) what constitutes the best or even a good interpretation of a given set of social practices, attention to performative commitments and role-taking limits on actual discourse will make for more responsive interpretations. There may also be other "rules of thumb" concerning valid social interpretation, but these will only emerge as we go along.

The second broad limit on justified constraints concerns the scope of dialogic justification, and we can think of it as the thesis of *weak universalism*. I suggested in the preceding chapter that the extension of principles of justice, however minimal in scope, should be limited to the participants in dialogue who exhibited certain common commitments, both to the success of their talk and to the project of justice itself, namely the sharing of a social space that is well-ordered and worthy of their support. Societies are the units to which the norms of justice *in the first instance* apply. We may want to extend these boundaries, especially in such forms as refugee and immigration policies, but even here we are—as well as dealing with interpretive issues concerning our self-image and current practices of mercy or openness—referring in principle to a desire on the part of citizenship candidates to share our social space.[1] In saying this, I am going some distance with the critics of Kantian liberalism who find "the set of all rational agents" a problematic, if not actually dangerous, place to locate issues of justification. The immediate demand for universal extension of norms and principles of justice makes the task of justifying them next to impossible; it may also lead us away from the actual tasks of political cohabitation.

Though there is no easy answer to this question—and, once more, no convincing theoretical or before-the-fact answer—I believe we may purchase political success at the price of rational limitation. I mean that we will want to limit the set of talkers for whom our justifications are meaningful, and by extension limit the amount of agreement or consensus we need to seek. In large part, it will be a straight matter of fact that our justifications only reach so far, and so this is a bargain about which we need not be excessively worried. If social coexistence and its shared values are the problems for which justice is the putative answer, some form of limitation on universalism is a rational one. And so we surrender certain strong universalist aspirations, but only pragmatically. I further believe that the notion of a well-ordered shared social space is theoretically open-ended. Norms of international interaction, for example, can be considered norms of justice, but only when we begin to conceive of international relations as a common project akin to the avoidance of civil war. Such a day will almost certainly come, and we will welcome it; it is nevertheless clear that it is not yet here.[2]

With these limitations in mind, the two final chapters of this book will be concerned to set out a more detailed version of the dialogue I think best suited to the articulation and justification of norms and principles of justice. In so doing, I am picking out a strain of already existing talk which, elevated

---

1. I thank Donald Moon for helping me to see this point more clearly.

2. This may, of course, be the wrong way to conceive of extranational justice. Bernard Williams has suggested, as have Walzer and Hampshire in their different ways, that some norms of justice—usually something to do with fairness—can be conceived of transnationally. I am not convinced, however, that fairness carries such weight in every culture, either as a matter of fact or as a result of being rational. The increasing globalization of contemporary political life complicates this conclusion, but it does not significantly improve the prospects for a transnational theory of justice.

to the status of a principle, acquires a force well beyond its usual connotation. By reconstructing the general interpretive commitments implied in
politeness and civility, in other words, I hope to show their availability as a
test of whether a given society may be judged well-ordered—that is, operating according to justified norms. It will turn out that civility, even understood stringently, can allow a number of different social organizations to pass
as just. I believe this is as it should be: we want a theory of justice that is
incisive, in that it picks out only a small number of justified configurations,
but we need not seek an exclusive theory, which picks out only a single
justified configuration. On this view, the ideal theory of justice is critical—
that is, able to show up existing states of affairs as unjustified—without
being either too formalistic to have content or too exclusive to be useful. As
we shall see, the civility theory also has the signal advantage of being both
structural (it governs interaction among rival conceptions of the good) and
rich (it stems from a deep-running and long-standing feature of our actual
dialogic interactions). It thus combines the political-pragmatic orientation
powerfully defended by Ackerman with a keener sense that dialogic constraints to make that orientation effective must arise from an interpretation
of *our* commitments and ideas of practical judgment.

Civility may seem an unlikely candidate for all these difficult tasks, and in
Chapter 7 I attempt to meet some powerful criticisms of the position. There I
answer critics who have found civility an ineffective, and perhaps a dangerous,
answer to the question of "What is just talking?" In the present chapter I
proceed as follows. The next section attempts to motivate a philosophical
understanding of civility by examining what sociolinguistics can tell us about
practices of politeness. Then I try to give the account content by isolating the
moral intuitions we have about sensitivity and self-restraint. Here I appeal to
hermeneutic and historical notions of politeness, particularly Gadamer's understanding of interpretive "tact" and the social and moral understanding of
politeness held by certain etiquette writers, the amateur philosophers of civility. These ideas in hand, I draw tighter the connection between the moral force
of civility and its role as a justified dialogic constraint in talk about justice.

A note about usage: I sometimes use the terms "politeness" and "civility"
interchangeably in what follows. I do this for two reasons: first, it is part of
my claim that the politically respectable virtue of civility is on a continuum
with politeness understood more prosaically; and second, the specifically linguistic aspects of the argument accept "politeness" as the term for conversational strategies of indirection, self-restraint, and face-saving, and so I have
followed that usage. There may indeed be divergences between the two terms

(and certainly between them and related ones like tact and manners), but there is no clear or generally accepted account of these divergences. The carving up of the terms I have adopted is, I believe, as good as any. In the context of dialogic justice and the present discussion, *civility* is centrally allied (if not strictly identical) to linguistic *politeness;* when understood as an orientation proper to citizenship, civility's two sides are self-restraint and *tact.* And civility is usefully distinguished, as we shall see below, both from *manners* (the rule-governed aspects of politeness) and from *etiquette* (the study and codification of manners). These terms, and the distinctions among them, will be clearer as we go along.

II. WHY CIVILITY?

Politeness and civility have typically received scant attention from philosophers, perhaps because the labor of untangling their conceptual strands cannot in their minds be justified by the apparent triviality of matters so untangled.[3] There *have* been, over the years, a number of attempts to define a "philosophy of etiquette," and these have made some headway in reclaiming the moral importance of manners or the status of politeness as a virtue. Yet most of these attempts have been made by writers that "serious" thinkers are likely to consider outsiders—novelists like Jane Austen, for example, or the etiquette mavens of high society; and, whatever the extensive merit of their efforts, these attempts usually lack rigor and precision. Some recent attempts by professional philosophers to reform a philosophy of etiquette often have the undesirable effect of sacrificing range and subtlety for strict rigor—they make politeness defensible, in other words, only by making it ethically less important than it ought to be.[4] At the same time, recent work in the field of

3. See, e.g., Philippa Foot's famous denunciation of etiquette, "Morality as a System of Hypothetical Imperatives," *Philosophical Review* 81 (1972): 305–16. Replies to Foot (e.g., Eugene Valberg, "Philippa Foot on Etiquette and Morality," *Southern Journal of Philosophy* 15 [1977]: 387–91; and Lawrence Becker, "The Finality of Moral Judgments: A Reply to Mrs. Foot," *Philosophical Review* 82 [1973]: 364–70) objected to her main argument that moral imperatives were hypothetical, but did not challenge the background assumption that imperatives of manners were not only hypothetical but also less important than those of morality.

4. See, e.g., Judith Martin and Gunther S. Stent, "I Think; Therefore I Thank: A Philosophy of Etiquette," *American Scholar* 59 (1990): 237–54, and Felicia Ackerman, "A Man by Nothing Is so Well Betrayed as by his Manners? Politeness as a Virtue," *Midwest Studies in Philosophy* 13 (1988): 250–58. While disagreeing on some details, both discuss politeness in its capacity as a

sociolinguistics has clarified the pragmatic goals of polite speech, but it has not, with a few important exceptions, preserved the normative stakes highlighted by an investigation of civility within the field of justice theory.[5] Systematic *and* sympathetic accounts of the range of phenomena covered by "civility," therefore, and of their moral and political significance, do not seem to exist in the philosophical literature. My central goal in this chapter is first to motivate and then to provide such an account.

Motivation first. I want to show why, and under what conditions, the following exchange does not involve a non sequitur:

> A: So what do you think of my new haircut?
> B: Did you see the Blue Jays game last night?

This will also entail showing why the conditions for such an exchange are rational, and therefore why the commitments evident in the exchange are in some sense normative. In *what* sense we shall see shortly. I approach these issues by discussing sociolinguistic analyses of politeness influenced primarily by H. P. Grice. My hope is that, in a manner similar to Habermas, I can conclude with a suggestion for a theory of communicative competence that includes politeness as a central element.

1. Is It Rational to Be Polite?

Suppose you have a friend—a philosophy colleague—who one day decides to devote herself entirely to practicing what she calls perfectly rational speech (PRS). In her jaundiced and cynical view, far too much of ordinary speech, even among philosophers, is taken up with superfluous additions and qualifications, little evasions and euphemisms, hemming and hawing—all of which waste energy and obscure understanding. She thinks people spend too much time not saying what they mean, indulging in pointless (sometimes even false) courtesy, and displaying other forms of "phoneyness." Her PRS program, by contrast, will involve full and frank disclosure of propositional states. It will

---

rule-bound limitation on offensive social behavior and conclude that politeness is a virtue, but not an important one.

5. Nevertheless, the range of these investigations is impressive and has not yet been fully considered by philosophers. See Geoffrey Leech, *Principles of Pragmatics* (London: Longman, 1983); Penelope Brown and Stephen Levinson, *Politeness: Some Universals in Language Usage* (New York: Cambridge University Press, 1987); and a special issue of the *Journal of Pragmatics* 14 (1990), esp. the contributions from Gabriele Kasper and Bruce Fraser. (I am grateful to an anonymous reader at the journal *Dialogue* for initial reference to these works.)

likewise call for direct and truthful responses to all posed questions. In bald terms—and what better?—your friend will adopt PRS because it is the truth, the whole truth, and nothing but the truth.[6] In view of these considerations, her reasons for choosing PRS can be summarized as follows: (1) she believes PRS will maximize the efficient exchange of information between speakers and so allow them to achieve their goals more easily; (2) she believes it will track the truth more faithfully than any other kind of speech; and (3) she concludes, on the basis of these reasons, that it will succeed in being normative with respect to whatever value issues might come under discussion. That is, it will issue in propositions that, given interlocutors' previous commitments to goal-seeking and truth, can be considered binding on the interlocutors.

It is clear that your friend has set herself an arduous task. As she begins implementing her PRS policy, restricting herself to true and direct questions and answers, she quickly discovers that her friends have melted away in alarm. She is no longer in demand at dinner parties. Acquaintances begin crossing the street to avoid her. Her students frequently leave her office in tears. She finds herself unable to enjoy the films she formerly admired or spend time reading her favorite novelists. Moreover, because she cannot convince any of her colleagues or friends to jump on the PRS bandwagon, except for quite short periods of time, she finds that the normative weight of her policy is not large. The propositions she frames prove not to be binding on her interlocutors because, while they do indeed share certain commitments about goal-seeking and truth-tracking, they don't share her conviction that full-time, on-principle true talking will in itself tease out normativity. They find that her value propositions, such as they are, are sterile and thin, largely unrelated to the concerns and travails of life as they try to live it. At about this time, they begin to suspect that your friend's life may be itself becoming sterile and thin, if not actually mad, and they start to treat her with elaborate solicitude. Typically, she begins asking direct questions about their apparent change in demeanor and, not satisfied with their evasive answers, retreats to her office, where she attempts to write a contemporary version of Wittgenstein's *Tractatus*.

I would like at this point, with your friend deposited neatly into apparent madness, to help myself to the conclusion that a policy of strict truth-telling

---

6. Though we frequently make a coherent distinction between "partial" and "whole" truth in certain matters (i.e., in condemning lies of omission), the notion of "full disclosure" per se is not meaningful. What, after all, could it mean for to me tell the whole truth? Saying all that I knew? All that I could remember? Or all that was relevant? My suspicion is that we always employ situation-specific guidelines on disclosure, usually concerning relevance. (My thanks to Chris Kutz for helping to sharpen this point.)

and truth-seeking is at odds with a life lived among other humans. I will forbear doing that, however, in order to add more weight to the claim. For it is easy enough to say that nobody does maintain a twenty-four-hour-a-day commitment to PRS, but that tells us little about whether one could if one chose to, or whether it would be rational to do so under any circumstances at all. And the quick empirical conclusion also tells us little about the desires that motivated your friend's PRS policy in the first place, desires that most of us can be taken to share in some degree or at some time. These times may be fleeting—after watching an election speech, for example, or going to a cocktail party in a bad mood—but they are significant in grounding our less severe commitments to truth-telling. They may also be long-term and deep, even if as a general program they remain the preserve of oddballs, Holden-Caulfield–style adolescents, and other "hopeless" idealists.

In fact, it is precisely because we can recognize your friend's desires as relevantly ours (or related to ours) that we accept claims, like Grice's, that conversation is rational just to the extent that it involves the efficient exchange of information and the goal-directed influencing of other people.[7] In Grice's work the claim is made almost by the way, as a background assumption, and this appears to square with a general philosophical view of language-use. Given that conversation is rational in this sense, Grice's Cooperative Principle (CP), the governing imperative of discourse, is relevant: "Make your conversational contribution such as is required, at the stage at which it occurs, by the stated purpose or direction of the talk exchange in which you are engaged."[8] So stated, of course, it sounds not simply relevant but trivially obvious, no more than reasonable.

Grice believes this CP yields four central maxims, as follows:[9]

MAXIM OF QUANTITY: Make your contribution as informative as is required, and not more.

MAXIM OF QUALITY: Do not say what you believe to be false or that for which you lack evidence.

MAXIM OF RELATION: Be relevant.

MAXIM OF MANNER: Avoid obscurity, ambiguity, prolixity, disorder.

7. See H. P. Grice, "Logic and Conversation," in *The Logic of Grammar*, ed. Donald Davidson and Gilbert Harman (Encino, Calif.: Dickenson, 1975), pp. 64–75. Though there are several others, this article, based on Grice's 1967 William James Lectures, is the clearest statement of the implicature thesis.

8. Ibid., p. 67.

9. Ibid. (adapted).

Grice then wants to claim that any deviation from these maxims is a mark of uncooperativeness—and hence irrationality—*except* in cases, which he explores at length, when the CP is implicated by certain features of what is said or done. In other words, if there is a reason for my apparent lack of cooperation, a reason that can be cashed out in terms of my *presumed* cooperation, my utterance is saved from a charge of irrationality. It might be suggested that uncooperative acts are not in themselves irrational, but I believe Grice is committed to the following entailment: if a speech-act appears uncooperative, and no good conversational reason can be found for that, it is an irrational speech-act. Nobody save a madperson is uncooperative *for no reason at all*.[10]

Most of us are familiar with how implicature functions in conversation. You ask me, for example, what time it is. I reply, "Well, the letter carrier has just gone." This reply is on the surface uncooperative, and therefore irrational, because it violates two, and possibly three, of the CP maxims. (It's ambiguous, apparently irrelevant, and with respect to a direct question uninformative.) Yet with the rational presupposition operating between us that direct questions will receive informative answers, the conversational implicature of my answer may well be clear. I have assumed that you know the mail always comes at or near eleven o'clock. Therefore you will know from my answer that it is around eleven, maybe just after. We assume implicature of this routine type all the time when faced with the nuanced indirectness of conversation. Indeed, the CP guarantees, and experience indicates, that (except when there is some previous evidence) we will long cast about for conversational implicatures before we will entertain the notion that an interlocutor is speaking irrationally. We usually move to the conclusion of irrationality unwillingly and only after prolonged inability to tease out mishearings, ironies, unknown allusions, context shifts, and the like.

Grice's subtle analysis of conversational implicature is attractive and useful, but it contains a troubling ambiguity with respect to the conversational tactics associated with politeness. He allows that there are, in addition to his stated four CP maxims, "all sorts of other maxims (aesthetic, social, or moral in character) such as 'Be Polite,' which are also normally observed by participants

---

10. Note that "reason" here will include the reasons for indulging such apparently uncooperative speech-acts as joking, irony, mimicry, and the like. The only exception I can think of to this rule is the occasion on which I, for no reason I can state to myself or anyone else, just break out into song or scat or word-salad. Yet even here we might, if challenged, give accounts of high spirits, the beautiful weather, or a new love-interest. Or we might say that, for a moment, I was mad—or anyway *feeling* mad. Madness may simply be that state in which reasons for acting, though present, cannot be straightforwardly articulated.

in talk exchanges, and these may also generate nonconventional implicatures."[11] His mentioning a possible CP maxim that commands "Be Polite" is troubling, I believe, precisely because many of the implicatures we associate with the original schema are going to be the conversational moves characteristic of politeness. That is, polite deflections and evasions, indirection and not-saying—including the sort of face-saving vagueness that was used to deal with your mad-seeming PRS friend—are obvious deviations from the four original maxims. We explain them, if we do, by reference to a general commitment to cooperation like Grice's CP.

A well-known example can make this clear. Asked to supply a letter of reference for a pupil, a professor sits down at his desk and writes the following brief message: "He always attended class and took copious notes." He signs it, puts it in a departmental envelope, and posts it to the pupil's graduate school of choice. In the context of a response to an implicit question (What do you think of the candidate?), this message makes no surface sense. It is surely irrelevant how many notes he took and, though attendance is not entirely irrelevant, it is not of central importance. So the implicature here carries the weight, as any admissions director would know, that the professor had nothing better to say. And if so, his opinion of the student must be extremely low: damning with the faintest possible praise. But what is also significant here is the form in which this implicature is made clear. The professor has told the truth, but he has not told the whole truth. He has politely evaded the question in just such a way that his true opinion can be made clear without saying it. We may not consider that this extreme example is very polite at all, but less extreme ones—of the kind we have probably all written—would make the point just as well. When we don't say all we could say, and do so in a certain polished manner, we have implicated our true opinions by calling attention to the fact that we have not spoken with maximum clarity, relevance, brevity, or truth. This is by no means the only kind of conversational implicature available under Grice's analysis, but it is a central one.

Yet, in his parenthetical remark, Grice has suggested that politeness can itself be considered a cooperative maxim—which would suggest that politeness involves not *deviation* from maxims but a *clash* of maxims, and a particularly troubling one at that. Polite speech does give us ways of saying what we don't like to say outright, but it is motivated by more other-regarding interests. When I fail to tell the whole truth in a reference letter, my primary concern may be not tipping a wink to the imagined reader but instead protecting the

11. Grice, "Logic and Conversation," p. 67.

interests of the poor student who insisted on the letter in the first place. I don't value those interests above the truth in general—I will not lie—but neither do I value them beneath a wholesale commitment to truth-telling. Indeed, that commitment would be positively inappropriate in such a case. (Imagine the reference letters your PRS friend would soon be sending around.) The issue may appear trivial, but it actually goes to the center of our question. Is politeness rational, in that it forms an aspect of some kind of general background principles of communication—and if so, exactly what sort of principles, and how would the maxim of politeness be cashed out? Or is politeness a surface deviation from a CP, and therefore something explicable only as implicature? The question may be phrased this way: Is tempering our speech in the interests of others part of our general rational commitments in conversation, or instead an apparent deviation from those commitments that can be explained only with the aid of implicature? If we choose the former option, it is clear that "rational commitments" will no longer mean something like PRS or the efficient exchange of information and influencing of people. It is likewise clear that we will have to cease regarding politeness as nonstandard usage and see it, instead, as standard usage.

Why concern ourselves with this question at all? I believe it carries enormous normative significance for any dialogic theory of justice. If linguistic civility is not a deviation from a presumed standard of rational speech, but instead a central aspect of it, then any theory that purported to extract normative juice from communicative competence—like Habermas's—would have to be recast. [12] That is, the reconstruction of rational presuppositions in communication would have to include the presuppositions associated with civility. Normativity could no longer be conceived as the unforced force of the better argument, but instead would involve the civil phrasing of arguments and concerns for the interests of other interlocutors. This would in turn make for a very different sort of ideal speech situation, one in which strict truth-telling would no longer succeed in getting all relevant interests in play and would indeed violate the maxims of cooperative speech. Whether such a reformation

---

12. It has been suggested that Habermas's model is not really at fault here, for the orientation to the better argument alone rules out force and deception, not sensitivity and openness. To such an objection I want to say (1) that we still need to capture some sense of the rationality of *self-restraint*, which I do not find in Habermas's model, and (2) that, as I argued in the previous chapter, the prorational claims in Habermas's model, like those in other Kantian-style models, make for the wrong focus in discussing justificatory talk. I do not mean that "civil discourse ethics" is *incompatible* with discourse ethics, just that the former is a crucial corrective to the latter.

of communicative normativity would solve any or all of the problems associated with Habermas's theory is a question I shall discuss in a moment. For now, I want briefly to examine the legacy of Gricean theory in the sociolinguistics of politeness.

2. Why Do We Speak Politely?

Though there is a good deal of theoretical difference among the linguists who make politeness their study, they are united on several points. Most, if not all, have (1) used Grice's CP and its associated maxims as a basis of polite pragmatics. They have done so largely in the manner I suggested earlier, using the implicature framework as a means of exposing the sense behind apparently superfluous or even mendacious speech-acts. This usually involves, as we shall see in a moment, the addition of some further notion or maxim that supplements the "bare" maxims of rationality inherited directly from Grice. It follows (2) that these investigators consider civility of central importance in pragmatic exchanges between persons, though the precise relationship between such potentially conflicting maxims as "Be clear" and "Be polite" is rarely stated, and firm definitions of politeness as a whole are conspicuously lacking in the literature. Yet strangely, given this presumed centrality, linguists are (3) united in asserting that normativity is not available in their detailed studies of the range of behaviors associated with politeness. True, the view that politeness reflects context-specific social norms is "generally embraced by the public within the English-speaking world"; yet, according to one linguist, "it is safe to say that the social-norm approach has few adherents among current researchers."[13] The aspiration that movitates the field's practitioners is, almost without exception, to frame an account of politeness, based on comparative empirical evidence, that will prove systematic in character, universal in scope, and value-free.

One of the earliest and most ambitious of these accounts was given in a 1978 study by Penelope Brown and Stephen Levinson.[14] In addition to a "minimalist" assumption of practical rationality, these authors gave their model person a sense of "face," using the notion as already explored and conceptualized by

13. Bruce Fraser, "Perspectives on Politeness," *Journal of Pragmatics* 14 (1990): 220–21
14. Penelope Brown and Stephen Levinson, "Universals in Language Usage: Politeness Phenomena," in *Questions and Politeness: Strategies in Social Interaction*, ed. Esther N. Goody (Cambridge: Cambridge University Press, 1978), pp. 56–289. Revised as *Politeness: Some Universals in Language Usage*.

Erving Goffman.[15] What they found in linguistic politeness was a staggering variety of strategies for coping with "face-threatening acts," or FTAs. Brown and Levinson adopted Grice's CP as a background assumption of "the rational and efficient nature of talk" and thus understood "polite ways of talking . . . as deviations, requiring explanations on the part of the recipient, who finds in the considerations of politeness reasons for the speaker's apparent irrationality or inefficiency."[16]

Thus politeness is implicated, first and foremost, by speech-acts that fail in some fashion to be rational or maximally efficient. This is in strict accord with Grice's stated analysis and the given CP maxims. Under Brown and Levinson's rubric, such speech-acts are directed toward saving positive face (the desire that others should want what I want) and softening blows to negative face (the desire that my actions should be unimpeded by others). These basic social desires give rise to a number of coping strategies, as mentioned, including going "off-record" (not-saying, changing the subject, etc.), "positive politeness" (emphasizing solidarity, e.g.), and "negative politeness" (softening an FTA blow with qualifications, requests, restraint, etc.). They are furthermore complicated by variables of social distance (D), relative power (P) between interlocutors, and the absolute ranking (R) of a given act along some accepted cultural spectrum. Thus the following formula:

$$Wx = D(s,h) + P(h,s) + Rx$$

That is, the "weightiness" of an FTA—the seriousness or estimated net loss of face—is equal to the social distance between speaker and hearer, plus the relative power imbalance between hearer and speaker, plus the absolute rank of the FTA in question. Weightier FTAs will call for more elaborate coping strategies than routine ones.[17]

The usefulness of this formula is limited in practice, however, and many commentators have found the rather paranoiac background of this analysis, with face in threat at every moment, unhelpful.[18] A more nuanced analysis was provided by Geoffrey Leech in his 1983 study *Principles of Pragmatics*. Following Austin and Searle as well as Grice, Leech's explicit aim was to outline a pragmatic theory of "interpersonal rhetoric" that would complement standard semantic (or in his term "grammatical") accounts of "textual rheto-

15. See Erving Goffman, *Interaction Ritual: Essays on Face-to-Face Behavior* (New York: Anchor Books, 1967), and *Relations in Public* (Harmondsworth: Penguin Books, 1971).

16. Brown and Levinson, *Politeness*, p. 4.

17. Ibid., pp. 78ff.

18. See Fraser, "Perspectives on Politeness," pp. 228–31, for a review of these arguments.

ric."[19] He hoped in this way to account for the relationship, demonstrated in conversation, between sense and force. So he rejected depth-grammar and linguistic competence accounts like Chomsky's and, using Grice as a stepping-stone, outlined several principles of conversational performance. The CP was retained, but added were an explicit Politeness Principle (PP), an Irony Principle, and other, subsidiary principles: a Banter Principle, an Interest Principle, and a Pollyanna Principle.[20]

Leech's PP clarifies what is obscured in Grice and unremarked in Brown and Levinson. The principles governing politeness in conversation *are themselves rational* in that they form part of the background of conversational performance. They may appear, under other analyses, mere deviations from the CP, but that indicates not that politeness is implicated but rather that the CP is not per se constitutive of conversational rationality. What normally appears in polite speech-acts to be a deviation from the CP is in fact, as suggested above, a clash of principles. The CP is still useful in seeing *that* indirection is used in speech, but only the PP can indicate *why* it is used; it is therefore "an important missing link between the CP and how to relate sense to force."[21] Leech's PP is stated as follows: "Minimize (other things being equal) the expression of impolite beliefs; maximize (other things being equal) the expression of polite beliefs." Like the CP, this principle comes with four associated maxims:

TACT MAXIM:	Minimize hearer costs; maximize hearer benefits
GENEROSITY MAXIM:	Minimize self-benefit; maximize other-benefit
APPROBATION MAXIM:	Minimize hearer dispraise; maximize hearer praise
MODESTY MAXIM:	Minimize self-praise; maximize self-dispraise

The most important of these, and the only one to receive detailed attention in Leech's study, is the Tact Maxim. In general, Leech attempts an account of interpersonal rhetoric that will demonstrate why persons are often moved to deviate from the strict efficiency of the CP in order to secure other goals *they consider equally rational*, that is, confirming group solidarity, considering the feelings of others, and restraining their own egos.

---

19. Leech, *Principles of Pragmatics*, introduction.

20. Ibid., pp. 149ff. The Banter Principle accounts for such conversational conventions as routinized insults and joshing among long-term friends; the Interest Principle suggests that saying something unusual or uncooperative may be justified in terms of being witty or nonbanal; and the Pollyanna Principle accounts for the value listeners place on prima facie positive accounts of speech acts—i.e., they want to see others as being nice and will move from that assumption only if forced.

21. Leech, *Principles of Pragmatics*, p. 104.

It is significant, then, that politeness does not always, or even usually, work as a devious means of securing goals in the narrow sense—goals that may elude me if I am direct ("If I ask nicely, I'll get more of what I really want"). That is, politeness is not a strategy justified by its ability to achieve the same set of ends by other means. It actually expands the set of rational ends pursued by interlocutors. So it is essential to see that the PP *clashes* with the CP, doesn't deviate from it; the clashes are resolved, if they are, by the relative tactfulness of our adopted speech. By contrast, there is no such clash in Leech's Irony Principle, with which the PP might superficially be confused. The Irony Principle states: "If you must cause offense, at least do so in a way that doesn't overtly conflict with the PP but allows the hearer to arrive at the offensive point of your remark indirectly, through implicature." As a subsidiary of the PP, irony amounts in Gricean terms to an *exploitation* of the CP rather than a clash with it. It follows that irony is only superficially polite, and despite appearances it is usually cooperative in that it ultimately conveys relevant information—however unpleasant.

It must be said, however, that Leech's account of when and how the CP and PP conflict is only partial. Leech offers nothing like the detail of examples of implicature given by Grice, nor does he provide any general rules for when speakers will opt for polite speech beyond a fourfold schema of situations (competitive, convivial, collaborative, conflictive). He suggests scalar variations for each PP maxim—that is, the relative called-for degree of tact, or generosity, etc.—but these do not finally prove much more helpful than the Brown and Levinson formula, though they are more detailed. The most significant aspect of Leech's analysis, for our purposes, is its insistence that politeness forms part of the background of goal-directed human action, not a deviation from that state that requires special pleading of one sort or another. The PP is an affirmation that we are often moved by goals that do not involve the rational and efficient exchange of information.

Yet this affirmation can lead to internal incoherences. Excessive politeness, as most of us know, can actually be impolite—both intentionally (in irony and sarcasm) and unintentionally (as, e.g., when a person I consider a friend persists in treating me with elaborate courtesy).[22] Leech also briefly examines what he calls "the practical paradox of politeness": a situation in which both interlocutors are so bent on upholding the PP at the expense of the CP

22. This may recall an infamous psychology experiment in which undergraduates were asked to treat their parents with formal politeness during a college vacation. Invariably, the parents experienced this treatment as viciously sarcastic.

that they back themselves into a noncooperative corner of inaction. Such a situation is invariably comic. For instance: as an undergraduate, I once found myself approaching a doorway at exactly the same time as another student. I was a visitor in his college, which had a reputation for a high standard of manners. So I politely offered him the way through. But he, recognizing a visitor, stood back and politely offered *me* the way. I then politely refused and repeated my offer. He did the same. We stood there for what seemed like an age, each of us unwilling to go first, acting out a scene from (as it might be) Noel Coward revised by Ionesco. We might be there still if one of us—me, as it happened—had not relented and walked through the doorway first.

I do not believe, however, that this paradox poses any serious problem. Sooner or later we realize that such ideally polite behavior is impractical, and the cycle breaks. This may be for practical reasons, backed by the CP (one of us has to get through the door first in order that both, or either, of us can), but it may also be for polite reasons, backed by what Leech calls the Tact Meta-Maxim: "Do not put others in a position where they have to break the Tact Maxim." I abandon my polite stance in the interests of something like a higher-order politeness, namely accommodating the other person.

What Leech's view suggests, finally, is that politeness is *not* best understood as a category of conversational implicature, except in the first or recognizing instance. A final strand of sociolinguistic research makes this point even more explicit by, in effect, redescribing the CP such that it includes a crucial polite-ness element.[23] Bruce Fraser's theory of "conversational contract" thus fulfills Grice's suggestion that a politeness maxim was part of the CP, but does so in a fashion that shows the CP to be no longer a matter of efficient exchange of information and influencing of interlocutors. Fraser's view is that "upon enter-ing into a given conversation, each party brings an understanding of some initial set of rights and obligations that will determine, at least for preliminary stages, what the participants can expect from the other(s)." These presupposi-tions of conversation, which may be conventional, social, or habitual, are anticipated by all participants. On this implied contract view, then, "politeness is not a sometime thing. . . . Politeness is a state that one expects to exist in every conversation." And so politeness is not noted as a deviation (it is not implicated), but instead expected as part of the background (it is anticipated). It

---

23. Fraser, "Perspectives on Politeness," pp. 232–35. See also Bruce Fraser and William Nolen, "The Association of Deference with Linguistic Form," *International Journal of the Sociology of Language* 27 (1981): 93–109.

is impoliteness, not politeness, that violates a background norm of conversation. "Being polite is taken as a hallmark of abiding by the CP," says Fraser.[24]

The implications of this view are many. First, it shows that politeness is not a superfluous flourish on speech, something that could be dispensed with in the "real" conversational interests of speakers. Nor is politeness either, as in Leech, simply a matter of making speakers "feel good" or, as in Brown and Levinson, avoiding making them "feel bad"—though these will clearly remain consequences of politeness. It shows likewise that, contrary to expectation, the CP is not thwarted by an independent PP but instead must be redescribed so that it includes politeness as a central element. Precisely how the resulting maxims will relate is not determined by Fraser, and this is a major drawback. We still lack what we most desire, a detailed account of just *when, how,* and *why* politeness might override or nullify concerns of efficiency or strict truth-telling. And this, after all, is the essence of polite speech, that it flouts any imagined maxims of "bald on-record" or maximally efficient truth-telling. It may be that such an account is impossible, or will prove impossibly complex. That politeness does in fact so override bald on-record truth-telling cannot remain in doubt, however. With Fraser's theory, and to a less explicit extent Leech's, we now have a linguistic basis for claiming that *it is rational to be polite*—if "rational" means conducting conversation in accordance with a set of background presuppositions that can be expressed as the principles of communicative competence. These principles will form either a CP/PP scheme like Leech's or (perhaps better?) a modified-CP scheme like Fraser's.

What are the normative stakes in such a claim, if any?

3. Normativity

I mentioned earlier that the sociolinguistics researchers, to a person, have rejected normative claims for their findings. This is mainly because they believe no valid scientific conclusions can proceed from the quicksand of social relations, the field in which norms are thought to reside. In other words, they are barred from being normative just to the extent that they want to make claims about universally valid patterns and strategies of linguistic politeness. This may strike us nonspecialists as odd, since politeness appears to our eyes a nonpareil example of social norms in action. Or, from another point of view, we may indeed regard politeness behavior as normative, but feel rather dismissive toward it, as belonging in the realm of so-called "petty morality"—

24. Fraser, "Perspectives on Politeness," p. 232.

the lesser do's and don't's of social interaction. In this section I want to suggest how we might achieve two goals that arise naturally from this situation of conceptual stand-off: we can, first, close the fact-value gap the sociolinguists are keen to maintain around politeness; and so at the same time, second, rescue politeness from the dismissiveness of petty morality and place it at the center of justificatory talk in general. This will have the coincidental benefit of strengthening a third claim, that it is rational *in a normative sense* to be polite—not merely something we do but something we *must* do.

Like Habermas, sociolinguists are critical of the grammatical-competence theory found in early Chomskian linguistics. Like him, they prefer to move from semantics to pragmatics, to speak of performative ability rather than of ability to utter well-formed sentences. In short, there is much common ground on the level of pragmalinguistic investigation. But the company parts on two issues: Habermas has nothing to say about politeness, and the sociolinguists find his ultimately normative project clearly wrongheaded. How can these strands be brought back together?

The obvious way is to attempt to build a politeness element into the ideal speech situation, revising the demands of discourse in a fashion similar to what Leech and Fraser did to Grice's theory. We saw in the previous chapter that Habermas, in an attempt to get his fingers on something normative, may have set too much store by an uncritical or elevated notion of rationality.[25] Worries about this may take many forms, as we also saw, but can be summed up as *a limit on the powers of cognition* to forge binding moral or political agreement. That is, it is not clear that my knowing more—for instance, about your interests and the arguments that seem valid from your point of view—will ever be enough for me to agree with you about some shared norm of, say, goods-distribution. From this point of view, the ideal speech situation is too ideal to do any work, too "Eurocentric" or "logocentric" or "phonocentric" or "phallocentric," or just centric in some other bad way. We were enjoined, among other options, to leave the "rational" out of rational agreement and, more radical still, to forget about agreement altogether and concentrate on solidarity.

Solidarity is indeed an important goal, and it is not coincidental that some of the politeness behaviors analyzed by the linguists appear aimed at just that

25. Criticism of this type comes from many quarters, including feminist philosophy especially. Nancy Fraser, e.g., thinks Habermas crucially omits discussion of gender; see "What's Critical About Critical Theory?" in her *Unruly Practices*. See also N. Fraser, "Towards a Discourse Ethic of Solidarity," *Praxis International* 5 (1986): 425–29.

goal. Though he speaks positively of solidarity, Habermas is perhaps, like Grice, too occupied with philosophical chimerae. Indeed, his communicative rationality may begin to resemble a version of the PRS that earlier led your friend into social disaster.[26] Communication, we want to say, is not simply about phrasing interests and arguments or the maximally efficient transfer of information; it is also about not hurting other people's feelings, not having mine hurt, not saying all we could say, oiling the wheels of mundane social interaction, and strengthening the ties that bind us together. Habermas's model of full disclosure, this unconstrained conversation in which the better argument wins just because it is better, is indeed too ideal—or rather, ideal in the wrong way—to be normatively useful. Getting interests into conversational play is not simply a matter of us all speaking our minds; it is also a matter of us sometimes restraining ourselves to listen, sometimes coaxing out the interests of the other through sensitivity and tact. If this is so, then clamoring after an impossibly ideal rational discourse can only end in frustration, if not actual oppression or injustice.

But by the same token an ideally polite discourse would, as the practical paradox of politeness demonstrates, have its own practical shortcomings. Hence, as with the purely empirical investigation of speech pragmatics, it is clear that only a *combination* of orientations can succeed in telling us all we want to know about normative language. I have suggested that such a combination could involve revisions of what we consider rational, such that politeness becomes part of rationality after all; or it could involve recognition that rational is not all we want speech to be, even *or especially* when we want it to be normative. Whether something like "civil dialogue" can be set out with sufficient precision to be useful in actual legitimation talk remains, for now, an open question. Whether the anticipation of politeness is, as Fraser avers, *a contract* is also an undecided issue, for it is not clear that the language of implicit contract is very helpful here, despite its obvious normative connotation. It might indeed appear, on this view, that we contract for politeness but not for rationality, since we can imagine opting out of the former but not out of the latter. Fraser's view is stronger if the presuppositions of polite speech are as firm, as deeply held within our competence as speech-actors, as those of rationality in the narrower sense. It is only thus that politeness will be not

26. For Habermas's views on solidarity and its relation to discourse ethics, see esp. "Justice and Solidarity: On the Discussion Concerning 'Stage 6.' " In general, Habermas here reiterates his argument that, because *Sittlichkeit* is secured within it, discourse ethics is not susceptible to the kind of Hegelian objections to Kantian moral theory that afflict other theorists.

simply something that we do but something that we must do—"must" meaning here that it would be irrational, incompetent in some respect, to do otherwise. Under such a description, then, it would be rational *in a normative sense* to be polite.

I said a few pages ago that the imagined exchange between A and B, concerning haircuts and baseball games, might not be a non sequitur. It was probably evident even then why this is so, since most of us have dealt like B with similar situations in our own lives. In this sense, having already had occasion to deal with some version of it, the exchange does not even *appear* to be non sequitur. We're only inclined to recognize it as one when we apply standards of entailment that are extrasocial in some important sense. Intrasocially, B's response follows A's question as the night the day. Why? Because B is being polite: without actively lying, he is not saying what he thinks about the haircut, instead changing the subject to something that presumably is a source of fellow-feeling between him and A.[27] Of course, if A is inclined to, he can see what B really thinks by means of Gricean implicature. He can see that B's reticence is tacit indication that he dislikes the new haircut. Indeed, if B is not adept at his politeness or, in a different sort of case, actually *wants* A to know what he thinks in a sarcastic or ironic way, A will be forced to draw the implied conclusion. (This would then follow Leech's Irony Principle.) But politeness done correctly—sincere insincerity, let us call it—has the special feature of allowing A not to face the conclusion. If he insists on drawing it out, contrary to B's intention, that is his own special kind of impoliteness or perversity. And I am certain that most of us would find it perverse, too, if our own version of A were suddenly to say, without irony: "Why do you say that? You're simply changing the subject! You really hate it, don't you? Why can't you just say it? Is it that bad, that you can't even bring yourself to say it? Oh my God! Is it that bad? Tell me!"

So the exchange involves a conversational implicature only, I want to say, from an odd point of view, a point of view that is defiantly antisocial. From this standpoint the exchange appears irrational, but the standpoint is itself irrational in an obvious respect. Why do we adopt it? For the most part, we do so

27. Donald Moon has suggested that the abruptness of the change of subject would fail to be polite because it would call for B to draw the implied conclusion that A does not like the haircut. But this is not so if there are features of the situation, which we could easily specify, that help to blunt the force of the indirection. For example, B allows a pause, looks out the window, consults his schedule of Blue Jays games, etc. (This is the sort of thing I mean by the "adeptness" of a given politeness act.) The central point holds: linguistically, what looks like a non sequitur, and a pretty bizarre one at that, is in fact not one at all.

because we believe it is the only way to secure certainty or efficiency. Yet such efficiency or certainty is of limited value if it cannot make its force felt elsewhere than in its special realm. Even there—as, say, in scientific or philosophical exchanges, where politeness is thought to be dispensable—empirical analysis shows that we are actually more moved by concerns of politeness than we might care to admit. And this can only indicate that we have values in play in such exchanges—the preservation of face, the health of a common culture—that are not straightforwardly related to efficient information-exchange and the unforced force of the better argument. If this is so, we abandon politeness only at our peril.[28] What I am suggesting, then, is that *contextual constraints* exist already within our competence as communicators, and these can frame a conversation that is both real (it is recognizably ours) and normative (its results are binding because they are rational in some expanded sense).[29] This, then, is what might be called *civil discourse ethics.*

III. GIVING CIVILITY CHARACTER

We still require, however, what sociolinguistic analysis could not give us, namely a firm and rich characterization of civility. In this section of the chapter, I draw on some historical and literary sources that go some distance in providing such an account. This will also serve to clarify the political stakes of civility, which will be finally assessed in the next chapter. One thing I think we find, in giving civility character, is further evidence for a point made earlier: writers of etiquette manuals, both contemporary and classical, are as a general thing better able than philosophers to defend the social and ethical significance of civility. Philosophers tend to get caught up in the apparently rigid rule-boundedness of "correct" behavior—and therefore they are too quick to dismiss the moral significance of politeness, classifying it (if

28. A lack of politeness is often taken, in scientific or philosophical culture, as a mark of hard-headedness. Yet it is neither a necessary nor a sufficient condition: there are many astute critics who are marvelously polite, and lots of rude people who could not spot a bad argument if it reared up and dealt them a blow to the head.

29. In an earlier version of this material, I used the phrase "natural constraints" where "contextual constraints" now appears. A number of commentators (including especially Robert Hanna and Donald Moon) pleaded confusion: weren't the constraints I had in mind social through and through? Yes. The contrast I was concerned with was not natural as opposed to social, but natural *as opposed to artificial or theorist-constructed constraints.* I hope the new phrase makes the point more clearly.

sympathetic) as a minor virtue or (if unsympathetic) dismissing it from the field. Writers who make the regulation of behavior their business do not make that their only business, and the best of them display a philosophical acumen that, while certainly untutored, gives us the initial means for taking politeness seriously.

Primers for "correct" behavior have been a publisher's staple since at least the Renaissance, with a great upsurge in examples appearing during the nineteenth century, especially in the United States. The concern to know "what's done" is basic to our social fears and ambitions, and it is heightened in times of social upheaval or mobility. Perhaps the oldest extant manuals of manners are two works from the thirteenth century, Thommin von Zirclaria's *Der Wälsche Gast* (c. 1210) and Bonvicino da Riva's *De le zinquanta cortexia de tavola* (c. 1290). Later works include Jacques le Grand's *Book of Good Manners* (1487) and Alexander Barclay's *Mirror of Good Manners* (1523), but the true gem of Renaissance manners manuals is Giovanni della Casa's *Galateo* (1558), a witty and sophisticated discussion of civil behavior.[30] Better-known examples, from the eighteenth century, are the Earl of Chesterfield's *Principles of Politeness and Knowing the World* (1774) and George Washington's *Rules of Civility and Decent Behavior in Company and Conversation* (c. 1745). Erasmus's *De Civilitate* (1530) is, according to one commentator, noteworthy as "one of the few etiquette books written by a philosopher." But consider James Forrester's little-known work *The Polite Philosopher; or, An essay on that art which makes a man happy in himself, and agreeable to others* (1734). Looking a little further afield, Castiglione's *Book of the Courtier* (1528) is, in some sense, a book of correct behavior, just as Machiavelli's *The Prince* (1513) and parts of Montaigne's *Essays* (1580) might be said to be. But these more elaborate and ambitious political guidebooks take us beyond the polite; indeed, politeness may be reductively instrumentalized in such works, whose *telos* is personal power and glory. In our own century there has been a large amount of interest in correct behavior, from Emily Post's writing on her own Connecticut–Manhattan–Long Island nexus in the 1920s, to Judith Martin's popular Miss

---

30. For example, "It is not polite," says Della Casa, "to scratch yourself when you are seated at table. You should also take care, as far as you can, not to spit at mealtimes, but if you must spit, then do so in a decent manner." It is, he adds, "unmannerly to fall asleep, as many people do, whilst company is engaged in conversation," for people who do "are generally obliged to doze in an uncomfortable position, and this nearly always causes them to make unpleasant noises and gestures in their sleep. Often enough they begin to sweat and dribble at the mouth." Giovanni della Casa, *Galateo; or, The Book of Manners*, trans. R. S. Pine-Coffin (Harmondsworth: Penguin Books, 1958), pp. 98, 31.

Manners guides to "excruciatingly correct behavior" (1982) and "manners for the end of the millennium" (1988).

Even a cursory study of these sources shows how deeply their authors take the consideration of why manners matter. So, for example, Amy Vanderbilt, the doyenne of 1950s politeness, notes an important distinction between "superficial" and "good" manners:

> The finest rules of behavior are to be found in Chapter 13 of First Corinthians, the beautiful dissertation on charity by Saint Paul. These rules have nothing to do with fine points of dress nor with those of superficial manners. They have to do with feelings and attitudes, kindliness, and consideration of others. Good manners have much to do with the emotions. To make them ring true, one must feel them, not merely exhibit them.[31]

And compare:

> Etiquette has to do with when you wear white gloves and how you unfold your napkin on your lap; *real manners* are being thoughtful toward others, being creative in doing nice things for people, or sympathizing with others' problems. . . . As our population grows and we are forced to live ever more closely together, never have manners been more desperately needed.[32]

Taken together, these passages seem to indicate that an argument in favor of manners can make claims on our more general social commitments. But this argument has force only when we have taken the time to distinguish—both conceptually and in practice—between outward conformity to a code of social behavior and the real thing. And "the real thing" involves, at the very least, feeling the pragmatic force of the argument that manners reduce social friction.

This distinction between "etiquette" and "real manners" (or, as it is sometimes expressed between "superficial" manners and "good" manners) is clearly meant to have some kind of normative force. Vanderbilt thus indicates what is not always apparent, even to readers of etiquette books—namely, why man-

---

31. Amy Vanderbilt, *New Complete Book of Etiquette: A Guide to Contemporary Living* (New York: Doubleday, 1952), p. 134.

32. Ibid., p. xi.

ners matter beyond the rather facile considerations of doing "what's done." But her account is, not unexpectedly, far from systematic. She confesses her frustration when she says: "The word 'etiquette' for all the things I have tried to discuss is really inadequate, yet no other will do. It covers much more than 'manners,' the way in which we *do* things. It is considerably more than a treatise on a code of social behavior."[33] But in what way is politeness more than a code?

The notion I think Vanderbilt is groping toward here is politeness in its moral-political sense, or the orientation to one's fellows I earlier called civility. This is that part of politeness we can understand as distinct from both manners (social behavior of particular kinds) and etiquette (the codified rules of that behavior). So the distinction Vanderbilt made between etiquette and real manners is one I shall express more clearly as between *manners* on the one hand and that part of social politeness we may call *civility* on the other. Various forms of the distinction can be found prominently in the etiquette literature, where it is employed to underline the difference between the details of mannerly acts (which can be governed by rules) and the general orientation to social cooperation that grounds them. "All acts of civility," wrote Lord Chesterfield rather cynically to his son, "are, by common consent, understood to be no more than a conformity to custom, for the quiet and conveniency of society, the *agremens* of which are not to be disturbed by private dislikes and jealousies."[34] Compare Obadiah Walker, who in his 1673 pamphlet *Of Education, Especially of Young Gentlemen*, offers this version of civility:

> Civility is not, therefore, punctuality of behaviour: I mean that which consists in certain modish and particular ceremonies and fashions, in clothes, gesture, mien, speech, or the like; is not using such discourses, words, phrases, studies, opinions, games, &c. as are in fashion in the Court: with gallants, ladies &c. This is a constrained formality, not civility; a complying with the times, not with persons; and varieth with the age or season . . . whereas the rules of civility, founded upon prudence and charity, are to perpetuity unchangeable.

33. Ibid., p. ix.
34. Between 1739 and 1752, Philip Dormore Stanhope, fourth Earl of Chesterfield, wrote a series of letters to his "natural son"—that is, bastard—as he helped advance the boy's career and education. They are collected in the treatise *On Manners and Morals*, published in various forms and editions. The quotation is from the letter of September 29, 1752, page 112 of a modern edition (Mount Vernon: Peter Pauper Press, 1936).

Consider, further, the anonymous author of a nineteenth-century etiquette work, *Decorum*, who declared that "morals lay the foundation of manners. A well-ordered mind, a well-regulated heart, produce the best conduct. The rules which a philosopher or moralist lays down for his own guidance, properly developed, lead to the most courteous acts."[35] "Politeness," he added, "has been defined as benevolence in small things. A true gentleman is recognized by his regard for the rights and feelings of others, even in matters the most trivial."[36] And Emily Post, whose "Blue Book" of etiquette was widely consulted in America in the 1920s and 1930s, notes that "[c]onsideration for the rights and feelings of others is not merely a rule for behavior in public but the very foundation upon which social life is built."[37]

I think, *pace* Walker, that the really useful distinction between manners and civility is not between the changeable and the eternal, but rather between the rule-bound and the rule-independent. This likewise accepts the concern of etiquette writers to show that true politeness is best understood as instinctive and judgmental, not conformist or stringent—a result, that is, of effective socialization, insight and intuition, not of slavish obedience to a code. The genuinely polite person shows himself or herself unfettered by rules and conventions, able to play with existing rules, invent new ones, and stretch the boundaries of manners with the assurance of social experience and concern for others, which always transcends the dictates of fashion. So it is not by following rules of good manners, however detailed, that one becomes polite.

Indeed, it appears that even the codification of such rules is ultimately an absurd task; one is reduced to providing a longer and longer list of examples and offering rules of the most basic sort—rules, in fact, of manners. The attempt, familiar from other practice-based accounts of social phenomena, would be similar to the task of writing down all the elements of "tacit knowledge" required to, say, play baseball. In addition to all the rules of the game, there are an indeterminate number of subrules, conventions, understood relations, and complexes concerning "what's done" in the game, all of which resist strict or even coherent codification. (In a complex game such as baseball, it is doubtless true that many players and managers do not know even the written rules of the game; still less can they articulate the tacit rules. This does not mean they cannot play the game well, even brilliantly.) What is systematically

---

35. The full title of this work is *Decorum: A Practical Treatise on Etiquette and Dress of the Best American Society*, by an anonymous author but revised by S. L. Louis (New York: Union Publishing, 1882). The quotation is from p. 19.

36. Ibid., p. 232.

37. Ibid., p. 37.

lacking in such accounts when applied to politeness, I want to say—the reason they fail to hold our moral attention—is a sense of the original or basic disposition of politeness. This is the disposition to (1) refrain from saying all one could say and (2) listen sensitively to what others are saying—it is a disposition, in short, to rise above one's own likes and dislikes and consider those of others. This disposition is through and through ethical; it has, moreover, a very significant political role to play. We must now examine what such a two-sided account of civility would look like.

1. Not-Saying

I have suggested that the identification of civility as a first virtue of dialogic citizens is pragmatically motivated: avoidance and resolution of social conflict are the goals it aims to achieve. The constraints modeled in civility will be those that make possible a collective project of living together well, while maintaining a principled moral noncognitivism. Civility, in short, is a civil goal; it has to do with getting along with one another in society, not with reaching the truth or articulating the best possible theory or moral vision. What are the implications of making such a distinction within *dialogic* theory of justice?

The most obvious point is that civility does not allow interlocutors to say anything they like, or all the things they might want to say. As I suggested above, it therefore encourages, and even demands, a kind of insincerity.[38] Examples of this form of insincerity are familiar. You come to dinner at my house wearing an ugly, ill-fitting suit. What is more, I *know* that your suit is ugly and ill-fitting, having cultivated a dress sense that is clearly, at least on present evidence, rather keener than yours. The judgment that your suit is ugly and ill-fitting is therefore both true and a sincere expression of my justified beliefs. Nevertheless, politeness bids me keep silent. I speak of the weather, offer you a drink, busy myself in the kitchen. I pass no comment on your suit. If you ask me what I think of your new outfit, I am noncommittal. I mention whatever good points it may have, or say something vague. As a

---

38. But not, it is significant, all kinds of insincerity. Without a sincere commitment to common understanding, for example, politeness will not be able to effect the combined tasks of social criticism and social justification. It will remain a fetish of certain segments of the population, often the dominant ones; and it will merely mask social conflicts with an appearance of civility. To be socially effective—to overcome the objection that it leaves everything as it is—politeness must be sincerely practiced by social actors.

result of these restraints on myself, I have succeeded in being polite, but I have clearly failed to say what I sincerely believe and what I know to be the case.

What kind of "failure" is this? Many people, some philosophers among them, would consider it a failure of nerve and a rather feeble one at that. On this view, civility is equivalent to being mealy-mouthed or inadequate. I am being a wimp; if I really think your suit is ugly and ill-fitting, by God I should just say so and stop pussyfooting around. More seriously, if I don't say what I think and what I moreover know to be the case, I may have failed in my commitments to the values of truth and sincerity. Every time I fail to tell the truth, the whole truth, and nothing but the truth, I am causing the stock of truth-telling to drop just a little bit. I may also tarnish my reputation for being a reliable reporter of truth and cause people to distrust everything I say. My failure can therefore be seen as both moral *and* epistemological. I did the wrong thing because I failed to be a perspicuous vessel of true propositions that I sincerely, and with good reason, believed. The failure might even be political in a broad sense. I held back on my judgments and consequently closed off the possibility of collective emancipation that might be thought to reside in a commitment to self-transparency and the whole truth.

The essence of my civil behavior, however, was not that I *lied* about the suit, but that I did not say all that I believed of it, namely that its check was loud and the sleeves too short. We can of course imagine cases in which not-saying *would* be judged a lie, and blamed on those grounds. And there are other cases in which not-saying might be blameworthy without being judged a lie—for example, I stagger up to you on the street, bleeding from a gun wound, and ask where the nearest hospital is; you say nothing and walk on. But I do not lie when, without quite unusual contextual constraints, I do not say what I know and believe to be the case about your suit. And I am here not simply being perverse. My silence is rationally motivated by pressing concerns other than truth-telling, concerns, namely, of smooth social interaction and putting you at your ease. These concerns, despite the possibly trivial example, are best understood as related to shared moral and political goals. On this view, my failure to tell you what I think of your suit is no failure at all; it is a success of good sense and concern for the continuing civil regard with which we treat each other—whatever our disagreements about fashion or anything else. Civility contributes to smooth social interaction, makes for tolerance of diversity, and conditions a regard for the claims and interests of others. It is a de-centering strategy that deflects concern from my beliefs and claims to take account of those held by persons with whom I am interacting.

Most of us are familiar with examples in which the morally responsible thing to do is not to tell the truth: the fugitive's protector confronted by a death squad, for example, who will not say where the fugitive has been hidden. But I am suggesting that a more general, and less extreme, version of not telling the whole truth can function as the basis of a specifically political dialogue. As we saw above, the concerns of that dialogue are clearly different from a dialogue oriented only to the truth. The ugly-suit example is meant to isolate a relatively straightforward intuition, but one that is nevertheless frequently misplaced in theories of dialogic justice. The intuition is that there are many cases in which telling the truth is not the first priority of participants in dialogue. Their first priority is rather the smooth management and, if possible, the resolution of those conflicts each may rationally expect to arise from interaction with the others. Such a dialogue retains its force by beginning with commitments that all participants in it can be assumed to share, including a basic commitment to have a well-ordered public space—or, in the example, to pass a pleasant evening together.

It is important in these cases that the distance between not-saying and lying be maintained.[39] Civil discourse, the goals of which are admittedly pragmatic and political, must not be actively deceitful. Deceit can undermine the possibility of a successful political dialogue: a dialogue oriented to understanding the claims of others and creating a political order that allows (some of) these claims to be judged normatively valid. Deceit creates opportunities for ideological manipulation and the practiced verbal hoodwinking long favored by smooth talkers. Vaclav Havel expressed the stakes of political dialogue clearly when describing some of the difficulties he, a poet, faced in his unexpected political career. "The *sine qua non* of a politician," Havel said,

> is not the ability to lie; he need only be sensitive and know when, to whom, what, and how to say what he has to say. It is not true that a person of principle does not belong in politics; it is enough for his principles to be leavened with patience, deliberation, a sense of proportion, and an understanding of others. It is not true that only the unfeeling cynic, the vain, the brash, and the vulgar can succeed in

---

39. In *The Journalist and the Murderer* (New York: Vintage, 1990), Janet Malcolm castigates journalists who deceive through not-saying; and pragmatic defenses of the practice by, among others, William Buckley are held up to ridicule. But a significant distinction is not drawn in her indictment of not-saying—namely, that between situations in which goals are shared and those in which goals diverge. If I fail to say something *for my own ends only*, I am acting strategically, not communicatively; if I do so for the sake of goals we both (all) share—e.g., smooth social interaction—blame may turn to praise.

politics; all such people, it is true, are drawn to politics, but in the end decorum and good taste will always count for more.[40]

A main problem for the current argument is that politeness has all too often in the past been the locus of just the kind of politically motivated deceit Havel mentions here. I believe the strongest objection to such deceitful strategies is not that they undermine truth in general, but rather that they make a defensible and just social order less likely. And yet this objection will not be convincing unless the pragmatic commitments to which it appeals can be shown to be shared by all participants in a social dialogue. One necessary facet of any convincing account of civility will therefore be a solution to the problem of deceit.

The most effective way of dealing with this problem, and incidentally giving a firmer characterization to civil dialogue, is to introduce the notion of *relevance criteria*.[41] Civility provides its practitioners with the ability to see which kinds of locution are appropriate to given situations—an ability, I suggested, socialized in the form of restraint on any general commitment to the whole truth. That sort of commitment has great potential for social harm: we have only to think of the policy of "brutal honesty" adopted by some PRS-minded people in a misplaced effort to get the whole truth "out in the open." This policy may succeed in exposing the fatuity of some kinds of social restraint, and may even bring to light things that ought to be known, but it possesses a debilitating defect in terms of the political dialogue of legitimation. It does not take difference seriously enough, working instead on the politically naive assumption that all conflicts of opinion can be resolved if enough talk is produced. (If we add the idealizing proviso of Habermas—enough talk *of the right kind*—we have a true principle without useful concrete application in hard cases.) There are some deep differences that are irreconcilable, and the social task relevant to these is not resolution but mediation. Mediation, like diplomacy, requires restraint; it likewise presumes a willingness, at some level of commitment, to negotiate. That commitment is more likely to be some kind of pragmatic desire for a well-ordered civil society than it is to be a deep commitment to the force of the better argument. And this commitment, as we saw above, is itself a rational one under an expanded and defensible description of "rational."

40. *New York Review of Books* (May 1992). I thank an anonymous reader for this reference.

41. Many, if not most, of the writers who concentrate their energies on defending dialogue have some notion of relevance in hand: Ackerman's neutrality, e.g., or Rorty's public/private distinction. These notions mark the often problematic limits of the politically sayable.

Within this sort of social commitment, then, relevance criteria are those that indicate which topics of discussion are appropriately addressed in a public, political dialogue—and which, because they cannot be effectively disputed, must be left to the private realm of deeper moral commitments. It would not be surprising, given this relevance division, if the dialogue on the public side were formal, stylized, and sometimes tricky. We are not born with the ability to talk effectively here, to address issues of legitimation and justice with the right sort of arguments—that is, the arguments that speak to the common concerns, however minimal, of all participants in the dialogue. Acquisition of the skill of social talk is not simply a matter of following rules, though there may well be rules for its successful performance. On the other hand, we might expect to habituate ourselves in the practices of such talk in the first instance by simply following the rules.

Of course, it is not obvious that all citizens will share the same view of the relevance criteria associated with social dialogue. Georgia Warnke suggests that democracy, fairness, and equality are the "criteria of relevance that we use for leveling the playing field on which interpretations are to compete." But she also suggests, *pace* Rorty, that we have a commitment to keep talking (and listening) to those who claim to *reject* those criteria. "Indeed," she says, "we have to assume that our task as interpreters is to understand the point in this rejection and to learn from it."[42] Let us say, for example, that the conventions of legal argument, or the rules of parliamentary procedure, represent one form of the kind of dialogue I am calling civil. What happens when a particular decision reached within these conventions—for example, *Roe v. Wade*— proves unacceptable to some, perhaps many, citizens? I believe there are three kinds of recourse open to them: they may challenge the decision within the existing conventions, using legal argument to overturn the precedent; or they may challenge the logically prior decision, concerning whether the matter under consideration was relevantly addressed by the social dialogue of legal decision; or they may, at the highest level, challenge the legitimacy—which is to say, the political relevance—of some or all of the conventions themselves.

All three courses serve to reinforce the existence of relevance criteria, even though it is likely that the marshaling of arguments in this sphere will not be free of confusion about those criteria. For example, employing *moral* arguments in favor of making abortion a matter of public policy (or in favor of

---

42. Warnke, *Justice and Interpretation*, p. 156. I have mentioned already that these criteria of equality, fairness, and democracy—while mostly unobjectionable—seem themselves too much open to varying interpretation to serve as ground rules for an interpretive conversation.

removing it from public policy) is not good strategy, for such arguments cannot be expected to have force for all interlocutors. Instead, the advocates must attempt to phrase their arguments in such a way that they can appear relevant to all concerned participants. The difficulty of the abortion debate shows that the boundaries presumed here are not fixed, or even easy to fix, but its very difficulty suggests why restraint is called for. A commitment to the whole truth, a public policy of brutal honesty, will in a case such as this lead only to acrimony and violence. By the same token, restraint in public dialogue does not indicate deceit or failure to express my interests, but instead indicates that we are doing the only thing possible when faced with an irreconcilable difference on a moral issue. We are searching for whatever common commitments, whatever shared interests, we can find, and building our way of living together on their foundation.

How different, finally, are the two kinds of discourse being contrasted here? On one hand we have a kind of truth-seeking, sincere discourse that we might associate with some idealized or stringent notion of philosophy and science. Here, in Habermasian language, only the unforced force of the better argument holds sway. In the Habermasian model, however, this ideal of full disclosure is not limited to science or philosophy, but is thought to be central in claims about normative rightness as well. The truth is reached when a self-transparent consensus about norms is achieved, and social emancipation results from the purgation of all hidden motivations, concealed agendas, and forced compliance. Complete openness in talk will make us free, in other words; unconstrained dialogue is the only kind equal to the tasks of truth *and* justice.[43] On the other hand, we have a kind of discourse that is willing to sacrifice the goal of seeking the whole truth in favor of a more mundane but perhaps more pressing goal: living together in a way that allows different visions of the good life to be pursued. This political or pragmatic conversation is willing, like Ackerman's, to let truth become only an auxiliary value by (1) postponing any search for the whole (philosophical or moral) truth to some other time or place and (2) insisting only that the locutions advanced in the conversation be true, not that they be the whole truth.

Thus nondeceitful yet civil dialogue becomes the nexus of decision-making about society's basic structure. This is constrained dialogue, true, but the constraints can be justified by reference to pragmatic commitments we all

43. I have already, in Chapter 5, alluded to the criticism that Habermas's "unconstrained dialogue" is constrained in many ways, making the general commitment to strict openness difficult to maintain. See Walzer, "A Critique of Philosophical Conversation."

perforce share: the need to inhabit a common social space while maintaining as many of our diverse personal and group commitments as such commonality will allow. It is, moreover, dialogue constrained not by strangely external means imposed from without, but rather on the basis of social practices that we all, to the degree we are citizens of a single society, take for granted. Though the details of manners may vary greatly over distances in time and space, the general regard for the interests of others that defines the polite is something we can expect to operate in all social structures. At the very least, within a single society we can appeal to standards of civil behavior that, while not always or everywhere practiced, constitute a kind of normative backdrop to social interaction. One goal of articulating a theory of justice based on dialogue is to bring that sometimes obscured background into clear view. Civil speech may leave many true and sincere things unsaid. It will not, as a result, be itself deceitful. [44]

2. Tact: Keeping One's Distance

But how exactly, *as citizens*, do we begin not telling the whole truth? Consider the following parable:

> One cold winter's day, a number of porcupines huddled together quite closely in order through their mutual warmth to prevent themselves from being frozen. But they soon felt the effect of their quills on one another, which made them again move apart. Now when the need for warmth once more brought them together, the drawback of the quills was repeated so that they were tossed between two evils, until they had discovered the proper distance from which they could best tolerate one another. Thus the need for society which springs from the emptiness and monotony of people's lives, drives them together, but their many unpleasant and repulsive qualities and insufferable drawbacks once more drive them apart. The mean distance which they finally discover, and which enables them to endure being together, is politeness and good manners (*feine Sitte*).

44. Bruce Ackerman's version of a constrained dialogue also orders society by leaving many things unsaid. Ackerman's catch-phrase of liberalism—"I'm at least as good as you are"—is in some ways a model of the basis for civil discourse; but as we saw, Ackerman's restraints, and the maintenance of a right-over-good priority, are enforced rather than socialized or cultivated.

This story appears near the end of the Schopenhauer's *Parerga and Paralipomena*.[45] Schopenhauer is unenthusiastic about this "mean distance" of politeness, but I want to take seriously the *political* implications of the parable. The simple but important question is still this one: Is civility an adequate basis for the kind of normative conversation that dialogic theories of justice aim to provide, a conversation judging a society well-ordered or just? I believe civility can be so defended, insofar as it is seen as a species of *understanding* achieved in conversation. We must see this point in two distinct but related respects.[46]

First, the stance assumed by interlocutors in civil discourse can be understood as a two-sided orientation: (1) as a self-imposed restraint on one's own claims, as discussed above and (2) as a cultivated ability to discern the force of others' claims, as well as context boundaries and common social goals. As I shall suggest in a moment, Gadamer's investigation of interpretive "tact" in *Truth and Method* adds to the not-saying example an element of cultivation and education that serves to round out its pragmatic orientation. In other words, the other side of self-restraint is the willingness to listen to my interlocutors with the genuine intention of understanding them. Civility, understood thus two-sidedly, may finally be seen as the justified constraint on talk about justice.

Second, and perhaps less obvious, the practice of civil discourse may itself assume a central role in a just society. Schopenhauer's parable suggests a kind of "reflective equilibrium" reached between strong individual claims and the forcible constraints of living together with others; the porcupines find the distance between them that best allows pursuit of both common pragmatic and individual goals. That equilibrium can be understood as an ongoing interpretive achievement about society's basic structure and what constitutes its justification. On this view, civility is therefore *both* the disposition governing talk about justice *and* a central fact of which the notion of justice is an expression, namely well-ordered social interaction.[47]

45. See vol. 2 (1851), §396. This story is alluded to by Nietzsche in *The Birth of Tragedy*, where he expresses his contempt for journalistic aesthetic criticism; it is used in Germany, he says, to unite "a vain, distracted, selfish and moreover piteously unoriginal sociability whose character is suggested by Schopenhauer's parable of the porcupines" (§22).

46. As indicated in the previous chapter, there are good reasons for concluding that Habermas's presumption of *agreement* in discourse is a practically ineffective result, whereas the achievement of *understanding*, which preserves plurality, may be so effective. Such a claim involves a further argument, which I am likewise assuming, that pragmatic rather than rational basic commitments are all we can presume in political conversation.

47. "Politeness" does not, coincidentally, derive from the Latin root *polis*, city, source of the English "political." It comes, rather, from the Latin *politus*, to polish. My conclusion is nevertheless that we need to put the civility back into civil society.

What, then, is tact? Emily Post provides us with a definition that seems to owe more to not-saying than to anything else. "The tactful person," she says, "keeps his prejudices to himself"[48]—not bothering to add the obvious point, that this person need not *surrender* any of those prejudices in so doing. But Post is not in doubt as to tact's centrality, for she goes on to define "tactless-ness" as itself "the polite word for unfeeling stupidity."[49] As usual, this sort of discussion does not get us very far in providing tact with a clear characteriza-tion. Nor does Post's prejudice-suppressing model add anything much to what we already have under the heading of civility. In trying to mint the obverse of the coin, seeing tact as an *interpretive disposition* is more helpful.

Early in *Truth and Method*, Gadamer notes the usefulness of the concept of interpretive tact. In the task of reaching understanding, tact may effectively replace the rules of strict entailment or inference, which, if available at all in real talk, are only so in a fairly narrow band of it. "By 'tact,' " Gadamer says, "we understand a particular sensitivity and sensitiveness to situations, and how to behave in them, for which we cannot find any knowledge from general principles. Hence an essential part of tact is its inexplicitness and inexpressi-bility."[50] Where general principles cannot be found, we rely instead on a more intuitive, possibly even subconscious, sensitivity to situations. More than this, though, tact implies a restraint exercised in choosing the sort of speech-acts appropriate to a given situation. "One can say something tactfully," Gadamer continues, "but that will always mean that one passes over something tactfully and leaves it unsaid, and it is tactless to express what one can only pass over. But to pass over something does not mean to avert the gaze from something, but to watch it in such a way that rather than knock against it, one slips by it. Thus tact helps one to preserve distance, it avoids the offensive, the violation of the intimate sphere of the person."[51]

Central here, as our porcupines would attest, is the notion of *distance* and the role tact plays in preserving it between persons. A good part of Gadamer's concern is aesthetic, building on Alexander Baumgarten's well-known sugges-tion that between spectator and artwork there exists an optimal (and for

48. Emily Post, *Etiquette: The Blue Book of Social Usage* (New York: Funk & Wagnalls, 1922), p. 52.

49. Ibid., p. 55.

50. Gadamer, *Truth and Method*, p. 16. It is worth noting that the word "tact" comes from the same Latin roots, *tactus/tangere*, that give us such English words as "tactile" and "tangible." Tact thus refers to a keen sense of *touch*, a sense that knows not only how to touch but also how and when not to—discrimination, in short.

51. Ibid., pp. 16–17.

Baumgarten precisely calculable) distance for the work's appreciation. Gadamer advances our understanding of distance by taking tact seriously as a *general* virtue of interpretation, a trained receptivity to the otherness of the work, the past, another person, or beliefs other than my own. It is a function, he says, of aesthetic and historical education (*Bildung*), a sophisticated awareness of difference and therefore of what should and should not be said in encounters with the other. Without being able to give reasons or rules, tact makes sure distinctions and evaluations. Tact means, above all, "to distance oneself from oneself and from one's private purposes, . . . to look at these in the ways that others see them."[52]

The cultivated and tactful person, then, is someone able to see beyond personal interests in the service of something ever more other-regarding and general. Tact is a basic requirement of civil discourse, the kind of talk in which politeness appears as an *orientation toward understanding*. By talking together in this restrained and receptive manner, two civil people can expect to understand one another and reach ever more general conclusions concerning their shared social space. Their dialogue serves to establish common ground between them, a basis for yet further understanding. Indeed, ongoing dialogue of this kind may even be expected to establish a "common sense" among them. Gadamer refers, rather hopefully, to the strain of *sensus communis* thinking prominent in the work of Vico, Shaftesbury, and the Scottish "common-sense" philosophers of the eighteenth century. "Here," he says, "*sensus communis* obviously does not mean only that general faculty in all men, but the sense that founds community"; it is "the sense of the right and the general good that is to be found in all men, . . . a sense that is acquired through living in the community and is determined by its structures and aims."[53] Civility is here the indication that a person is engaged in the continuing project of smooth social interaction, performed not for the sake of show or even for particular social rewards (though these may well accrue to the person), but instead because civility is a mark of concrete commitment to the common goals of society, including in the first place a commitment to the social dialogue of legitimation.[54]

Well and good. But I take it that the parable of the porcupines is also meant to emphasize the *difficulty* of reconciling individual goals with the presence of

52. Ibid., p. 17.
53. Ibid., pp. 21–22.
54. For a more detailed discussion of this point in its historical context, see my examination of the Rev. William Robertson and the Moderate clerics of eighteenth-century Edinburgh, in "Politics and the Polite Society in the Scottish Enlightenment."

others whose goals might be contrary to mine.[55] How does restraint and sensitivity in dialogue provide a basis for ordering a pluralistic and perhaps deeply riven society, or for judging whether such a society could be called "just" or "well-ordered"? Let us agree that rules or norms of justice are assessed and justified, if anywhere, in some kind of social talk. Taking the rationality of politeness together with the kind of character I have been trying to show in civility, I believe we are justified in seeing civility as the governing virtue of a social conversation that is oriented toward understanding and the mediation of social conflict. Total agreement is not necessary in this conversation, nor even perhaps desirable, since vigorous dissent must be part of what we mean by a well-ordered society. It is true that the pragmatic aspect of civility will leave many things unsaid in the social conversation. But no one will be forced to say anything he or she does not believe, and no *external* constraints will be necessary. A cultivated sensitivity to context will play a large part in any sense of the civil, indicating when it is appropriate to use this argument, this turn of phrase, this image—and when not.

Civility, which is both rational and *sittlich*, therefore does two things in governing social interaction. First, it provides the awareness of what it means to play more than one language-game, and how to tell one from another.[56] This is reflected in our internalized relevance criteria, including the ability to say the things appropriate to a given context, and not to say others. But civility also

---

55. That is, more precisely, justice on a prevailing liberal model. The civility model of justice is structural and pragmatic, but, because it locates its restraints in an already rich feature of our form of life, it is more justifiable than many versions of this kind of justice. Schopenhauer, of course, meant his story as a negative one. The parable does not end at the identification of the "mean distance" with "politeness and good manners." "Whoever does not keep to this," Schopenhauer continues, "is told in England to 'keep his distance.' By virtue thereof, it is true that the need for mutual warmth will be only imperfectly satisfied, but, on the other hand, the prick of the quills will not be felt. Yet whoever has a great deal of internal warmth of his own will prefer to keep away from society in order to avoid giving or receiving trouble and annoyance." This last exception describes Nietzsche, if not Schopenhauer, well enough. The point from the vantage of political theory is that such exceptional individuals cannot be part of the general reckoning about society's basic structure.

56. Civility could amount, on this reading, to something like a theory of language-games, or at least an intuitive guide to which game is which. The failure by Wittgenstein and his followers to articulate such a theory is part of what drives Habermas's discussion of communicative action. This practice-based account of politeness may also remind us of Oakeshott's use of civility as an underlying norm of social interaction. See, e.g., Michael Oakeshott, "Political Education," in his *Rationalism in Politics and Other Essays* (London: Methuen, 1962), where he notes that the game of cricket preserves, beyond its stated rules, an implication of what is proper to the practice of playing it—an implication that spills into other spheres in the notion, now considered quaint, that something is "not cricket."

means something like what another kind of theory (and, incidentally, the unsystematic authors of the etiquette manuals) would call "respect for persons" or "taking difference seriously" or simply "tolerance." We might indeed be inclined to see civility as a matter of "respecting the rights of others," but persons who use rights-talk typically speak as if they were drawn from some ultimate metaphysical source, control of which lies somewhere beyond question; at base in many disputes about rights are conflicting groups, each convinced that *their* access to rights in the disputed sphere is more legitimate.[57] The idea of civil dialogue gives a better sense of the common, ongoing task that creating and maintaining a just society must be. Civility is something we learn, if we learn it at all, as we become competent users of language, fully functioning and communicating members of our society. It therefore comes neither from above nor from below; it is part of what it means to be communicatively rational—which is to say, rational together with others, never in a kind of monological Kantian sense. As we further saw, any strict codification of it will of necessity fail.

I said earlier that civility, as well as being the conversational orientation in which we achieve decisions about principles of justice, might also be an indication of what a just pluralistic society looks like. Schopenhauer's porcupines find the mean distance most effective in realizing shared and individual goals—that is politeness. In my terms, the impolite thus becomes the use of language or arguments demonstrably inappropriate or irrelevant to the given language-game or context: now your quills prick me, you are being offensive. (Demonstrating this inappropriateness or irrelevance, if necessary, then becomes part of the social discourse, but at a higher level.) Keeping our distance means leaving room for the realization of individual goals within a field of more general communicative interaction that does not impinge on them. Such a reading of our porcupines' civility understands the problem of justice as, once more, a question of ordering individual or group pursuit of goods within a field of social interaction that allows goods to be pursued and prevents interference by those pursuing other goods. This is the priority of right revisited, but now in communicative and interpretive terms that make the central liberal thesis more compelling than ever—and more responsive to the contextualizing challenges of liberalism's recent critics.

I have accepted throughout this discussion that the field of social interaction

---

57. An especially illuminating assessment of this tendency in contemporary political discourse is in Mary Ann Glendon's *Rights Talk: The Impoverishment of Political Discourse* (New York: The Free Press, 1991). See also Ian Shapiro, *The Evolution of Rights in Liberal Theory* (Cambridge: Cambridge University Press, 1986).

is ruled by dialogue; it is a place where persons of diverse aspiration meet to talk with one another and, when possible, reach some manner of collective decision. I have now suggested, in what I hope are convincing terms, that this talk can be fundamentally ordered by civility. Civility should now be understood in (broadly) hermeneutical terms: it is an orientation toward not agreement but understanding; it makes for a political conversation in which we try to sharpen our self-interpretation as common citizens of a society in need of justification. A civil orientation on the part of citizens finds the arguments and statements of every interlocutor worthy of some sensitive appreciation. Further, it restrains a talker from saying all that might be said at a given time.[58] And finally, because it both shapes political talk and functions (as a result) as a first virtue of citizens, civility is thus *both* the governing value of the legitimation conversation *and* one of the principles justified within that talk.

Civility is, in short, the basis of a truly civil society that pursues its collective goals only by allowing individuals and groups to pursue theirs. And a civil society in this sense is one, therefore, that has found its distance.

58. It is essential to distinguish kinds of pragmatic restraint in dialogue. Civility does not mean the preclusion of certain *issues* from the social conversation, but rather the preclusion of certain *justifications*. In this respect I follow Bruce Ackerman in believing that issue-preclusion would screen out too much. If it is uncivil for me to wonder why you earn twice as much as me for doing the same work, justice talk never gets going. What *will* be uncivil, on my view, is for you to refuse to reply to such a question with a reason open to assessment by all of us. See Ackerman, "Neutralities"; for an opposite view, see Stephen Holmes, "Gag Rules; or, The Politics of Omission," in Elster and Slagstad, *Constitutionalism and Democracy.*

7

The Limits of Civility

I. CIVILITY AND CENSORSHIP

"It's not enough to be against censorship or self-censorship," Susan Sontag said recently, advertising a public lecture. "In a free society, you must be for the right to offend."[1] I think this provocative statement, at once sane and subversive, captures the essence of objections to views, like mine, that justice demands some kind of self-restraint. Too often, it is suggested, political programs of self-restraint have the force of denying voice to the oppressed. When there is a situation of unequal political power, especially, the demand for civility may seem just another strategy of ideological continuance. As long as we can force subordinate groups to adopt the nostrums of "proper behavior," perhaps even making them complicit in adopting perversities like "good girl" or "good nigger" roles, the perpetuation of our system of dominance is assured. Armed with a theory of justice turning on propriety, we can

1. *The Globe and Mail* (Toronto), March 6, 1993. Sontag's lecture "The Writer's Freedom: Literature and Literacy" was delivered in Toronto on March 29, 1993.

always (can we not?) indulge the luxury of labeling threatening political behavior "uppity." It is no surprise that writers—particularly, in our society, feminist, native, and black writers—find theories of justice of this type objectionable. For them, such theories do no more than recapitulate the systems of oppression already in place, and do so in such a way that their true nature remains invisible. The arguments for restraint act both to maintain the status quo *and* to disguise the fact that the status quo is oppressive. They are ideological through and through, the white glove of politeness concealing power's iron fist.

Yet Sontag's statement, and its demand for a right to offend, goes deeper even than this judgment. It begins to indicate why the issue of civility is not as simple as it may at first appear. At the time I am writing this, there is a debate on many U.S. and Canadian college campuses about whether to adopt "speech codes" that would regulate discourse within the public spaces of universities—not the classrooms, which are presumed to have rules of conduct already inscribed, but rather the shared corridors and cafeterias and walks of the campus. These debates are complex, and frequently poorly thought out, but a number of points arise with vivid regularity. The first is a laudable concern about speech that is offensive, and a desire to do something about it. For many young people tasting true intellectual and political freedom for the first time, it is unconscionable that institutions allegedly devoted to the free exchange of ideas should be subject to the *ad hominem* slurs and recriminations typical of the outside world. So the second frequent commitment in these debates is to a wide-ranging tolerance of differences in race, gender, sexual orientation, age, physical ability, economic class, and even weight and height. There is then, third, usually a more-or-less convincing argument that the making of such statements is in some way linked to violence, oppression, or economic subservience. The speech codes that supporters want would ban any statements, jokes, or epithets that turn on pointing out, or making fun of, such differences. "Civil" speech will be defined as speech that is not offensive in this fashion, speech that is suitable to the shared public spaces of institutions of higher learning. Because criteria of offense are notoriously intractable, many advocates of these codes have settled on a procedure of enviable simplicity. Speech is offensive, they argue, if *someone* finds it so.

I hope I am not giving the impression, so easy to give here, that I am using caricature in a sly effort to make these arguments appear ridiculous. Many writers have done just that in commenting on the tyranny of tolerance contained within recent demands for civil speech on campus, and I have no desire either to join them or to rehearse their comments here.[2] My concern is, rather, to show why civility need not be understood the way the most stringent of these campus speech codes defines it—as a blanket ban on what anybody finds offensive. First and most obvious is that as a criterion of judgment, that one is too wide. As long as offense is a function of there being (or being imagined) just one person for whom a locution or epithet appears objectionable, it will be in practice impossible to say anything that is more than bland and innocuous. Less obvious, it may prove impossible even to *quote* views with which one is not in total agreement, say for the sake of argument or example or study. In the wake of tolerance, therefore, comes intolerance. Civil speech, here, is indeed nothing more than censorship. Gone is Sontag's right to offend; gone also is any right to speak one's mind and engage in debate about issues over which there is as yet no general agreement—and may not be, as in the case of those "essentially contested concepts" that lie at the heart of so much political, religious, and moral disagreement. Gone, in short, is intellectual life, the very goal for the sake of which the realm of speech regulation was first entered into. Gone also is any notion of a university shared community, arguably the only notion strong enough to provide motivation for adopting civility.[3]

It is usually replied, at this point, that these demon scenarios of campus censorship are overstated, and that the things speech codes of civility seek to ban are simply those most of us would agree are unacceptable: racial slurs,

2. But see, e.g., the collection of essays and comments entitled *Debating P.C.: The Controversy over Political Correctness on College Campuses*, ed. Paul Berman, (New York: Dell, 1992). See also Nat Hentoff, " 'Speech Codes' on the Campus and Problems of Free Speech," *Dissent* 38 (Fall 1991): 546–49, and Robert Hughes's bracing *Culture of Complaint: The Fraying of America* (New York: Oxford University Press, 1993). The debate concerning "political correctness," which occupied a good number of column inches in North American newspapers and magazines during 1990 and 1991, provided a good example of—among other things— just how the university impinges on the common social consciousness in the media. Under cover of ridiculing the warring factions of left-wing and right-wing students (and professors), a number of conservative writers furthered their own antitolerance agenda. I was myself implicated in this phenomenon. Having published a newspaper comment on the superficiality of current campus left-wing politics ("Enter the Campus Thought Police," *The Globe and Mail* (Toronto), April 15, 1991), I was unwillingly championed by several reactionary correspondents. With friends like these. . . .

3. It has been my concern to show that a desire for community, and its continuance, is what provides the motivation for accepting the strictures of civility in the justice conversation. A good argument of this kind concerning campus civility is made by Ivan Strenski in his "Recapturing the Values That Promote Civility on the Campuses," *Chronicle of Higher Education*, June 23, 1993, p. A36. Strenski's argument is that a loss of seriousness and sense of community, combined with student individualism concerning education and membership in subgroup communities *within* a university, contribute to the current incivilities and to the external speech-codes thought adequate to deal with them.

misogynist jokes, cheap shots of the kind that link physical inadequacy with stupidity or shortness with impotence. Perhaps. But what is lost in these demands is a division between form and content, and it is just here that civility can be recovered from those who would do it damage—both those in favor, like the campus activists, and those apparently against, like Sontag's right-to-offend followers. What I want to argue in this final chapter is that civility must concern, first and foremost, the manner in which a statement or argument is made, and not its content. Once we see this, we can indeed defend civility as a primary virtue of citizens.

I say "first and foremost" because, to be sure, the phrasing of arguments or statements in civil terms will, in fact, cause them to admit some content and not others. There will prove to be a *de facto* content limitation on speech—a limitation already present, for example, in the legal decisions to exempt hateful, inflammatory, or dangerously mischievous speech from general freedom-of-expression protections. Not all statements or points of view can be phrased in such a way as to make them part of a political discourse of legitimation, which is what the relevance criteria of justice as civility demand. But this limitation does not depend on any problematic criterion of individual offense, however, nor does it in principle rule out the possibility that I might say lots of offensive and politically challenging things. Civility is not to be understood as a set of gag rules, and it is not politically conservative by definition. Certainly many demands for public justification are going to be offensive to those who have interests to protect. But no society that wants justice can allow that feeling of offense to keep the demands off the public agenda.

Objections that civility is politically conservative need a more lengthy reply than just these assertions, however. The next section of this chapter deals with the two most powerful aspects of that objection. In replying to this objection, which is the most common charge against justice as civility, I show that civility is, so far from being an implicit defense of the status quo, a notion that is both critical and politically liberating. By clarifying the stakes and duties of citizenship, and by reemphasizing the idea of a vigorous public dialogue—the desire for which, we may recall, began this investigation and has driven it throughout—civility can produce citizens who are both critical and sensitive, both restrained and articulate. These will be citizens who are just. In pursuit, still, of these just citizens, I conclude the present chapter—and this study—by examining the pitfalls and prospects for what one writer has called the "democratization of politeness." Only by divorcing civility from its exclusive uses, making it not a fetish of the dominant classes (and thus a weapon of domination), but instead a common property, a tool of dialogic liberation, can we hope to go on, talking all the while, into a better social future.

II. SUPPORTING THE STATUS QUO

I have said before that I am aware of the oddness of this discussion. Placing civility in such close proximity to the serious subject of justice seems not just tendentious, but possibly perverse. We need to rehearse only a few of the reasons. The historical study of civility appears to show not a salutary political role for it but rather its central place in the tactics of oppression. Norbert Elias, in his widely influential history and sociology of European manners, has argued with some force that the standards of courtly behavior are, almost without exception, used to keep subordinates in their place and to keep questions of social legitimacy off the public agenda by denying the untutored a voice in which to articulate them.[4] That is one common view of civility. Equally common, though at odds with this first view, is the view that civility is merely an adjunct of slave morality: manners are meant to show deference, and this they certainly do—but at the expense of my real interests. Here civility is not an active tool of oppression but, on the contrary, an indication, in the oppressed, that they are in a subordinate position to those to whom deference is shown.

So, on the one hand, as Richard Duffy has noted, "the polished gentleman of sentimental fiction has so often served as the type of smooth and conscienceless depravity that urbanity of demeanour inspires distrust in ruder minds"; while, on the other hand, "the words etiquette and politeness connote weakness and timidity—their notion of a really polite man is a dancing master or a man milliner."[5] If civility is commonly considered an expression both of strength and of weakness, it might well be time to dispense with these common considerations and make of civility just what I have been suggesting: a

---

4. Norbert Elias, *The History of Manners*, vol. 1 of *The Civilizing Process*, trans. Edmund Jephcott (New York: Pantheon Books, 1978). Elias's general thesis is that restraints on mannerly behavior fluctuate with the degree of social anxiety about loss of control. Margaret Visser's survey of table manners, *The Rituals of Dinner* (Toronto: HarperCollins, 1991), suggests in a similar fashion that table manners, in all their variety, are universally founded on a desire to comport oneself nonviolently toward eating companions—that is, to have dinner with them rather than make dinner of them.

5. From "Manners and Morals," introduction to Emily Post's *Etiquette*, pp. xi, xii.

central feature of successful political dialogue. As one author notes, repeating and stretching one side of the common view: "Good manners were perhaps originally but an expression of submission from the weaker to the stronger, and many traces of their origin remain; but a spirit of kindliness and unselfishness born of a higher order of civilization permeates for the most part the code of politeness."[6]

That is good rhetoric, but I fear it is bad argument, and not many critics will be so easily convinced. I want to consider two fairly powerful objections that can be brought against the conception of justice as civility. They are rooted in a similar source, the worry that civility has no critical bite because it *leaves everything as it is.* It does this, the charge goes, in either of two ways.

First, civility as a principle of dialogic interaction may take for granted a certain problematic picture of the human agent, specifically that picture of the individual associated today with liberalism. You and I meet on a field of civil interaction, perhaps, but this is only possible once our individual interests and abilities have already been fixed conceptually in place. We can talk together civilly only on the basis of a shaky self-understanding of ourselves as collections of claims and counterclaims, loci of individual interests and desires, a self-understanding that is thought to predate the critical discussions. Civil dialogue may mediate our interaction, but it cannot perform the serious critical task of challenging the preunderstanding of human agents as individual collections of interests and desires. Nor, even in a case where we accept this model of the self, can it challenge the extension of the set of interests I take to be mine. Civility therefore leaves no room for putting into question this so-called liberal or "thin" view of the self or for any kind of *collective* decision-making about what our interests really are, or should be.

Justice as civility thus seems to lack critical bite because it hypostatizes a faulty conception of the individual.[7] It may also, however, be seen to hypostatize certain kinds of social relation. Civil dialogue comes into play, it might be objected, only when real power relations are no longer up for grabs—that is, when social roles are already highly defined and immune from routine questions about their legitimacy. It is no coincidence that civil behavior has in the past been the preserve of the rich and powerful; they are the ones who can afford to indulge in good manners, who do not have to be rude to get what

6. *Decorum,* p. 16.

7. I need not go into here the reasons for and against this objection that the liberal conception of self is faulty. But see, e.g., Sandel, *Liberalism and the Limits of Justice,* chap. 1. Since I take such criticisms to be at least partially effective in showing the limitations of the traditionally conceived liberal self, I cannot meet this charge against politeness by quarreling with their source.

they want. Civility is, on this view, *both* evidence of deep-running colonizing strategies, by which persons (or groups) in a superior position maintain that position vis-à-vis some other persons (or groups), *and* the medium by which such hierarchies are maintained. Linguistic colonization is both a reflection and an instance of the more general social and political colonization effected between persons or groups. It is an unlikely place to look for the dialogue that may achieve justice. The behavior of "polite society" merely reflects the preferences of a dominant social ideology, say that of the landed gentry or some other social elite.

These objections have a common source, and they merit a common reply. In offering it, I am helped by Habermas's notion of how the critique of ideology is carried on in dialogue. Take the second version of the objection as more serious. It seems plausible that politeness need not hypostatize the hierarchical domination of one person (or group) by another *if* all participants in the social dialogue are in fact oriented toward understanding. The well-mannered aristocrat condescending to his servant is not an instance of dialogic civility, I want to say, only a sham performance of good manners whose surface barely masks the structural domination in play. The aristocrat is not oriented to understanding the claims of the servant, and moreover his speech-act is not relevantly dialogic—it does not operate reciprocally, or preserve the interests of communication. Examples of a less extreme kind are easily imaginable, and not so obviously subject to criticism, but Habermas suggested that the *sincerity* of interlocutors is one feature of communicative action that will show itself forth in the dialogue oriented toward understanding.[8]

On my reading this sincerity is not, significantly, the sincerity of full disclosure that was separated from polite speech in the pragmatic analysis of civility—where, it will be remembered, civility was defended as a kind of *insincerity* about deep commitments known in advance to be controversial. The difference is that the insincere dialogue of civility can succeed in framing justice only if at least one—and probably only one—value is sincerely shared by the interlocutors, namely the value of finding solutions to political conflict in talk. If I am not sincerely open to the political legitimacy of your claims, our dialogue is distorted. I am acting instrumentally and not communicatively; no

---

8. This sincerity in assessing your claim and believing what I say to be true need not be the same as sincerity-as-full-disclosure. I suggested the latter could actually defeat the goals of civil dialogue. The distinction that is once more crucial here is between situations in which we share goals and those in which our goals diverge. I must sincerely share the goals of smooth social interaction; that does not imply that I must sincerely say all I believe. Indeed the second kind of sincerity will in many cases cut against the first.

amount of such talk can be expected to reach the pragmatic agreement neces-sary for justifying the norm under discussion.

This is an example, as Habermas has indicated, of the distortion to which communication is sometimes prey. Without needing to agree with Habermas's other commitments to full and frank discussion, we may still use the notion of therapeutic assessment of one's commitment to dialogue in this instance. If I am not committed to social dialogue in the minimal sense of thinking that through it, and only through it, will we as citizens succeed in forging a society for ourselves, civility will no longer work as a critical and effective principle of justice. This is what the objection attempts to motivate: civility will, in such a case, be a means of oppression or an expression of power, not a restrained and open orientation to understanding. Our dialogue will lack legitimate force unless and until we repair the faults of this instrumental superordinate-subordinate talk—we must find again the common goals, or shared orienta-tion, that can make our civil dialogue politically effective. So in order to continue our political project of living together well, we must first seek to solve our communicative difficulties.

The solution is something I mentioned briefly in the previous chapter. Though it may seem paradoxical, we must agree to be *sincerely insincere:* we may hide our deep disagreements about certain issues, but circumstance com-pels us to agree on one crucial point, that we must go on talking together if we are going to succeed in living together. The real force of this response is to get us to see that social life is, in some sense, a matter of finding our full interests only by talking to one another, not conceiving them as fixed beforehand and therefore as ammunition in a conflict among voices. Our word "politeness" comes from the Latin "to polish"; the hermeneutical reading of politeness I have been attempting to give shows why polishing one another, smoothing and reflecting one another in the rough-and-tumble of social interaction, is the real task not only of justice theory but also of politics itself.[9]

We may be inclined to doubt this. Yet the reply shows how civility, under-

9. Joseph Addison, one of the great eighteenth-century defenders of politeness, used this image of mutual polishing extensively in his writings on the social role of politeness. "In the *Spectator* essays," notes historian J.G.A. Pocock, "politeness becomes an active civilizing agent. By observa-tion, conversation, and cultivation, men and women are brought to an awareness of the needs and responses of others and how they appear in the eyes of others; this is not only the point at which politeness becomes a highly serious practical morality. . . . It is also the point at which Addison begins to comment on the structure of English society and the reconciliation of its diverse 'inter-ests.' " See "The Varieties of Whiggism from Exclusion to Reform: A History of Ideology and Discourse," part 3 of *Virtue, Commerce, and History* (Cambridge: Cambridge University Press, 1985), p. 236.

stood in dialogic terms, can fold itself reflectively into justificatory talk. When you suspect that my civility hides an instrumental end, that suspicion must itself become part of the discussion. And when it does, our conversation will not carry on just as before; we must be able to assess the sincerity of our commitments to the more general goal of justifying norms and procedures— for instance, of distribution—however insincere our speech-acts within that justification conversation itself may be. Power relations are therefore not allowed to lie *beneath* conversation, there to be obscured or covered up by strategically fine talk. Power relations are mediated in, and established by, talk itself. Talk governed by civility can criticize norms, rules of distribution, and patterns of interpersonal relation, precisely because, as dialogue, it can reflectively assess the conditions of its own possibility. It is true that talk may come to an end, and one or other of us may resort to violence. Then the matter is no longer a question of justifying a social organization we share, or desire to. In war, civility ceases to have any meaning. But so does dialogue more generally.

This reply also meets the concern about the picture of the individual. In civil dialogue of the political kind, interests are not conceived as fixed beforehand or irreducibly individual. Indeed, interests are precisely what the dialogue is there to identify and put into play. I come to know what I want at least partly as a collective matter of discussing it with you (and others), by testing arguments against one another, justifying the best available norms through the generation of workable compromises. There will remain things that I want to keep out of this process of testing and arguing, and you must give me that freedom—unless there are compelling reasons to do otherwise, reasons that show my private beliefs oppressing other citizens. Civility is the orientation in dialogue that best allows generation and justification of social norms. It is also, I suggested, the *result* of such a dialogue, since we cannot expect that universal norms will emerge from civil dialogue. Instead we can expect to find a mean distance, which will almost certainly vary with time and more discussion, such that each of us (or groups of us) can pursue particular aims without tyrannizing the others.

Of course, the ability to speak civilly will not be evenly distributed throughout a society, and that poses its own problems. We can meet some of these problems with institutions of advocacy or trusteeship that deal with nontalkers and bad talkers,[10] but these solutions are only stand-ins for the real solution:

---

10. Briefly, trusteeship would work to preserve and articulate the interests of those who cannot, or cannot yet, participate in political conversation. Advocacy would be a different sort of structure, whereby we find, appoint, or hire practiced talkers to help us phrase interests we could

that civility not be the preserve of one person or group, but the common social property of all citizens. It is only thus, after all, that civility will mark its advance over the excessive idealization of Habermas's rational reconstruction, which I suggested asked too much of citizens when they came to discuss political questions. Is the democratization of politeness a plausible goal?

III. THE DEMOCRATIZATION OF POLITENESS

In 1985, the columnist Judith Martin—better known as Miss Manners—gave a series of lectures at Harvard University that were intended, she said, to "solve the problem that baffled Mr. Jefferson."[11] "The problem with which Mr. Jefferson wrestled," Martin says in the published version of these lectures, "and which promptly defeated him, was how to adapt European systems of etiquette and protocol, based on court life and hereditary social class, in order to make them appropriate for a democracy."[12] Jefferson's main concern was to find appropriate manners for his new republic, but in my view the issue of making politeness democratic cuts more deeply than this (admittedly fascinating) project. The problem of how politeness can be "democratized" is in a sense the one that has been exercising my discussion, especially with regard to the objection sketched above and others of a similar mind. How can the structures of civility, apparently so deeply bound up with deference and restraint and aristocratic privilege, be put in the service of justice in a society of democratic interests? In concluding my consideration of this problem, I shall look at what

---

not ourselves phrase as well. We might consider animals, children, and madpeople as trustees; we might consider anyone, including ourselves, as needing an advocate. In short, I do not think the undeniable fact of variance in dialogic ability is a prima facie—and still less a crippling—objection to dialogic justice generally. Many structures of trusteeship and advocacy already function in this manner in our society, allowing us to bring into the conversation the interests of those who cannot speak for themselves.

  11. Judith Martin, *Common Courtesy* (New York: Atheneum, 1985). Though Martin is concerned chiefly with etiquette and manners suitable for a democracy, her discussion serves more widely (and with greater success) to draw out the importance of civility for a successful democratic society. But her concerns are less ambitious than mine, for she wants only to vindicate a democratically acceptable code of manners, while I want to place civility at the heart of democratic talk about justice. It should be noted that Martin has a cognate version of the distinction I made earlier between etiquette and manners. The former, she says, is "the codification of social ideals," "the rules of behavior," while the latter is "the social premises from which the[se] are derived" (pp. 7–9).

  12. Ibid., p. 3.

we can learn from Miss Manners's proposal to solve the problem that baffled Mr. Jefferson.

There is little doubt that Jefferson's infamous Pell Mell Etiquette system, which simply abolished all distinctions of rank, however based, was a failure. "This novel democratic etiquette," Martin comments, "succeeded chiefly in giving everyone equal offense."[13] Unfortunately, though Martin is possessed of a finer touch and reflects much more sophistication about current problems in discussing manners, her own solution is ultimately no more successful. It consists mainly in a proposal to make firmer the distinction between the "commercial" world and the "private" one, the former being that place in which hierarchy is allowed and necessary, and the latter being one where we can all enjoy the equality of consideration that is our democratic birthright.

Martin's reasoned defense of politeness is marshaled against powerful opposing forces, at least two of which are worth mentioning here. The first is what she labels "the California school" of openness in communication, with its belief in the value of "unwavering, literal truth."[14] This version of unconstrained communicative action works on the politically naive supposition that no difference between talkers is great enough that it cannot be overcome by prolonged and sincere talk (probably mediated by a therapist or facilitator). This openness thesis has, I argued earlier, the pernicious effect of trivializing difference and the organic structures we adopt for dealing with it. "Many forms of etiquette are employed exactly to disguise those antipathies that arise from irreconcilable differences, in order to prevent mayhem," Martin notes,[15] implying (correctly) that a pragmatic desire for social order may be the only commitment operative here, a commitment that embraces structures of negotiating difference, not overcoming it. "A standard set of manners," she continues later, "also disguises the fact, *inevitable and desirable in a democracy*, that not everyone agrees on every issue."[16]

Yet this fact of disagreement, the starting point of liberalism, leads to a second consideration that might seem to threaten a democratization of politeness from the opposite side. The plurality of goods, if fostered rather than overcome, can serve to diminish political equality. If not everyone can agree on a single answer to moral questions, lines will be drawn over controversial issues, lines used to show some people inside the consensus of right thinkers (and therefore equal)

13. Ibid., p. 7.
14. Ibid., pp. 12, 25.
15. Ibid., p. 12.
16. Ibid., p. 64 (emphasis added).

and some outside it (and therefore deluded or impossibly stubborn). If such exclusions are likely in political life—and they are—then any structures that reinforce difference, or at least refuse to challenge it, would seem to cut against equality. As we saw in the previous sections of this chapter, this is just what people have always said about politeness: it destroys equality, instead of fostering it. Martin admits, as she could not fail to do, that politeness can be and often is used on a principle of exclusion. "The best way to play In and Out is to keep devising new rules of etiquette so that only the nimble can keep up, as was done in the court of Louis XIV," she says. "This is the sort of thing that gives etiquette a bad name. It is a wonderful instrument of class warfare. . . . [But] those who conclude that manners are therefore merely an affectation of the rich to annoy the poor also overlook the fact that codes of manners are employed by classes going in different directions."[17] Her example of a viciously exclusive class is a good one: teenage street gangs. "The rationale that etiquette should be eschewed because it fosters inequality does not ring true in a society that openly admits to a feverish interest in the comparative status-conveying qualities of sneakers," she notes wryly.[18]

The central point here is that etiquette and manners are not, in themselves, the natural property of any particular class. They are in fact morally and politically neutral properties, employed by all classes, in their different ways, to reinforce exclusions. Seeing this ought to be enough to defeat the dismissive objections of those who feel equality threatened by structures of negotiating difference, including those of civility as I have been discussing it. The point is even more vivid if we recall the distinction between the details of manners and the virtue of civility as I interpreted it. Martin admits that there is a great deal of confusion these days about what good manners consist in—indeed, it is this confusion that provides her livelihood, answering the letters of the confused in a syndicated and widely read newspaper column. It is also arguable that manners are changing more rapidly today than ever before, the result of a highly accelerated social and cultural mobility. A middle-aged American man holding open a door to allow a woman to pass is doing only what his parents taught him was correct, and yet he is odds-on likely to be insulted for his trouble. These changes, whatever doubt they may cast on the usefulness of a given example of manners, do not succeed in throwing the value of civility itself into doubt. That value is succinctly expressed by Martin in a hope that reflects the liberal character of politeness, once democratized. "I hope," she says, "we can

17. Ibid., pp. 16–17.
18. Ibid., p. 19.

take it for granted that individual freedom must be tempered somewhat by the need for maintaining a harmonious society."[19] So stated, that hope is unfounded—we cannot take it *for granted*—but it is nevertheless open to rational vindication.

We can, then, observe two respects in which the democratization project is significant. First, it shows that the concern to make politeness pluralistic originated with, or nearly with, liberalism itself. Jefferson's central worry was how visiting persons ought to be addressed at state functions, but Martin draws out the wider implications: in a society based on a principle of equality, how do we justify the indispensable social lubrication of politeness, which appears to vindicate social differences? The second point, then, hints at the right approach to this issue—a solution lies in where the principle of equality is meant to apply. Martin is right to insist on a public/private separation, but she makes the wrong kind of emphasis: the crucial distinction is not commercial identity versus social identity, as she argues here, but instead political identity versus moral identity. We are relevantly equal in the *public* realm—that is, before the law, in political debate, in the voting booth. The private realm, where distinctions based on rank and wealth and worth will dominate, is whatever social space is governed by particular conceptions of the good: not just the private home or church, but all places where formal equality—the claim that one is (in Ackerman's words) at least as good as anyone else—is not necessary for social cohesion.[20] This line is not fixed or even necessarily clear, as I emphasized earlier; nevertheless, it remains crucial for a successful conversation concerning political legitimacy.

Armed with this emphasis, it is possible to argue, as I have done, that civility is not only justifiable socially within a democracy, but also is in fact a crucial aspect of democracy, an internalization of the priority of right that is reflected in civil restrained conversation and the openness of tact—what I have labeled civil dialogue. To engage in this dialogue is the right and responsibility of every citizen. More than this, the ability so to engage can be viewed as the criterion by which persons may begin to consider themselves citizens, for what

19. Ibid., p. 32.
20. Martin has a version of this claim to equality, expressed in the Ackermanian-sounding notion that I am "just as good as anyone else" (p. 54). But she argues, oddly in my view, that this claim should be honored in what she calls, somewhat paradoxically, the private social realm. Martin's central concern is that persons should act socially on their own merits, not as a reflection of what they do in the commercial world. She is led to this conclusion by the evident fact that social distinctions are too frequently a function of wealth. While sharing this concern, my wider political point must diverge from her reformation of social manners at this juncture.

else is this ability except the socialized recognition that person and citizen are not the same thing?

What results from the discussion of civility is perhaps not very different from certain extant conceptions of the liberal state. On my reading, however, liberalism is given the benefit of identifying a normative basis for dialogue that requires no external justification and instead finds restraint deeply embedded in our cultured selves. This embeddedness, and the *gebildet* character of civility generally, likewise possesses the advantage of giving us a richer picture of the self than that typically associated with liberalism. External constraints were thought to work on liberal selves largely because those selves were conceived as loci of preexisting interests who needed "merely" to regulate their conflicts in the search for individual gratification—or whatever level of such gratification is possible consistent with the claims of other individuals.

The richer picture of the self, and of political dialogue, I have been defending throughout this work begins with a different set of premises than unreconstructed liberalism. Though deep moral conflict is inevitable in a pluralistic society, that does not warrant the conclusion that no common goals can be discerned among a body of citizens. At the very least, insofar as they are citizens they will share the goal of wanting to have a well-ordered society. Achieving that goal is not simply a matter of generating consensus, or simple coexistence, out of a plurality of competing claims. It is instead a matter of engaging in a dialogue that is willingly restrained in the service of determining (some of) our interests collectively. It therefore already presumes a strong cluster of political virtues that will regulate any and all discussions. Disagreement may well persist in these discussions—we would all be amazed if it did not—but the thrust of civil dialogue is that social interest is, sometimes anyway, a fluid thing. And so it may be that only in talk with others will I come to see what my, and their, interests really are.

How is this possible? We may recall that in Chapter 3 I agreed with William Galston's argument that political argument was rarely, if ever, a matter of simply stating a position and then remaining silent about any subsequent disagreement. Argument, he said, is instead often a matter of using any means available in an attempt to change the other person's mind. I want to agree with this claim, but only if by "any means" we understand means that stop short of coercion, deception, or manipulation. These qualifications may seem no more than obvious, but they are at the heart of the notion of political relevance I introduced in the preceding chapter. Indeed, they are at the center of civility's ability to restrain (without yet saying anything about civility's ability to make people listen): a justification is acceptable if and only if it can be phrased in such a way as too avoid force, deceit, or manipulation. Galston, among others, objects to Ackerman's constraints of neutrality because he thinks they are preclusionary; he likewise objects to Larmore's more Habermasian liberalism because he thinks it too rationalistic. My belief is that civility avoids both of these limitations by in some sense combining the virtues of each. Civility as I interpret it still allows ample room for giving offense and for making politically unpopular or even dangerous claims. But these must be claims that are offered as part of an ongoing dialogue of justification—that is, open to further assessment by interlocutors. They must be *claims*, in short, and not simply abuse or insult. Or, if one is moved to perform a political act that is not itself a claim, it must be something in principle open to translation into politically relevant claims.

James Fishkin—who speaks of the goal of an "unmanipulated dialogue" of "participatory civility" in a "self-reflective society"—gives a vivid example of the last possibility. "We might," he says, "imagine a countercultural theatrical troupe that performs a variety of acts in public considered disgusting by mainstream society—and that articulates a political message according to which those apparently disgusting acts can be considered symbolic contributions to political dialogue."[21] The key point here is that the message, though expressive and not rational in form, remains *in principle* capable of entering a public debate as a claim. (He mentions that the troupe members may hand out long and boring pamphlets explaining how.) It is therefore open to the base-level restrictions—foremost, considering its effect on others—that motivate civility. It is also something that, as a claim, must be open to reply. The power of anger and the shocking are not things we should readily surrender in political dialogue (consider the abortion posters, with their strong symbolic messages—dead fetuses, bloody coat hangers). We can only demand that, for the sake of the dialogue, expressive shocks and symbolic actions remain always in principle translatable into political claims. "We should aspire," Fishkin says, correctly, "to a culture of participatory civility—a political culture where people learn to listen and respond on the merits in an atmosphere of mutual respect."[22]

Respect is the sort of motherhood value that few reasonable people would allow themselves to challenge. It might be to the point to address why I believe civility and mutual respect are not coextensive values, and thus to distinguish

---

21. James Fishkin, *The Dialogue of Justice*, p. 191. Fishkin's use of civility as a central pillar of the "conditions of activist liberty" (see part 3 of his book) parallels my arguments for civility as a combination of openness and restraint.

22. Ibid., p. 190.

my view from Fishkin's, and Larmore's, while noting that these two "reconstructed" liberals are close in orientation to my own commitments. Fishkin's notion of mutual respect combines, in a way similar to Larmore's, with a grounding notion of rationality to form the basis of a legitimate political dialogue. Like Larmore, too, it is the "self-reflective" character of this rationality, and not its reference to some metaphysically fixed external standpoint, that gives it critical purchase in actual political debates. Though the continental debts are less obvious than in Larmore's explicit discussion, Fishkin's concept of rationality is significantly Habermasian. Combining a basic commitment to rational vindication of claims with a practical orientation to listen and participate, both theories are promising revisions of liberal aspiration. Indeed, the critical aspects of these theories—Larmore's reintroduction of "moral complexity" and Fishkin's circumvention of the conflicting values of contemporary liberalism[23]—are timely and valuable correctives on the arid and seemingly endless debates that have recently afflicted North American political philosophy. (Those debates that led John Gray to the denunciation of contemporary political philosophy that began my discussion.) They bring ethical substance back into the theoretical picture without surrendering the ability to address the basic normative questions that motivate political theory in the first place.

Yet there are limitations. Fishkin, though he speaks eloquently of respect and civility, does not sufficiently specify the dialogue of justice. His account of interests and their civil articulation is one-sided, failing as it does to account for the sincere expression of false consciousness. And finally, his theory fails meaningfully to problematize the public/private distinction, leaving it a controversial but presumed feature of political debate. It was in response to the first difficulty—a difficulty that was obvious well before Fishkin's contribution to the recent debates, and indeed thematized in this book from its very beginnings in the hermeneutical turn—that I introduced some historical and cultural substance to the category of civility. For it is this actual interpretive task that now confronts us: what is civil dialogue? I labor under no illusions that the characterization of civility defended in this book is complete, or even fully convincing in its present form. What I do claim is that only by clarifying the contours of civility itself will we be in any better position to say what just talking will be for us. In particular, we can do that best by conceiving civility as a *virtue*, a character trait cultivated and practiced by citizens; in other words, a

---

23. See part 2 of *The Dialogue of Justice*, in particular "Criteria for an Acceptable Theory" and "Political Thought Experiments." Fishkin's deft, critical discussion of Rawls, Ackerman, and Nozick amply demonstrates the structural limitations of consent-based theories of political justification.

deep feature of our ethical life susceptible to variation but always present, learned by imitation yet clarified by theory, acquired by way of habituation but defended philosophically.

Viewing civility thus also serves to distinguish it from the more obvious, and more freqently defended, liberal virtue of respect. It is true that civility as I characterize it is related to mutual respect, but there is a crucial difference: genuine respect is too strong a value to demand of a justice dialogue in a deeply pluralistic society. The relative advantage of civility is that it does not ask participants to do anything more than treat political interlocutors *as if* they were worthy of respect and understanding, keeping their private thoughts to themselves. It might be replied that mutual respect, as conceived and defended by Larmore for example, is really no more than this. The version of respect championed by liberals is typically Kantian respect for persons, of course, and not the strong and invidious quality of respect that entails relative differences in virtue or worth. But even this Kantian notion of respect, which grants all persons an intrinsic worth based on (some form of) rational agency, seems to ask too much of us when we consider the vastness of moral differences. We need not grant interlocutors any metaphysical status in order to speak to them civilly; we need only see them as members, actual or prospective, of a social organization to which we too belong. I do not want to overstate the difference here: many liberals defend respect in contingent and socialized terms that move them closer to what I regard as the forms and orientation of civility. And certainly civility as I have defined and defended it does involve regard for the other talker. But it is a regard that falls some way short of moral approval or metaphysical ascriptions—and is, in my view, the more defensible for doing so.

Philosophical liberals, especially ones chastened by the impasse of recent liberal theory, also seem too inclined, like Habermas, to invest their normative hopes in the structures of rationality. We cannot abandon altogether the idea that debate, to be considered normative, must depend on the making and testing of criticizable validity claims. But we do well to remember, as Galston and Warnke do, that the bare structures of rational argumentation are rarely, if ever, practically effective in guiding discussion of vexed political questions. Whether or not we can reach a final account of the rational anticipation of civility or politeness in social speech-action, it is a more fruitful place to concentrate our hopes of specifying a justice conversation that is both real and normative—a conversation that is recognizably ours, carried on by citizens with real foibles and limitations but also with real virtues and desires.

A society guided by civility will allow a political debate that is vigorous, even fractious, while retaining a goal we should all consider binding: the possibility that minds can be changed. And if our political dialogue is in fact as lively, as challenging, as this, we can finally vindicate the hope held out by the dialogic model. I come to know who I am, and what I care about, in large measure as a result of talking with my fellow citizens. This will prove an unsettling conclusion, certainly, but it is also an enormously liberating one. Guided by a civility that forces me, no less than my interlocutors, to make claims available for public assessment, I enter into the public domain as someone in search of my own, and my society's, identity. I need not, and often cannot, put all my present beliefs and interests into play. Yet when I argue, I argue to convince—remaining ever aware that others have arguments that move them and that may well come to have some hold on me too. It is for these reasons that I have emphasized throughout this discussion the double-sided character of civility, its nature as both listening and restraining. I can hear what may move me only if I am silent long enough to listen. My silence is not passivity, it is active participation in a social project that is at once personal and political. I do not in silence surrender my ability to make claims; I simply purchase that ability at the price of a willingness to listen to the claims of others.

A civil model of dialogic justice builds on other models of just talking by taking from them a collection of defensible points and molding these into a new model, a model deployed under the rubric of a rather surprising moral category. By thus avoiding the flaws of these other models, and yet retaining their strengths, we achieve a worthy goal—the most defensible answer to the question "What is just talking?" Such an answer is rich and interpretive; it is at the same time realistic about social conflict, the limitations of justice, and our own compelling interest in a vigorous and meaningful social discourse— our interest, that is, in political community. It tells us that justice, so far from being an insurmountable social task, is within the reach of any body of citizens; yet it also possesses enough critical bite to show that being a citizen is hard and serious work.

There has been an inevitable degree of abstraction in this discussion, and the reader may be forgiven for wondering just where civility should be put into practice. I have used the words "public" and "political" almost interchangeably in suggesting where civility should have a hold over us, but that seems to cover a lot. My conviction here—and it is no more than a conviction, for I have no compelling argument to back it up—is that public discourse, a discourse ruled by civility, should be found in many places in a truly just society. Perhaps most obvious is that it will govern constitutional and juridical structures concerned with articulating the principles or norms according to which a society will function. Here codified versions of civility already have a hold, in the form of rules of order or legal procedure. But since most of us have no access to the forums where such principles or norms are formally discussed, we cannot confine political discourse to these rarefied realms. Instead we should pursue our vigorous public debate in as many places as possible—remembering always that some arguments from private conviction carry no force when brought to the attention of others, and may even offend. It may well be that these lower-level debates will have to appeal to the higher-level structures for adjudication—in appeal-court decisions and elections, for example—and may sometimes even be backed by state-sanctioned force. But the essence of a well-ordered society is that its citizens are engaged in an ongoing conversation—a conversation taking place on street corners and talk shows, in newspaper columns and lecture theaters, in town-hall meetings and candidates' debates—that addresses their deep concerns about social life, the shared problems and issues of cohabitation. Only this conversation will make it possible for them to live together well.

Of course my argument for civility as the first virtue of citizens should not be conceived as a naive plea to be nice, to just sit down and *talk* about things. "Pious calls for civility will fall on deaf ears unless there are compelling reasons to be civil," Ivan Strenski recently noted, quite correctly. "And imposing civility with speech codes from on high or legal action from the aggrieved may punish certain flagrantly uncivil behavior, but will never foster long-term sincere civility."[24] In working through the prospects of a dialogic theory of justice, I have, on the one hand, identified at least some of the compelling reasons why we need a civil public discourse. I have also, on the other hand, avoided the contradiction of imposing civility through force or threat of punishment. The only meaningful threat of punishment here is this general one: when civility fails, we all lose, because as citizens we lose the possibility of justice, and of a genuinely shared political community. Civility is, according to certain conceptions of the good, too little to ask of our public debates about justice. And yet, considering the difficult task of framing a just society in a world of pluralistic interests and conceptions of the good life, I nevertheless believe it is enough.

And now, having said all this, I will finally fall silent and invite polite comment.

---

24. Strenksi's argument is made in the context of campus incivilities and the speech codes lately constructed to deal with them; see his "Recapturing the Values That Promote Civility on the Campuses."

Bibliography

English translations of foreign-language texts have been used, where available. In general, the most readily available sources and editions for variously reprinted works have been relied on.

Ackerman, Bruce. "Neutralities." In *Liberalism and the Good*, ed. R. Bruce Douglas, Gerald R. Mara, and Henry S. Richardson. New York: Routledge, 1990.
———. "Why Dialogue?" *Journal of Philosophy* 86 (1989): 5–22.
———. "What Is Neutral About Neutrality?" *Ethics* 93 (1983): 372–90.
———. *Social Justice in the Liberal State*. New Haven: Yale University Press, 1980.
Ackerman, Felicia. "A Man by Nothing Is so Well Betrayed as by His Manners? Politeness as a Virtue." *Midwest Studies in Philosophy* 13 (1988): 250–58.
Alexy, Robert. "Probleme der Diskurstheorie." *Zeitschrift für Philosophische Forschung* 43 (1989): 81–93.
———. "Eine Theorie des Praktischen Diskurses." In *Normenbegründung, Normendurchsetzung*, ed. W. Oelmüller. Paderborn: Schöningh, 1978.
Apel, Karl-Otto. *Understanding and Explanation: A Transcendental-Pragmatic Perspective*. Translated by Georgia Warnke. Cambridge, Mass.: MIT Press, 1984.
———. *Kommunikation und Reflexion: Zur Diskussion der Tranzendentalpragmatik*. Frankfurt: Suhrkamp, 1982.
———. *Dialog als Methode*. Göttingen: Vandenhoeck & Ruprecht, 1972.
Austin, J. L. *Philosophical Papers*. Oxford: Clarendon Press, 1979.
———. *How to Do Things with Words*. Oxford: Oxford University Press, 1962.
Barber, Benjamin R. "Unconstrained Conversation: A Play on Words, Neutral and Otherwise." *Ethics* 93 (1983): 330–47.
Beatty, Joseph. "'Communicative Competence' and the Skeptic." *Philosophy and Social Criticism* 6 (1979): 267–88.
Becker, Lawrence. "The Finality of Moral Judgments: A Reply to Mrs. Foot." *Philosophical Review* 83 (1973): 364–70.
Bencivenga, Ermanno. "Rorty and I." *Philosophical Forum* 24 (1993): 307–18.
Benhabib, Seyla. "In the Shadow of Aristotle and Hegel: Communicative Ethics and Current Controversies in Practical Philosophy." *Philosophical Forum* 21 (1989–90): 1–31.
———. "Liberal Dialogue vs. a Critical Theory of Discursive Legitimation." In *Liberal-

ism and the Moral Life, ed. Nancy Rosenblum. Cambridge, Mass.: Harvard
    University Press, 1989.

———. *Critique, Norm, and Utopia: A Study of the Foundations of Critical Theory.*
    New York: Columbia University Press, 1986.

Benhabib, Seyla, and Fred Dallmyer, eds. *The Communicative Ethics Controversy.*
    Cambridge, Mass.: MIT Press, 1990.

Berman, Paul, ed. *Debating P.C.: The Controversy over Political Correctness on Col-
    lege Campuses.* New York: Dell, 1992.

Bernstein, Richard J. "One Step Forward, Two Steps Back: Richard Rorty on Liberal
    Democracy and Philosophy." *Political Theory* 15 (1987): 538–63.

———. "From Hermeneutics to Praxis." In *Hermeneutics and Modern Philosophy,* ed.
    Brice Wachterhauser. Albany: SUNY Press, 1986.

———. "What Is the Difference That Makes a Difference? Gadamer, Habermas, and
    Rorty." In *Hermeneutics and Modern Philosophy,* ed. Brice Wachterhauser.
    Albany: SUNY Press, 1986.

———. *Beyond Objectivism and Relativism: Science, Hermeneutics, and Praxis.* Phila-
    delphia: University of Pennsylvania Press, 1983.

———. "Philosophy in the Conversation of Mankind." *Review of Metaphysics* 33
    (1980): 745–76.

———, ed. *Habermas and Modernity.* Cambridge, Mass.: MIT Press, 1985.

Bloom, Allan. "Justice: John Rawls vs. the Tradition of Political Philosophy." *American
    Political Science Review* 69 (1975): 648–62.

Brown, Penelope, and Stephen Levinson. *Politeness: Some Universals in Language
    Usage.* New York: Cambridge University Press, 1987.

———. "Universals in Language Usage: Politeness Phenomena." In *Questions and
    Politeness: Strategies in Social Interaction,* ed. Esther N. Goody. New York:
    Cambridge University Press, 1978.

Carter, Stephen. *The Culture of Disbelief: How American Law and Politics Trivialize
    Religious Devotion.* New York: Basic Books, 1993.

Civility and Citizenship in Liberal Democratic Societies. New York: Paragon House, 1992.

Clarke, Thompson. "The Legacy of Skepticism." *Journal of Philosophy* 69 (1972):
    754–69.

Comay, Rebecca. "Interrupting the Conversation: Notes on Rorty." *Telos* 69 (1986):
    83–98.

Connolly, William. "Mirror of America." *Raritan* 3 (1983): 124–35.

Daniels, Norman. "Reflective Equilibrium and Archimedean Points." *Canadian Jour-
    nal of Philosophy* 10 (1980): 83–103.

———. "Wide Reflective Equilibrium and Theory Acceptance in Ethics." *Journal of
    Philosophy* 76 (1979): 255–82.

———, ed. *Reading Rawls.* New York: Basic Books, 1974.

Davidson, Donald. "A Coherence Theory of Truth and Knowledge." In *Truth and
    Intepretation: Perspectives on the Philosophy of Donald Davidson,* ed. Ernest
    LePore. Oxford: Basil Blackwell, 1986.

———. "On the Very Idea of a Conceptual Scheme." In *Inquiries into Truth and
    Meaning.* New York: Oxford University Press, 1986.

———. "Communication and Convention." *Synthese* 59 (1984): 3–18.

Decorum: A Practical Treatise on Etiquette and Dress of the Best American Society.
    New York: Union Publishing, 1882.

Della Casa, Giovanni. *Galateo; or, The Book of Manners.* Translated by R. S. Pine-
    Coffin. Harmondsworth: Penguin Books, 1958.

Derrida, Jacques. *Limited Inc.* Translated by Samuel Weber. Evanston, Ill.: Northwestern University Press, 1988.

Douglas, R. Bruce, Gerald R. Mara, and Henry S. Richardson, eds. *Liberalism and the Good.* New York: Routledge, 1990.

Dustin, Christopher. "Ethics and the Possibility of Objectivity." Ph.D. dissertation, Yale University, 1991.

Dworkin, Ronald. *Law's Empire.* Cambridge, Mass.: Harvard University Press, 1986.

———. *A Matter of Principle.* Cambridge, Mass.: Harvard University Press, 1985.

———. *Taking Rights Seriously.* Cambridge, Mass.: Harvard University Press, 1978.

Elias, Norbert. *The History of Manners.* Volume 1 of *The Civilizing Process.* Translated by Edmund Jephcott. New York: Pantheon Books, 1978.

Elster, Jon, and Rune Slagstad, eds. *Constitutionalism and Democracy.* Cambridge: Cambridge University Press, 1988.

Fish, Stanley. "Play of Surfaces: Theory and the Law." In *Legal Hermeneutics: History, Theory, and Practice,* ed. Gregory Leyh. Berkeley and Los Angeles: University of California Press, 1992.

Fishkin, James S. *The Dialogue of Justice.* New Haven: Yale University Press, 1992.

———. "Can There Be a Neutral Theory of Justice?" *Ethics* 93 (1983): 348–56.

Fisk, Milton. "The Instability of Pragmatism." *New Literary History* 17 (1985): 23–30.

Flathman, Richard E. *Willful Liberalism: Voluntarism and Individuality in Political Theory and Practice.* Ithaca: Cornell University Press, 1992.

———. "Egalitarian Blood and Skeptical Turnips." *Ethics* 93 (1983): 357–66.

Fleicher, Josef, ed. *Contemporary Hermeneutics.* London: Routledge & Kegan Paul, 1980.

Foot, Philippa. *Virtues and Vices.* Berkeley and Los Angeles: University of California Press, 1978.

———. "Morality as a System of Hypothetical Imperatives." *Philosophical Review* 81 (1972): 305–16.

Forrester, James. *The Polite Philosopher; or, An Essay on that Art which makes a man happy in himself, and agreeable to others.* Edinburgh: Robert Freebairn, 1734.

Fraser, Bruce. "Perspectives on Politeness." *Journal of Pragmatics* 14 (1990): 219–36.

Fraser, Bruce, and William Nolen. "The Association of Deference with Linguistic Form." *International Journal of the Sociology of Language* 27 (1981): 93–109.

Fraser, Nancy. *Unruly Practices: Power, Discourse, and Gender in Contemporary Theory.* Minneapolis: University of Minnesota Press, 1989.

———. "Towards a Discourse Ethics of Solidarity." *Praxis International* 5 (1986): 425–29.

Gadamer, Hans-Georg. "On the Scope and Function of Hermeneutic Reflection." In *Hermeneutics and Modern Philosophy,* ed. Brice Wachterhauser. Albany: SUNY Press, 1986.

———. *Truth and Method.* Second edition. Translated by Garrett Barden and John Cumming. New York: Crossroad, 1975.

Gaita, Raimond. "Virtues, Human Good, and the Unity of a Life." *Inquiry* 26 (1984): 407–24.

Galston, William. *Liberal Purposes: Goods, Virtues, and Diversity in the Liberal State.* New York: Columbia University Press, 1991.

———. "Defending Liberalism." *American Political Science Review* 76 (1982): 621–29.

———. *Justice and the Human Good.* Chicago: University of Chicago Press, 1980.

Geuss, Raymond. *The Idea of a Critical Theory: Habermas and the Frankfurt School.* Cambridge: Cambridge University Press, 1981.

Giddens, Anthony. "Reason Without Revolution? Habermas's *Theorie des kommuni-kativen Handelns*." In *Habermas and Modernity*, ed. Richard Bernstein. Cambridge, Mass.: MIT Press, 1985.

Gilligan, Carol. *In a Different Voice*. Cambridge, Mass.: Harvard University Press, 1982.

Glendon, Mary Ann. *Rights Talk: The Impoverishment of American Political Discourse*. New York: The Free Press, 1991.

Goffman, Erving. *Relations in Public*. Harmondsworth: Penguin Books, 1971.

———. *Interaction Ritual: Essays on Face-to-Face Behavior*. New York: Anchor, 1967.

Grant, George. *English-Speaking Justice*. Sackville, N.B.: Mount Allison University Press, 1974.

Gray, John. "Against the New Liberalism: Rawls, Dworkin, and the Emptying of Political Life." *Times Literary Supplement*, July 3, 1992, pp. 13–15.

Green, Leslie. *The Authority of the State*. Oxford: Clarendon Press, 1988.

Grice, H. P. "Logic and Conversation." In *The Logic of Grammar*, ed. Donald Davidson and Gilbert Harman. Encino and Belmont, Calif.: Dickenson, 1975.

Gutmann, Amy. *Liberal Equality*. Cambridge: Cambridge University Press, 1980.

Gutmann, Amy, and Dennis Thompson. "Moral Conflict and Political Consensus." *Ethics* 101 (1990): 64–88. Reprinted with revisions in chapter 7 of *Liberalism and the Good*, ed. R. Bruce Douglas, Gerald R. Mara, and Henry S. Richardson. New York: Routledge, 1990.

Habermas, Jürgen. *Justification and Application: Remarks on Discourse Ethics*. Translated by Ciaran P. Cronin. Cambridge, Mass.: MIT Press, 1993.

———. *Moral Consciousness and Communicative Action*. Translated by Christian Lenhardt and Shierry Weber Nicholsen. Cambridge, Mass.: MIT Press, 1990.

———. *The Philosophical Discourse of Modernity: Twelve Lectures*. Translated by Frederick G. Lawrence. Cambridge, Mass.: MIT Press, 1990.

———. "Justice and Solidarity: On the Discussion Concerning Stage 6." *Philosophical Forum* 21 (1989–90): 32–52.

———. *The Theory of Communicative Action*. Vol. 1, *Reason and the Rationalization of Society*, and Vol. 2, *Lifeworld and System: A Critique of Functionalist Reason*. Translated by Thomas McCarthy. Boston: Beacon Press, 1984 and 1987.

———. "Habermas: Questions and Counter-Questions." *Praxis International* 4 (1984): 229–49.

———. "Modernity Versus Postmodernity." *New German Critique* 22 (1981): 3–14.

———. *Communication and the Evolution of Society*. Translated by Thomas McCarthy. Boston: Beacon Press, 1979.

———. "On Systematically Distorted Communication." *Inquiry* 13 (1970): 205–18.

———. "A Review of Gadamer's *Truth and Method*." In *Zur Logik der Sozialwissenschaften*. Frankfurt am Main: Suhrkamp, 1970.

———. "Towards a Theory of Communicative Competence." *Inquiry* 13 (1970): 360–76.

Hampshire, Stuart. *Innocence and Experience*. Cambridge, Mass.: Harvard University Press, 1989.

Heidegger, Martin. *Being and Time*. Translated by John Macquarrie and Edward Robinson. New York: Harper & Row, 1962.

Heller, Agnes. *Beyond Justice*. New York: Basil Blackwell, 1987.

Hentoff, Nat. " 'Speech Codes' on the Campus and Problems of Free Speech." *Dissent* 38 (1991): 546–49.

Holmes, Stephen. "Gag Rules; or, The Politics of Omission." In *Constitutionalism and Democracy*, ed. Jon Elster and Rune Slagstad. Cambridge: Cambridge University Press, 1988.

Honderich, Ted, ed. *Morality and Objectivity*. London: Routledge & Kegan Paul, 1984.

Horkheimer, Max, and Theodor W. Adorno. *Dialectic of Enlightenment*. Translated by John Cumming. New York: Continuum, 1993.

Hughes, Robert. *Culture of Complaint: The Fraying of America*. New York: Oxford University Press, 1993.

Hume, David. *A Treatise of Human Nature*. London, 1739–40.

Hurley, S. L. "Objectivity and Disagreement." In *Morality and Objectivity*, ed. Ted Honderich. London: Routledge & Kegan Paul, 1984.

Ingram, David. "The Possibility of a Communication Ethic Reconsidered." *Man and World* 15 (1982): 149–61.

Kasper, Gabriele. "Linguistic Politeness." *Journal of Pragmatics* 14 (1990): 193–218.

Kelly, Michael. "MacIntyre, Habermas, and Philosophical Ethics." *Philosophical Forum* 21 (1989–90): 70–93.

Kingwell, Mark. "The Plain Truth About Common Sense: Skepticism, Metaphysics, and Irony." *Journal of Speculative Philosophy* (forthcoming).

———. "Let's Ask Again: Is Law Like Literature?" *Yale Journal of Law and the Humanities* 6 (1994): 317–52.

———. "Madpeople and Ideologues: An Issue for Dialogic Justice Theory." *International Philosophical Quarterly* 34 (1994): 59–73.

———. "The Polite Citizen; or, Justice as Civil Discourse." *Philosophical Forum* 25 (1994): 241–66.

———. "Interpretation, Dialogue, and the Just Citizen." *Philosophy and Social Criticism* 19 (1993): 115–44.

———. "Is It Rational to Be Polite?" *Journal of Philosophy* 90 (1993): 387–404.

———. "Politics and the Polite Society in the Scottish Enlightenment." *Historical Reflections/Réflexions Historique* 19 (1993): 363–87.

Kohlberg, Lawrence. *Essays on Moral Development*. Vol. 1, *The Philosophy of Moral Development*—Moral Stages and the Idea of Justice; Vol. 2, *The Psychology of Moral Development*—The Nature and Validity of Moral Stages; Vol. 3, *Education and Moral Development*—Moral Stages and Practice. New York: Harper & Row, 1981–84.

Kuhn, Thomas. *The Structure of Scientific Revolutions*. Chicago: University of Chicago Press, 1962.

Kymlicka, Will. *Liberalism, Community, and Culture*. New York: Oxford University Press, 1989.

Larmore, Charles. "Political Liberalism." *Political Theory* 18 (1990): 339–60.

———. "Alasdair MacIntyre: *Whose Justice? Which Rationality?*" (review). *Journal of Philosophy* 86 (1989): 437–41.

———. *Patterns of Moral Complexity*. Cambridge: Cambridge University Press, 1987.

———. "Tradition, Objectivity, and Hermeneutics." In *Hermeneutics and Modern Philosophy*, ed. Brice Wachterhauser. Albany: SUNY Press, 1986.

Lear, Jonathan. *Love and Its Place in Nature*. New York: Farrar, Straus & Giroux, 1990.

———. "Ethics, Mathematics, and Relativism." In *Essays on Moral Realism*, ed. Geoffrey Sayre-McCord. Ithaca: Cornell University Press, 1988.

———. "The Disappearing 'We.'" *Proceedings of the Aristotelean Society*, suppl. vol., 1984.

Leech, Geoffrey. *Principles of Pragmatics*. London: Longman, 1983.

Lentricchia, Frank. *Criticism and Social Change*. Chicago: University of Chicago Press, 1983.

———. "Rorty's Cultural Conversation." *Raritan* 3 (1983): 136–41.

Leyh, Gregory, ed. *Legal Hermeneutics: History, Theory, and Practice*. Berkeley and Los Angeles: University of California Press, 1992.

Lyotard, Jean-François. *The Postmodern Condition: A Report on Knowledge*. Translated by Geoff Bennington and Brian Massumi. Minneapolis: University of Minnesota Press, 1984.

Lyotard, Jean-François, and Jean-Loup Thébaud. *Just Gaming*. Translated by Wlad Godzich. Minneapolis: University of Minnesota Press, 1985.

MacIntyre, Alasdair. *Some Rival Versions of Moral Enquiry: Encyclopaedias, Genealogies, and Traditions*. Notre Dame, Ind.: University of Notre Dame Press, 1990.

———. *Whose Justice? Which Rationality?* Notre Dame, Ind.: University of Notre Dame Press, 1988.

———. *After Virtue: A Study in Moral Theory*. Second edition. London: Duckworth, 1985.

———. *Against the Self-Images of the Age: Essays on Ideology and Philosophy*. Notre Dame: University of Notre Dame Press, 1978.

———. "Epistemological Crises, Dramatic Narrative, and the Philosophy of Science." *The Monist* 60 (1977): 453–72.

———. *A Short History of Ethics*. New York: Macmillan, 1966.

Mackie, J. L. *Ethics: Inventing Right and Wrong*. Harmondsworth: Penguin Books, 1977.

Mackie, John. "Competitors in Conversation." Review of Bruce Ackerman's *Social Justice in the Liberal State*, 1980. *Times Literary Supplement*, April 17, 1981.

Malcolm, Janet. *The Journalist and the Murderer*. New York: Vintage, 1990.

Martin, Judith. *Common Courtesy: In Which Miss Manners Solves the Problem That Baffled Mr. Jefferson*. New York: Atheneum, 1985.

Martin, Judith, and Gunther S. Stent. "I Think; Therefore I Thank: A Philosophy of Etiquette." *American Scholar* 59 (1990): 237–54.

McCarthy, Thomas. "Reflections on Rationalization in *The Theory of Communicative Action*." *Praxis International* 4 (1984): 177–91.

———. "Rationality and Relativism: Habermas's 'Overcoming' Hermeneutics." In *Habermas: Critical Debates*, ed. John B. Thompson and David Held. London: Macmillan, 1982.

———. *The Critical Theory of Jürgen Habermas*. Cambridge, Mass.: MIT Press, 1978.

———. "A Theory of Communicative Competence." *Philosophy of the Social Sciences* 3 (1973): 135–56.

McDowell, John. "Virtue and Reason." *The Monist* 62 (1979): 331–50.

Mellers, Barbara, and Jonathan Baron, eds. *Psychological Perspectives on Justice: Theory and Applications*. New York: Cambridge University Press, 1993.

Misgeld, Dieter. "Discourse and Conversation: The Theory of Communicative Competence and Hermeneutics in Light of the Debate Between Habermas and Gadamer." *Cultural Hermeneutics* 4 (1977): 321–44.

Mitchell, W.J.T., ed. *Against Theory: Literary Studies and the New Pragmatism*. Chicago: University of Chicago Press, 1985.

Moon, J. Donald. *Constructing Community: Moral Pluralism and Tragic Conflicts*. Princeton: Princeton University Press, 1993.

———. "Constrained Discourse and Public Life." *Political Theory* 19 (1991): 202–29.

Müller-Vollmer, Kurt, ed. *The Hermeneutics Reader*. New York: Continuum, 1990.

Murdoch, Iris. *The Sovereignty of the Good*. London: Routledge & Kegan Paul, 1970.

Nagel, Thomas. "Agreeing in Principle." Review of MacIntyre's *Whose Justice? Which Rationality?* 1988. *Times Literary Supplement*, July 14, 1988.

——. *The View from Nowhere*. New York: Oxford University Press, 1986.

Nietzsche, Friedrich. *The Birth of Tragedy*. Translated by Walter Kaufmann. New York: Vintage, 1967.

Norris, Christopher. "Philosophy as a Kind of Writing: Rorty on Post-Modern Liberal Culture." In *The Contest of the Faculties*. London: Methuen, 1986.

Novick, Peter. *That Noble Dream: The "Objectivity Question" and the American Historical Profession*. New York: Cambridge University Press, 1988.

Nozick, Robert. *Anarchy, State, and Utopia*. New York: Basic Books, 1974.

Nussbaum, Martha. *The Fragility of Goodness: Luck and Ethics in Greek Tragedy and Philosophy*. Cambridge: Cambridge University Press, 1986.

Oakeshott, Michael. *On Human Conduct*. Oxford: Oxford University Press, 1975.

——. *Rationalism in Politics and Other Essays*. London: Methuen, 1962.

Okin, Susan Moller. *Justice, Gender, and the Family*. New York: Basic Books, 1989.

O'Neill, Onora. "Kant After Virtue." *Inquiry* 26 (1983): 387–405.

Paden, Roger. "Post-Structuralism and Neo-Romanticism; or, Is MacIntyre a Young Conservative?" *Philosophy and Social Criticism* 13 (1987): 125–44.

Peck, M. Scott. *A World Waiting to Be Born: Civility Rediscovered*. New York: Bantam, 1993.

Pitkin, Hanna. *Wittgenstein and Justice: On the Significance of Ludwig Wittgenstein for Social and Political Theory*. Berkeley and Los Angeles: University of California Press, 1972.

Pocock, J.G.A. "The Varieties of Whiggism from Exclusion to Reform: A History of Ideology and Discourse." Part 3 of *Virtue, Commerce, and History*. Cambridge: Cambridge University Press, 1985.

Post, Emily. *Etiquette: The Blue Book of Social Usage*. New York: Funk & Wagnalls, 1922.

Pushing the Faith: Proselytism and Civility in a Pluralistic Society. New York: Crossroad, 1988.

Putnam, Hilary. *Reason, Truth, and History*. Cambridge, Mass.: Harvard University Press, 1981.

Rajchman, John, and Cornel West, eds. *Post-Analytic Philosophy*. New York: Columbia University Press, 1985.

Rasmussen, David. "Communication Theory and the Critique of the Law: Habermas and Unger on the Law." *Praxis International* 8 (1988): 155–70.

Rasmussen, David, ed. *Reading Habermas*. Cambridge: Basil Blackwell, 1990.

——. *Universalism vs. Communitarianism: Contemporary Debate in Ethics*. Cambridge, Mass.: MIT Press, 1990.

Rawls, John. *Political Liberalism*. New York: Columbia University Press, 1993.

——. "The Priority of Right and Ideas of the Good." *Philosophy and Public Affairs* 17 (1988): 251–76.

——. "The Idea of Overlapping Consensus." *Oxford Journal of Legal Studies* 7 (1987): 1–25.

——. "Justice as Fairness: Political Not Metaphysical." *Philosophy and Public Affairs* 14 (1985): 223–51.

——. "Kantian Constructivism in Moral Theory" (Dewey Lectures). *Journal of Philosophy* 77 (1980): 515–72.

——. "The Basic Structure as Subject." *American Philosophical Quarterly* 14 (1977): 159–65.

————. "Fairness to Goodness." *Philosophical Review* 84 (1975): 536–54.

————. "A Kantian Conception of Equality." *The Cambridge Review*, 1975, 94–99.

————. *A Theory of Justice*. Cambridge, Mass.: Belknap Press, 1971.

————. "Justice as Fairness." *Philosophical Review* 67 (1958): 164–94.

Raz, Joseph. *The Morality of Freedom*. New York: Oxford University Press, 1986.

————. "The Claims of Reflective Equilibrium." *Inquiry* 25 (1982): 307–30.

Richardson, Henry S. "The Problem of Liberalism and the Good." In *Liberalism and the Good*, ed. R. Bruce Douglas, Gerald R. Mara, and Henry S. Richardson. New York: Routledge, 1990.

Ricoeur, Paul. "Hermeneutics and the Critique of Ideology." In *Hermeneutics and Modern Philosophy*, ed. Brice Wachterhauser. Albany: SUNY Press, 1986.

————. *Interpretation Theory*. Fort Worth: Texas Christian University Press, 1976.

————. *The Conflict of Interpretations*. Evanston, Ill.: Northwestern University Press, 1974.

Rorty, James. *Where Life Is Better*. New York: n.p., 1936.

Rorty, Richard. "Putnam and the Relativism Menace." *Journal of Philosophy* 90 (1993): 443–61.

————. *Essays on Heidegger and Others: Philosophical Papers, Volume Two*. Cambridge: Cambridge University Press, 1991.

————. *Objectivity, Relativism, and Truth: Philosophical Papers, Volume One*. Cambridge: Cambridge University Press, 1991.

————. *Contingency, Irony, and Solidarity*. Cambridge: Cambridge University Press, 1989.

————. "Habermas and Lyotard on Postmodernity." *Praxis International* 4 (1984): 32–44.

————. "Postmodernist Bourgeois Liberalism." *Journal of Philosophy* 80 (1983): 583–89.

————. *Consequences of Pragmatism*. Minneapolis: University of Minnesota Press, 1982.

————. *Philosophy and the Mirror of Nature*. Princeton: Princeton University Press, 1979.

Rosenblum, Nancy. *Another Liberalism: Romanticism and the Reconstruction of Liberal Thought*. Ithaca: Cornell University Press, 1987.

————, ed. *Liberalism and the Moral Life*. Cambridge, Mass.: Harvard University Press, 1989.

Rousseau, Jean-Jacques. *On the Social Contract* and *Discourses*. Translated by Donald A. Cress. Indianapolis: Hackett, 1983.

Ruddick, Sara. "Remarks on the Sexual Politics of Reason." In *Women and Moral Theory*, ed. Eva Feder Kittay and Diana T. Meyers. Totowa, N.J.: Rowman & Littlefield, 1987.

Sandel, Michael J. "The Procedural Republic and the Unencumbered Self." *Political Theory* 12 (1984): 81–96.

————. *Liberalism and the Limits of Justice*. Cambridge: Cambridge University Press, 1982.

Sayre-McCord, Geoffrey, ed. *Essays on Moral Realism*. Ithaca: Cornell University Press, 1988.

Schneewind, J. B. "Moral Crisis and the History of Ethics." *Midwest Studies in Philosophy* 8 (1983): 525–39.

————. "Virtue, Narrative, and Community: MacIntyre and Morality." *Journal of Philosophy* 79 (1982): 653–63.

Schopenhauer, Arthur. *Essays from the "Parerga and Paralipomena."* Translated by T. Bailey Saunders. London: Allen & Unwin, 1951.

Searle, John R. *Expression and Meaning: Studies in the Theory of Speech Acts.* Cambridge: Cambridge University Press, 1979.

———. *Speech Acts: An Essay in the Philosophy of Language.* Cambridge: Cambridge University Press, 1969.

Searle, John R., and Daniel Vanderveken. *Foundations of Illocutionary Logic.* Cambridge: Cambridge University Press, 1985.

Shapiro, Ian. *Political Criticism.* Chicago: University of Chicago Press, 1990.

———. *The Evolution of Rights in Liberal Theory.* Cambridge: Cambridge University Press, 1986.

Shklar, Judith. *The Faces of Injustice.* New Haven: Yale University Press, 1990.

———. *Ordinary Vices.* Cambridge, Mass.: Harvard University Press, 1984.

Smith, Adam. *The Theory of Moral Sentiments.* Edinburgh, 1813.

Smith, Barbara Herrnstein. *Contingencies of Value: Alternative Perspectives for Critical Theory.* Cambridge, Mass.: Harvard University Press, 1988.

Smith, Steven B. *Hegel's Critique of Liberalism: Rights in Context.* Chicago: University of Chicago Press, 1989.

Stanhope, Philip Dormore (Earl of Chesterfield). *On Manners and Morals.* White Plains, N.Y.: Peter Pauper Press, 1936.

Stout, Jeffrey. "Homeward Bound: MacIntyre on Liberal Society and the History of Ethics." *Journal of Religion* 1 (1989): 220–32.

Strenski, Ivan. "Recapturing the Values That Promote Civility on the Campuses." *Chronicle of Higher Education,* June 23, 1993, p. A36.

Taylor, Charles. *Sources of the Self: The Making of the Modern Identity.* Cambridge, Mass.: Harvard University Press, 1989

———. *Human Agency and Language: Philosophical Papers, Volume One.* Cambridge: Cambridge University Press, 1985.

———. *Philosophy and the Human Sciences: Philosophical Papers, Volume Two.* Cambridge: Cambridge University Press, 1985.

Thompson, John B. "Universal Pragmatics." In *Habermas: Critical Debates,* ed. John B. Thompson and David Held. London: Macmillan, 1982.

Thompson, John B., and David Held, eds. *Habermas: Critical Debates.* London: Macmillan, 1982.

Tinder, Glenn E. *Tolerance: Towards a New Civility.* Amherst: University of Massachusetts Press, 1976.

Toulmin, Stephen. *The Uses of Argument.* Cambridge: Cambridge University Press, 1958.

Unger, Roberto Mangabeira. *The Critical Legal Studies Movement.* Cambridge, Mass.: Harvard University Press, 1983.

Valberg, Eugene. "Philippa Foot on Etiquette and Morality." *Southern Journal of Philosophy* 15 (1977): 387–91.

Vanderbilt, Amy. *New Complete Book of Etiquette: A Guide to Contemporary Living.* New York: Doubleday, 1952.

Visser, Margaret. *The Rituals of Dinner: The Origins, Evolution, Eccentricities, and Meaning of Table Manners.* Toronto: HarperCollins, 1991.

Wachterhauser, Brice R. "Must We Be What We Say? Gadamer on Truth in the Human Sciences." In *Hermeneutics and Modern Philosophy,* ed. Brice Wachterhauser. Albany: SUNY Press, 1986.

Waldron, Jeremy. "A Perfect Technology of Justice." Paper presented at the Yale Legal Theory Workshop, February 1989.

Wallace, James D. *Virtues and Vices.* Ithaca: Cornell University Press, 1978.

Walzer, Michael. "A Critique of Philosophical Conversation." *Philosophical Forum* 21 (1989–90): 182–96.

———. "Two Kinds of Universalism." Paper delivered to a conference on justice and interpretation, Cardozo School of Law, New York, October 1989.

———. *Interpretation and Social Criticism.* Cambridge, Mass.: Harvard University Press, 1987.

———. *Spheres of Justice.* New York: Basic Books, 1983.

———. "Philosophy and Democracy." *Political Theory* 9 (1981): 379–99.

Warnke, Georgia. *Justice and Interpretation.* Cambridge, Mass.: MIT Press, 1992.

———. "The Hermeneutic Turn in Recent Political Philosophy." *Yale Journal of Criticism* 4 (1990): 207–29.

———. "Rawls, Habermas, and Real Talk: A Reply to Walzer." *Philosophical Forum* 21 (1989–90): 197–203.

———. "Social Interpretation and Political Theory: Walzer and His Critics." *Philosophical Forum* 21 (1989–90): 204–26.

———. *Gadamer: Hermeneutics, Tradition, and Reason.* Stanford, Calif.: Stanford University Press, 1987.

Wartofsky, Marx. "Virtue Lost, or Understanding MacIntyre." *Inquiry* 27 (1983): 235–50.

Weinsheimer, Joel. *Gadamer's Hermeneutics: A Reading of "Truth and Method."* New Haven: Yale University Press, 1985.

Wellmer, Albrecht. "On the Dialectic of Modernism and Postmodernism." *Praxis International* 4 (1985): 337–62.

White, Stephen K. *Political Theory and Postmodernism.* Cambridge: Cambridge University Press, 1991.

———. *The Recent Work of Jürgen Habermas: Reason, Justice, and Modernity.* Cambridge: Cambridge University Press, 1988.

Williams, Bernard. "Modernity." Review of MacIntyre's *Whose Justice? Which Rationality?* 1988. *London Review of Books*, January 5, 1989.

———. *Ethics and the Limits of Philosophy.* London: Fontana, 1985.

———. "Space Talk: The Conversation Continued." *Ethics* 93 (1983): 367–71.

———. *Descartes: The Project of Pure Inquiry.* New York: Penguin Books, 1978.

Wittgenstein, Ludwig. *Philosophical Investigations.* Translated by G.E.M. Anscombe. New York: Macmillan, 1953.

Wolff, Robert Paul. *In Defense of Anarchism.* New York: Harper & Row, 1970.

Wolgast, Elizabeth H. *The Grammar of Justice.* Ithaca: Cornell University Press, 1987.

Index